COLONIAL
THE TOURNAMENT

60 YEARS OF GREATNESS

Published by

PANACHE
PARTNERS LLC

13747 Montfort Drive, Suite 100
Dallas, Texas 75240
972-661-9884
972-661-2743
www.panache.com

PUBLISHERS: Brian G. Carabet and John A. Shand
EXECUTIVE PUBLISHER: Steven Darocy
SR. ASSOCIATE PUBLISHER: Martha Morgan
ASSOCIATE PUBLISHER: Julianna Galloway
ART DIRECTOR: Michele Cunningham-Scott
WRITTEN BY: Dennis Roberson
EDITOR: Elizabeth Gionta
CONTRIBUTING EDITORS: Mike Rabun, Dan Jenkins and Russ Pate
Tournament Partners Photography: Gittings Photography

Printed in Fort Worth, Texas

Distributed by Gibbs Smith, Publisher
800-748-5439

PUBLISHER'S DATA

COLONIAL: 60 YEARS OF GREATNESS

Library of Congress Control Number: 2006901822

ISBN Number: 1-933415-30-4
978 1 933415 30 7

First Printing 2006

10 9 8 7 6 5 4 3 2 1

Previous Page: 1962 Colonial champion Arnold Palmer with
Marvin Leonard.

This Page: A view of Colonial's clubhouse, overlooking the scenic
18th hole.

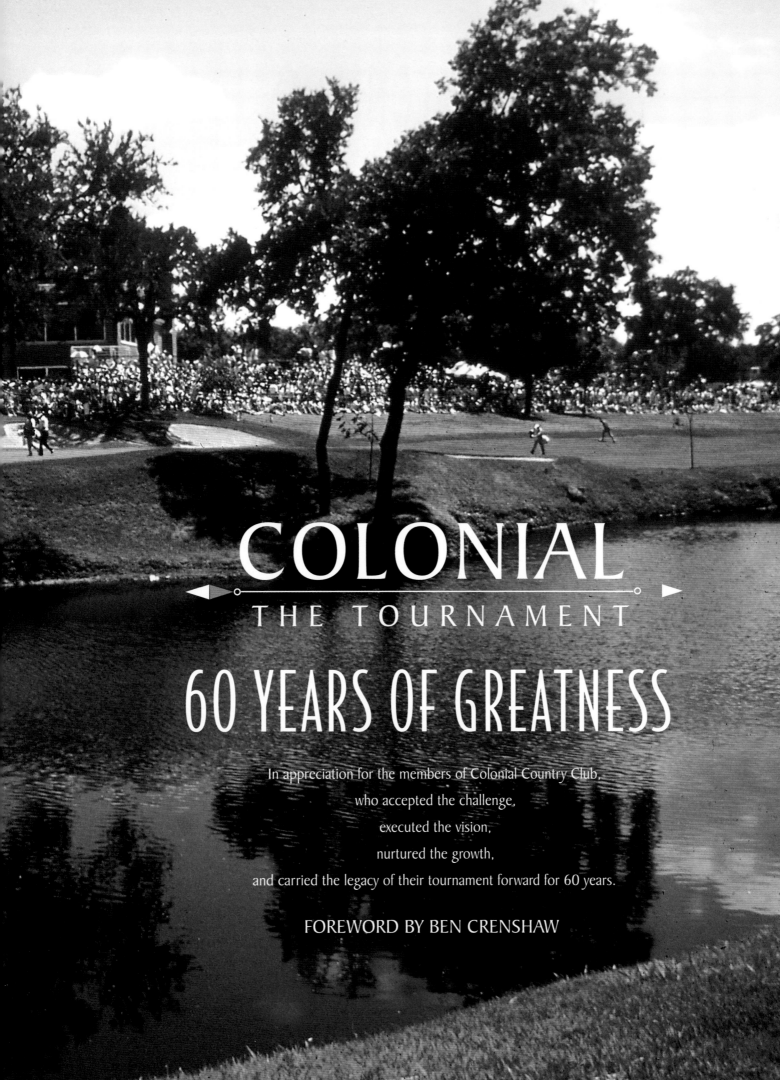

COLONIAL

THE TOURNAMENT

60 YEARS OF GREATNESS

In appreciation for the members of Colonial Country Club,

who accepted the challenge,

executed the vision,

nurtured the growth,

and carried the legacy of their tournament forward for 60 years.

FOREWORD BY BEN CRENSHAW

TABLE OF CONTENTS

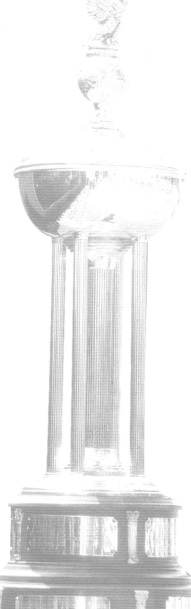

FOREWORD

60 YEARS OF GREATNESS

Very few professional golf tournaments survive for 60 years, and none at the same golf course — except for Colonial and The Masters. That is a wonderful testament to the enduring legacy of Marvin Leonard, who dedicated his passion for golf to building a championship golf course in Texas with bentgrass greens, and then bringing in the world's best golfers to play it.

The annual Colonial tournament is his ongoing gift to us all. I am honored to have played in 32 of them, and to have won it twice. Many wonderful memories are recounted here, and it is always fun to relive those moments. The great golf course, Ben Hogan and his five titles, Fort Worth hospitality, all the great champions and other golfers that have enlivened the tournament over the years — these are the things I will always cherish.

While change is inevitable, in golf as in everything, it is important that we honor our past and our traditions. Colonial is one of the few remaining places that can do that on the PGA Tour. Our thanks go to the members who lend us their course for a week each year. Being a Texan, I am certainly a little biased, but you don't have to be from here to find plenty to love, and remember, about Colonial. I'm sure the next 60 years will be just as great.

Ben Crenshaw

CLUB ACKNOWLEDGEMENTS

It is with great enthusiasm that we celebrate the 60th anniversary of the Colonial PGA TOUR event. Colonial Country Club was founded in 1936, and the Colonial National Invitation Tournament began 10 years later in 1946. Thus we also proudly celebrate the 70th birthday of Colonial Country Club, in addition to the anniversary of our great tournament.

Tremendous growth and impressive changes have occurred over the last sixty years in professional golf, but the constant of "greatness" has always been reflective of Colonial Country Club and our great TOUR event. Whether it is great players, a great golf course, great competition, or great hospitality, they all have been part of our history and tradition from the beginning. None of this greatness or longevity would have been possible without the dedicated members of Colonial Country Club, thousands of valuable hard-working volunteers, a devoted club staff, hundreds of loyal sponsors, our special Fort Worth community, unbelievably loyal golf fans, and, of course, exceptionally talented professional golfers.

We are grateful for the many lasting friendships we have made with countless people over these many years. We especially want to recognize the PGA TOUR, the CBS network, and, of course, our champions, all of whom epitomize the greatness of our event. We also want to pay special tribute to Ben Hogan, who, as a five-time champion of our event and close friend of our founder, Marvin Leonard, became the hometown "host" of our tournament; Mr. Hogan's name has become synonymous with Colonial Country Club, and we take great pride in being identified with him.

Many thanks also go to our title sponsors over the years: Southwestern Bell, MasterCard International and Bank of America. These great partners have supported this event from 1989-2006, and we are eternally grateful to all of these valued corporate supporters who became part of the fabric of our tournament.

Colonial Country Club and its Tournament are both the vision of one man, Marvin Leonard, who founded the Club and this historic tournament. Although Mr. Leonard likely would not have imagined what "his" tournament would look like today, we are confident that he would be extremely proud that his legacy has continued. Our tournament is the longest-running event on the PGA TOUR that is still held at the original course where it commenced; this is an unparalleled achievement.

We join all of you in celebrating "Sixty Years of Greatness," and we thank each of you for being an invaluable part of our history and an essential part of our future.

Bill Bowers
President, Colonial Country Club

Elliott S. Garsek
Tournament Chairman

CLUB LEADERSHIP

2006 BOARD OF GOVERNORS

Bill E. Bowers, Club President
Marty V. Leonard, Vice President
John E. Anderson, Vice President
Harold Turney Jr., Secretary
Ben L. Matheson, Treasurer

OTHER GOVERNORS

Jeffrey B. Luz	W.R. McHargue	Bruce W. Simpson	James W. Thigpen	Robert C. Wood
Scott Mahaffey	Jeffrey A. Moten	Chris W. Stenholm	Pamela J. Wood	William W. Wood

2006 BANK OF AMERICA COLONIAL TOURNAMENT COMMITTEE

Elliott S. Garsek, Tournament Chairman

Platt Allen III, Standard Bearers	Don Gerik, Carts	Chuck Scherer, Sponsors Chairman & Package Sales
John E. Anderson, Leaderboards	Don Gillespie, Parking	Pat Schmuck, Player Registration
Mike Ball, Player Concierge	Steve Gray, Pro-Ams	Wallace Schmuck, Patron Safety & Admissions
Dr. Bill Barnes, Hogan Award	Rob Hood, Volunteer Headquarters	Barry Smith, Corporate Sales
Sandy Barnes, Junior Clinic	Rick Hopwood, Vehicles	Ross Stephenson, Communications
Lance Barrow, Players & Media Advisor	Jim Hunt, Professional Caddies	Chris Tabor, Victory Dinner
Mark Barrow, Entertainment Night	Bob Lansford, Administration Chairman	James W. Thigpen, Golf Course Planning
Bill E. Bowers, Legal Advisor	Jim Leito III, Operations Chairman	Michael R. Thomas, Title Sponsor Advisor
John Cockrell, Marshals	Kathi Mahaffey, Player Child Care	Phil Thomas, Pride of the Plaid
Corrine Collins, Player Transportation	Mike Moore, Operations Chairman	Trish Thomas, Player Housing
Scott Corpening, Players Chairman	Jeffrey A. Moten, Financial	Wes Turner, Cook Charity Outing
Craig Crockett, Scoring & SHOTLink	Harold Muckleroy Jr., Special Events Chairman	Jody Vasquez, Practice Range
Jay Dill, Credentials	Craig Nicholson, Charitable Programs	David Walker, Media Center
Rob Doby, Will Call	Susan Nix, Programs & Pairings Sheets	Bill Whitman, Medical Services
Dee Finley, Advisory Chairman & Champions Dinner	Robert Patton, Starters & Scoring Tents	Jim Whitten, Player Hospitality

Joe Cauker, Former Tournament Chairman	Rodney Johnston, Former Tournament Chairman	Dr. H. Wallace Schmuck, Former Tournament Chairman
Sam R. Day, Former Tournament Chairman	Foist Motheral, Former Tournament Chairman	Floyd Wade, Former Tournament Chairman

PAST PRESIDENTS

Marvin Leonard, Founder, 1936-1943	Judge Charles J. Murray, 1968	Bill E. Bowers, 1986-87, 2006
Berl E. Godfrey, 1943-47	Jack W. Melcher, 1969-1970	Sam R. Day, 1987-89
Jonathan Y. Ballard, 1948-1949	Douglas Forshagen, 1971	Dr. H. Wallace Schmuck, 1990-91
Lacy Boggess, 1950-51	Michael R. Thomas, 1992	Michael R. Thomas, 1992
W.J. Laidlaw Sr., 1952-54	Charles H. Haws, 1973	Jay Lesok, 1993-94
S. Scott Teel, 1955	Vance C. Minter, 1974-75	Harold Muckleroy Jr., 1995-96
C. Victor Thornton, 1956	Ted C. Salmon, 1976-77	W. Clark Martin Jr., 1997-98
George P. Hill, 1957-61	Paul D. Cato Jr., 1978-79	Stephen S. Sikes, 1999-2000
William C. Conner, 1962	Charles T. Floyd, 1980-81	Elliott S. Garsek, 2001-2002
Ralph L. McCann, 1963-65	Darrell R. Lester, 1982-83	James W. Thigpen, 2003-04
Cecil A. Morgan Sr., 1966-67	M.C. Hamilton Jr., 1983-85	Jeffrey B. Luz, 2005

A VISION BECOMES REALITY

THE FOUNDING OF COLONIAL

COLONIAL COUNTRY CLUB and its 60-year-old PGA Tour event were the vision of John Marvin Leonard, the older of the merchant brothers who founded and operated the Leonard Bros. store on Houston Street in downtown Fort Worth. The store, a fore-runner of the discount stores that swept the United States after World War II, became a symbol of the vitality of the city of Fort Worth.

Both Marvin Leonard and his brother, Obadiah, were shrewd businessmen, possessed with instinctive minds that knew how to make money. Their business philosophy was simple: give the customer more merchandise for less money and make profits from volume instead of margins.

ABOVE:
Marvin Leonard helps celebrate Colonial Country Club's fourth birthday in 1940.
FACING PAGE:
Aerial photo of the course circa 1941. In lower center of the picture, original holes 3, 4 and 5 are visible.

ABOVE:
The original Colonial clubhouse.

The Leonards were builders, men of vision who could not only see the present but also anticipate the future. Especially Marvin, whose associates claimed had an uncanny ability to see the long-range implications of business decisions before anyone else.

The Leonard brothers, sons of an East Texas farming family, knew the value of hard work. Had the term "'workaholic" existed in the 1920s, when Marvin and Obie were building a family empire that would extend to oil and gas, ranching, banking, and real estate development, it could have been aptly applied to them.

All work left little time for play. In 1923, Marvin Leonard had accepted an invitation to join the Glen Garden golf club in Fort Worth, but after a few rounds he stashed his golf clubs in a closet with the comment that his time was too valuable to be wasted chasing a little white ball.

By 1927, though, the pace of business had begun to exact a physical price and Marvin Leonard's doctor ordered him to strike a balance between work and leisure activities. So Leonard pulled his golf clubs out of the closet and took up the sport.

Leonard, then 32, became enamored with the game. He began playing regularly at both Glen Garden and Rivercrest, building time into his daily routine for at least nine holes. Leonard often squeezed in nine holes at Glen Garden very early in the morning prior to heading to the office. There he met a young caddy named Ben Hogan, a scrappy boy who walked

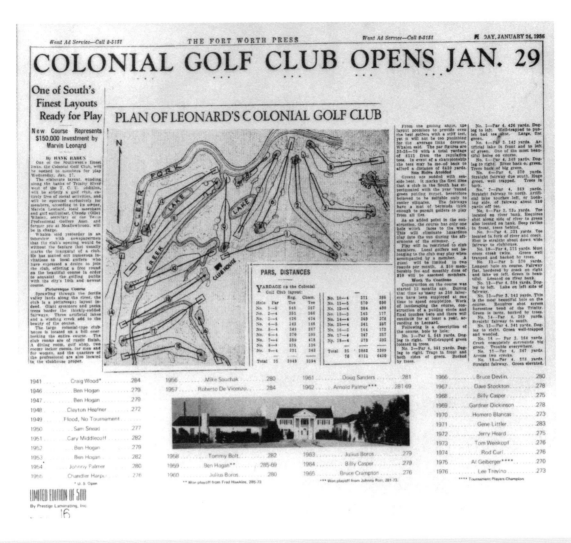

ABOVE:
Newspaper announcement of Colonial's opening in 1936

miles across town in the dark each morning in order to get a bag ahead of the bigger and older caddies at the club. The two hit if off in what was the beginning of a lifelong friendship.

Leonard developed his own game to the point where he shot in the low 80s consistently and dipped into the 70s when his putter was hot. His interest in golf became intense. He began to study all aspects of the sport, including golf courses. How they were built. How holes were designed. All about grass and sand. On family vacations to California, where Leonard scheduled a fair share of hours on the links, he developed an affinity for the qualities of bent grass greens.

Unlike the bumpy native bermuda greens back in Texas, bent greens were as smooth as billiard tables. On bent grass, if a player struck a putt true, he likely would be rewarded for this effort. On bermuda, the player was often at the mercy of the bump. Leonard made up his mind Texas courses should have bent grass greens. He'd see to it himself if necessary.

When Leonard brought his idea back to Rivercrest Country Club in Fort Worth, his associates scoffed at the suggestion. Everyone told him that bent grass was too fragile to withstand the unforgiving Texas heat. Bermuda, which thrived in the sun, was the natural grass for Texas greens. Sorry, Marvin.

ABOVE:
Byron Nelson and Ben Hogan relax prior to an exhibition at Colonial in 1939.

Dean and the St. Louis 'Gashouse' Gang baseball champions, but Marvin Leonard had little time to think about the Cardinals. The only birdies he was thinking about were putts to be sunk on bent grass greens.

Leonard had his eye on a piece of property in southwest Fort Worth, near Forest Park and the Texas Christian University campus. He acquired the land, roughly 157 acres, in late 1934 and at once went to work on designing his golf course. Leonard engaged the services of noted golf architects John Bredemus of Texas and Perry Maxwell of Oklahoma to assist with the layout.

Bredemus had been involved with courses all over Texas and in Mexico, and was instrumental in founding the Texas PGA. He had also been experimenting with bentgrass in Texas. Maxwell was finishing up work on the heralded new Southern Hills course in Tulsa. Leonard asked Bredemus and Maxwell each to submit five alternative plans for the course. He reviewed their recommendations then asked for five more. Marvin then started picking and choosing elements for his overall plan. He borrowed from both designers to mold the Colonial tapestry. Bredemus signed on to oversee the project, assisted by his foreman, Ralph Plummer, who later became a noted architect himself, building Champions Golf Club in Houston and more than 80 courses in all.

Leonard persisted in trying to sell his associates on bent grass greens. He told the Rivercrest Governing board that if they'd let him convert two or three greens to bent grass, he'd underwrite the cost. If the experiment didn't work, he'd pay for the conversion back to bermuda.

The story goes that the President of Rivercrest grew weary of Leonard's harping about bent grass greens and finally told him, "Marvin, if you're so sold on bent grass, why don't you go build your own golf course and put them in?"

"Thank you very much I may just do that." replied Leonard. That night he vowed to build a championship course. The year was 1934. The nation was captivated by the antics of Dizzy

On May 3, 1935, announcement of the golf course appeared in the local newspaper. "We intend to make this course the best links in the Southwest," said Leonard. "No cost will be spared in construction. Mr. Bredemus will design into the course all the latest improvements in golf architecture in making it one of the most picturesque in the country."

Marvin Leonard awards golfing great Babe Didrickson Zaharias the trophy for winning the Texas Women's Open at Colonial in 1940.

Construction of the golf course began in earnest. With the help of Claude Whalen, who would serve as the club's first manager, golf pro and greens superintendent, and R.L. 'Bob' Alexander, more than two dozen laborers, using mule teams and fresnoes (a sharp cutting instrument that overturned the earth), began sculpting the fairways, bunkers and greens. One of the first hired hands was a teenager named Joe Cano, who brought his mama's kitchen knife to the course to pull up weeds. Cano would work on the course for more than 40 years; many as golf course superintendent.

To develop the bent grass greens, Bredemus planted a combination of seaside bent grass, then popular on California courses, mixed with sand and cow manure. To combat heat, bent

grass' worst enemy, the ground crew kept the greens watered frequently. Marvin Leonard kept close watch on the proceedings.

By late 1935, the golf course and stately clubhouse highlighted by large white columns associated with the Colonial style architecture, neared completion. Marvin Leonard stayed busy contacting friends and business associates in Fort Worth to extend a personal invitation to enjoy the bent grass greens at his 'Colonial Golf Club.'

Legendary architect A. W. Tillinghast, who designed such championship layouts as Winged Foot, Baltusrol, and San Francisco Golf Club, toured the new Colonial course on January 12, 1936, with Leonard and Whalen. "Mr. Leonard deserves high

ABOVE:
Aerial photo of the course in foreground in 1940s.

praise for his experiment here," said Tillinghast. "He is pulling away from the belief that only native grasses can be used for greens. We have long felt that there was no reason why other grasses couldn't be grown in the section if the greens were properly prepared and cared for, that has been done here, and the entire Bermuda grass belt will watch the result with much interest.

"I never like to make comparisons, of course, but I will say that this is a lovely layout," Tillinghast continued. "And the bold experiment on bent grass cannot be praised too highly. We're all hoping it will succeed, and believe that it will."

The first Colonial members were charged no membership fee, but had to put up $50 as security deposit against charges to the club. By January 29, 1936, when the club officially opened, roughly 100 Fort Worth residents had joined Colonial

Golf Club. Marvin and his wife moved into the sleek Forest Park Apartments tower nearby his new golf course about this time, and soon they were joined in the building by a newlywed couple named Ben and Valerie Hogan. Hogan was one of the first players privileged to play the new Colonial tract. He was still struggling to succeed as a touring golf professional, and Leonard staked him expense money during this time period. Hogan never forgot that generosity, and his loyalty to Leonard and Colonial never waned.

Marvin Leonard's travels across the country and his keen appreciation of golf had given him the insight needed to put the Colonial Club on par with the best courses in the nation. He staged numerous golf exhibitions with Hogan and other top players, and he hosted Texas tournaments, PGA section tournaments and even U.S. Amateur Qualifying tournaments.

In 1940, the great Babe Didrickson Zaharias won a thrilling 36-hole match play final to claim the Texas Women's Open title at Colonial. All the while, Leonard visited with top players, constantly looking for ideas to improve his course. He tweaked bunkers, greens and anything else he deemed necessary. Leonard wanted nothing more than to put his club on the national map of golfdom.

He had a plan, of course. In the late 1930s, Leonard began lobbying the United States Golf Association to conduct the U. S. Open, America's national championship and golf's most prestigious event, at Colonial. Not only did he want to showcase the brightest jewel in Southwest golf, Leonard wanted Fort Worth golf fans to witness the shotmaking prowess of the world's best players.

Leonard enlisted the help of Amon Carter Sr., another of Fort Worth's visionaries and a man well-connected with the leading sportswriters and sports figures in the nation, and Dr. Alden Coffey, the president of the Fort Worth Golf Association and the so-called 'Father of Fort Worth Golf,' to help him spur the USGA's interest. They in turn enlisted the help of golfers and businessmen throughout the state.

Getting the USGA's attention was no mean feat. The group typically rotated the U.S. Open among courses in the Northeast like Winged Foot, Merion and Baltusrol. Never once had the Open championship been played in the South.

ABOVE:
The 9th green in the 1940s.

Leonard's effort to sell the USGA included a 60-minute phone call to Harold Pierce, the USGA president, who lived in Boston. When Pierce pointed out that the conversation was getting expensive (it cost Leonard $17.40), the Fort Worth merchant replied, "That's okay. This is important."

Later, meeting with Open officials in New York in April, Leonard put his bid in proper perspective. Leonard and some of his friends in Fort Worth would personally guarantee the USGA a sum of $25,000 to hold the event at Colonial. That figure, a king's ransom in its day, immediately turned the USGA's heads towards Texas.

Although Leonard was expecting a decision that summer after the 1940 U.S. Open, he received an unexpected phone call on Wednesday, May 8 from USGA officials. The 1941 Open would indeed be headed to The Lone Star State.

Leonard, Colonial and Fort Worth were ecstatic. Leonard was having quite a happy Spring indeed, as his young friend Hogan had finally broken through in March, winning his first professional tournament in record fashion, and then winning two more to place him atop the Tour's money list.

"Yes, I started out with the idea that some day we might get the Open," Leonard said. "Fort Worth and Texas have been very good to us, and the fact that I've been able to give them a course good enough to land the biggest tournament of all is most gratifying."

Before the U.S. Open unfolded at Colonial, however, a USGA committee reviewing the golf course for suitability of play recommended toughening a two-hole stretch on the front nine that it felt wasn't up to par. Their report stipulated that holes 4 and 5 needed to be upgraded. Otherwise, the USGA officials found a demanding test of golf forged from the pecan trees and hackberry bushes on bottom land along the Clear Fork of the Trinity River. The aesthetics of the course came from the pecan trees overhanging the fairways and greens and the river, which meandered along nearly half of the holes.

Marvin Leonard may have gone overboard in meeting the USGA's request for improvements to the front nine. He bought several acres adjacent to the boundary of the golf course on Rogers Road, on which a nursery and dairy were operated. Leonard was so eager to acquire the additional land he reportedly paid the owner several times the property's value.

He then brought in noted golf architects Perry Maxwell and Dean Woods, who incorporated the new acreage into a three-hole stretch that would later be dubbed the 'Horrible Horseshoe' both for its configuration and its degree of difficulty. Woods, who was hired for the year leading up to the Open to oversee all improvements, also worked on bunkers and greens elsewhere on the course. With the assistance of Colonial greenskeeper Bob Alexander, Woods created Colonial's world famous par 4 fifth hole, quickly dubbed throughout golfdom as 'Death Valley.' They also lengthened the par 4 third hole by some 50 yards and extended the par 3 fourth hole to its present gargantuan self (246 yards).

The fifth hole, which doglegs around the banks of the Trinity River, is universally regarded as one of the great holes in golf. It regularly appears on lists of 'best holes.' Arnold Palmer, who included the fifth on his personal list, once wrote, 'Nearly every great player has experienced the rigors of the hole and many wish they hadn't. I consider it a great hole because, sooner or later, you must play a difficult shot. I'll take par there any time.'

With the changes, which added roughly 300 yards to the course, Colonial presented a challenging 7,035 yard, par 70 layout that placed a premium on accurate driving. The shape of the holes, doglegs left and right, and their varying lengths and degrees of difficulty tested a player's proficiency with every club in the bag.

In late 1940, Marvin Leonard showed the proposed redesign to USGA official Joseph Dey. Dey assumed the holes would have to be completed after the Open, which was then only six months away. Leonard assured him, however, that the new holes would be ready for the Open.

Marvin Leonard could move mountains. Or in this instance, mountains of dirt. When the USGA and the game's best players rolled into Texas in the first week of June 1941 for the U.S. Open, the new and improved Colonial golf course awaited them.

OFFICIAL PROGRAM

Forty-Fifth

OPEN CHAMPIONSHIP

United States Golf Association

COLONIAL CLUB

FORT WORTH, TEXAS

JUNE 5-6-7, 1941

Price 50c.

THE 1941 U.S. OPEN CHAMPIONSHIP

THE GREATEST SPORTS EVENT
IN FORT WORTH HISTORY

The Fort Worth Star-Telegram was especially effusive about the 1941 U.S. Open coming to town, proclaiming it "the greatest athletic event in her history" and "golfdom's gaudiest carnival." For months preceding the Open that June, both Colonial and Fort Worth prepared diligently for the event. Fans paid $6 for weekly tickets; less for daily tickets.

Visiting sportswriters and newsmen received royal treatment. Star-Telegram publisher Amon G. Carter Sr. wined and dined media at his Shady Oaks Farm and on his cruiser at Eagle Mountain Lake. CBS broadcasters Jimmy Nolan and Harry Nash arrived to give a stroke-by-stroke description of the 45th U.S. Open to a nationwide radio audience. Famous 1913 Open champ Francis Ouimet oversaw the proceedings as a USGA official. Even the immortal Bobby Jones came for the festivities and commented on the largest U.S. Open practice round crowds he had ever seen.

ABOVE:
1941 U.S. Open Champion Craig Wood hoists the trophy.

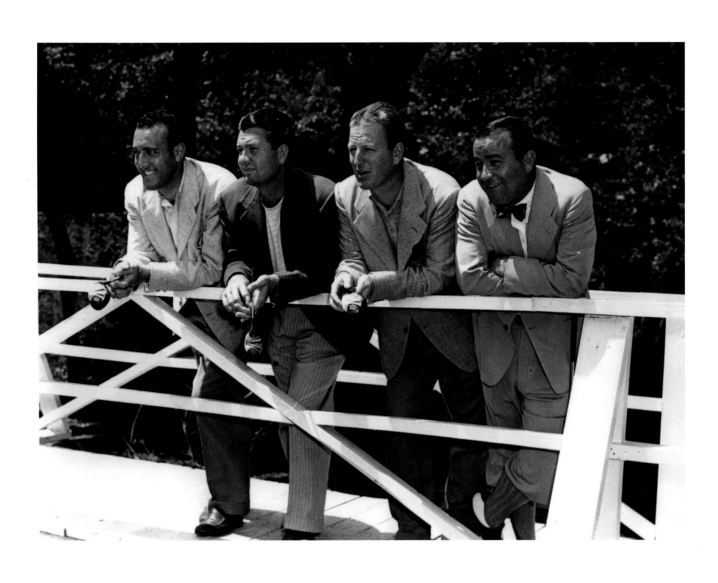

Official Score Card

Forty-Fifth Open Championship
of the United States Golf Association

Questions as to the Rules of Golf shall be referred to the Rules Committee

, 1941

HOLES	1	2	3	4	5	6	7	8	9	OUT	10	11	12	13	14	15	16	17	18	IN	TOTAL
YARDS	569	395	468	250	469	395	418	198	343	3505	403	593	400	192	455	447	207	406	427	3530	7035
PAR	5	4	4	3	4	4	4	3	4	35	4	5	4	3	4	4	3	4	4	35	70

Scorer's Signature

Competitor's Signature

TOP:
Top pros Vic Ghezzi, Jimmy Demaret, Craig Wood and Gene Sarazen pose at Colonial before the 1941 U.S. Open.
BOTTOM:
1941 U.S. Open official scorecard.

Marvin Leonard received able assistance from the ranks of the Colonial membership in seeing his U.S. Open dream come true. Volunteers Dr. Alden Coffey (General Chairman), E.M. Highfill and Harold Wilson (Ticket Sales), J.A. Gooch (Publicity and Press), W.L. Stewart (Tournament Program), Clarence Kraft (Gallery), Reuben Allbaugh (Tournament Director), Scott Teel (Scoring), J.M. Zachary (House and Grounds), and Johnny Ballard (Registrations) helped produce golf's greatest show. The budgeted committee expenses for the championship totaled $27,500, including a generous donation to the Fort Worth Golf Association from gate receipts.

Early attention that week focused on star Harold "Jug" McSpaden, who wowed the practice crowds Monday with a 66. Other early favorites were Fort Worth's own Ben Hogan and Byron Nelson, and boisterous Texan Jimmy Demaret. Big and popular Lawson Little was defending Open champion, and perpetual bridesmaid Craig Wood had finally broken through with a Masters victory earlier that year. Other former Open champions in the field included Gene Sarazen, Tommy Armour, Ralph Guldahl, Sam Parks Jr., Billy Burke, Olin Dutra, Johnny Goodman, Chick Evans and Tony Manero. All the players were quite impressed with the young Colonial course, and the treacherous new fifth hole received a great deal of buzz.

Here's how a UPI sports editor deliciously described the fifth hole just prior to the event, while nicknaming it 'Death Valley': "All week, survivors wet and weary have been straggling out of 'Death Valley' bearing horrible tales of the fate that awaits any man who ventures there armed only with driver, putter and irons," Harry Ferguson wrote. "Hole No. 5 combines the worst features of the Johnstown Flood, the forest primeval and the African trail that Stanley followed to find Livingstone. The only fair thing to do is to station Red Cross tents along the fairway, equipped with smelling salts, stretchers and life rafts to rescue players who hurl themselves into the Trinity River in despair.

ABOVE:
Spectators and players endure rain during the 1941 U.S. Open.

"The fairway is only about 35 yards wide in spots, and is as hard to hit from the tee as a mosquito in a dark bedroom," he continued. "Trees lie beyond the rough, ready to send slices and hooks bouncing in crazy directions. Along the right side of the fairway runs the Trinity River and along the left side is a swampy piece of land that will gobble any ball hit into it. Last evening a youngster killed a water moccasin on the bank, and for all anyone knows the Loch Ness monster may be swimming to and fro in the murky waters figuring on eating the first threesome that comes past tomorrow for breakfast."

Masters champ Wood of New York came to town with an unusual back injury. A few weeks prior, he dropped his razor while shaving one morning. As he stooped down to pick it up, he sneezed and painfully dislocated a vertebra in his back. Arriving for the tournament, he said, "I don't know if I can make it or not." He hadn't hit a shot in 10 days. Wrapped in a polo corset, though, he played.

Championship play began at 8:15 a.m. Thursday, June 5, with the first ball driven by Fort Worth's own Iverson Martin, an amateur who had qualified to compete with the big boys.

One hundred and sisxty three players joined the party. Former British Open and PGA champ Denny Shute led the first round with a sizzling 69. No one else broke par, and only two players managed a 70. Wood made a seven on the first hole but settled down from there.

The second round, however, was a different matter altogether. Play was suspended on two separate occasions as Fort Worth was hit with an honest-to-goodness Texas gully-washer, and lightning danced around the acreage. At one point during the storms, Wood, who was excited about neither the weather nor his back condition (he'd opened with a 73), threatened to withdraw, as several players, including Jimmy Demaret chose to do. But Wood's playing partner, Tommy Armour, talked him into staying around.

The rains created standing water on the fairways and puddles on the green. Byron Nelson recalled that playing the new fourth green was like 'putting on waves.' Ben Hogan remembered that the water rushing across the greens forced the players to use irons and try to "pitch" into the hole, since putting was useless. Meanwhile, a quagmire developed around the ninth green. Spectators were losing their footing and sliding down the slope. The Colonial grounds crew finally put out a combination of cottonseed hulls and manure to provide firm footing for spectators slip-sliding around the green. While the mixture served that purpose, it raised an aroma more familiar to the denizens of the stockyards on the city's north side.

At one point USGA officials Francis Ouimet (who won the Open as an amateur in 1913 by stunning the great Harry Vardon) and Joseph Dey left the clubhouse with a hand-cranked siren to signal a suspension of play. Players on the front side of the course, farthest from the clubhouse, didn't hear the alarm and continued to play. When Armour and Wood reached the 18th hole later, Armour spied Dey and shouted "Joe, you cost me $5. I bet you'd stop play." When told the siren had in fact sounded, Armour said he thought that noise was made by cars passing by on Rogers Road.

Despite the delays, most of the field completed their rounds and the leader board showed Wood, who shot a 71 after all, was tied for the top spot at 144 with Denny Shute, defending champ Little, and Clayton Heafner. Yet not even a downpour could dampen the enthusiasm Fort Worth area residents showed for championship-caliber golf. Tension and excitement ran high for the 36-hole Saturday finish.

A consistent ballstriker and a good putter, Wood won his fair share of pro tournaments, more than 20 altogether. But before 1941, fate always seemed to intervene whenever he neared a major championship. In 1933, Wood tied for the British Open title at St.Andrews but lost in a 36-hole playoff with Shute. (It was in that tournament that Wood unleashed one of the most massive shots in golf history: teeing off on the 530-yard fifth hole, Wood rocketed his ball into a fairway bunker 100 yards short of the green. That's a 430-yard drive.)

In 1935, Wood appeared to have sewn up the green jacket awarded to the Masters champion, only to fall victim to Gene Sarazen's double-eagle on the par-five 15th. Sarazen caught Wood in regulation play and whipped him by five strokes in an 18-hole playoff. Most golf fans remember Sarazen's shot. Few recall it was made at the expense of Craig Wood.

In 1934, Wood made it to the finals of the PGA's match-play format, but saw his title bid thwarted by Paul Runyan. Runyan, who had been one of Woods pupils at Winged Foot, turned the tables on his teacher with a 1-up win on the 38th hole. In 1938, Wood tied for the U.S. Open championship at Spring Mill C.C. near Philadelphia with Denny Shute and Byron Nelson. Wood looked to be a winner in the 18-hole playoff

until Nelson sank a birdie putt on the final hole to match Wood's 68. The next day, in a second 18-hole playoff, Nelson shaved Wood by four strokes.

In 1941, though, Craig Wood had his Cinderella season. The April Masters win was just the beginning. After Saturday's morning round at Colonial (the Open featured a 36-hole final day), Wood had moved two shots ahead of the nearest competitors, Shute and Runyan. As he approached the 18th hole of the final round, Wood was still two strokes ahead of the field. A crowd estimated at 10,000 waited to see the champ finish. His approach shot fell 30 feet right of the pin. Wood responded to the applause from the Texans ringing the 18th hole at Colonial with a warm wave, a broad smile and a tip of his hat.

He then calmly stroked the twisting sidehill putt into the hole for a birdie. The spectators erupted with cheers. The putt cinched the $1,000 first-place money for Wood, who finished

with a 284 total four-over-par. "I don't see how it would have been possible to have had a more popular champion," USGA President Howard Pierce told the crowd afterwards. Shute finished second, three strokes back, and won $800. Hogan and Johnny Bulla tied for third for $650 apiece. Only Hogan, whose 68-70 finish earned the tie for third, had a better final day than the new champion.

But the real winner that week was Colonial. Sportswriters had predicted the pros would "knock the brains" out of the 7,000-yard plus layout, the pride of Fort Worth. Yet despite repeated assaults by golf's best, only two players managed to record sub-par rounds in the entire tournament — Shute's opening 69 and Hogan's remarkable 68 in the third round. Pierce compared the "great triumvirate" of Amon Carter, Marvin Leonard and Alden Coffey to "Brutus, Caesar and Cassius" in producing "this great tournament."

ABOVE:
The great Bobby Jones shares a moment with golfer Sam Byrd and writer O.B. Keeler outside Colonial's clubhouse.

The two-time PGA Champion Runyan wrote a letter to the USGA after the event, saying "I thought Marvin Leonard's Colonial Club is the fairest and best test of golf of any course over which a National Open has been held."

The '41 Open was so popular with both players and fans that Colonial officials vowed to start a tournament of their own. Marvin Leonard began making plans to have the Colonial members host an annual event that would become part of the professional tour. It would be a very special tournament, too, by invitation only.

But six months to the day after Wood's victory at Colonial, the Japanese attacked Pearl Harbor and the United States was pulled into war. Craig Wood would become known as the "champion for the duration," as the U.S. Open Championship would not resume play until 1946. An annual Colonial golf tournament, too, would have to wait out the war.

1941

results

June 5-7

Rank	Player	1R	2R	3R	4R	Total	Money
1	Craig Wood	73	71	70	70	284	$1,000.00
2	Denny Shute	69	75	72	71	287	800.00
3T	Ben Hogan	74	77	68	70	289	650.00
3T	Johnny Bulla	75	71	72	71	289	650.00
5T	Herman Barron	75	71	74	71	291	412.50
5T	Paul Runyan	73	72	71	75	291	412.50
7T	E.J. "Dutch" Harrison	70	82	71	71	294	216.66
7T	Gene Sarazen*	74	73	72	75	294	216.66
7T	Harold McSpaden	71	75	74	74	294	216.66
10T	Ed Dudley	74	74	74	73	295	125.00
10T	Lloyd Mangrum	73	74	72	76	295	125.00
10T	Dick Metz	71	74	76	74	295	125.00
13T	Sam Snead	76	70	77	73	296	100.00
13T	Henry Ransom	72	74	75	75	296	100.00
13T	Harry Todd	72	77	76	71	296	--
13T	Horton Smith	73	75	73	75	296	100.00
17T	Lawson Little*	71	73	79	74	297	50.00
17T	Byron Nelson*	73	73	74	77	297	50.00
19	Victor Ghezzi	70	79	77	72	298	50.00
20	Gene Kunes	71	79	74	75	299	50.00
21T	Ralph Guldahl*	79	76	72	73	300	50.00
21T	Johnny Palmer	74	76	76	74	300	50.00
21T	Clayton Heafner	72	72	78	78	300	50.00
24	Jimmy Hines	75	74	76	76	301	50.00
25	Joseph Zarhardt	74	76	77	75	302	50.00
26T	Henry Picard	77	79	72	75	303	50.00
26T	Johnny Morris	72	73	81	77	303	50.00
26T	Herman Keiser	74	77	76	76	303	50.00
26T	Sam Byrd	76	78	75	74	303	50.00
30T	Jerry Gianferante	76	77	74	77	304	--
30T	Marvin Ward	76	77	75	76	304	--
30T	Jim Ferrier	77	71	81	75	304	50.00
33T	Toney Penna	75	77	76	77	305	
33T	Abe Espinosa	76	75	72	82	305	
33T	Jimmy Turnesa	74	80	77	74	305	
33T	Marvin Stahl	77	76	73	79	305	
33T	Sam Parks Jr.*	73	82	74	76	305	
38	Bill Kaiser	72	78	80	76	306	
39	Willie Klein	73	80	78	76	307	
40T	William Turnesa	75	77	75	81	308	
40T	Bunny Torpey	72	79	78	79	308	
42T	Felix Serafin	76	79	78	76	309	
42T	Jim Foulis	78	78	74	79	309	
42T	Mike Turnesa	77	79	75	78	309	
45T	Jack Ryan	71	82	80	77	310	
45T	Charles Farlow	79	77	77	77	310	
45T	Bob Hamilton	76	79	80	75	310	
45T	Henry Castillo	84	72	77	77	310	
49T	Pat Wilcox	80	75	79	78	312	
49T	Richard Chapman	76	80	76	80	312	
51	Raymond Gafford	76	78	82	77	313	
52	Al Watrous	79	75	81	79	314	
53	Bill Nary	77	76	83	79	315	
54	J. J. Jacobs III	74	77	82	83	316	
55	Verne Stewart	76	78	80	83	317	
56	Tom O'Connor	73	78	79	88	318	
57	Jock Hutchison Jr.	78	78	83	80	319	

Others:

	Billy Burke*	74	77	78	WD	
	Emerick Kocsis	78	78	81	WD	
	R. E. Barnes	80	76	81	NC	
	Fred Haas Jr.	78	76	83	WD	
	Otey Crisman	76	79	83	WD	
	Ray Mangrum	80	76	82	NC	
	Billy Bob Coffey	73	80		WD	
	Bruce Coltart	75	79		NC	
	Jack Munger	74	81		WD	
	George Fazio	77	79		NC	

DID NOT MAKE CUT

157   Chick Harbert, David Goldman, Johnny Goodman*, Steve Kovacs, Charles Penna, George Slingerland, Cliff Spencer, Stephen Warga Jr., Edward White

158   Sam Bernardi, Rut Coffey, Leonard Dodson, Mario Gonzalez, J.C. Hamilton Jr., Bill Jelliffe, Ted Kroll, Leo Mallory, W. A. Stackhouse, Jimmy Thomson

159   William Clark, Jerry Douglas, Lee Roy Garrett, Beard Mims, Iverson Martin, Buddy Pofeet, Sam Schneider, Wilfred Wehrle, Lew Worsham

160   Tommy Armour*, Joe Burch, John Burke, Gene Dahlbender, Andy Gaspar, Jim Milward, Don Schumacher, H.A. Van Sickle, Jack Winney, Roble Williams

161   Vincent Eldred, C. J. Gaddie, Andrew Gibson, Tony Manero*, Mike Pavella, George Picard

162   Johnny Farrell*, Henry Pabian, Bennie Toski, Leo Walper, Buck White

163   Ted Huge, Joe Bernolfo Jr., Frank Higgins, Leonard White

164   Charles Kocsis, Bill Souter, H. O. Young

165   Sal Di Buono, Tom Sockwell, Marshall Springer

166   James Black

167   Don Erickson, Lloyd Gullickson, Morgan Hampton

168   Chick Evans*

169   Gene Battistoni

172   Don Malarkey, Lloyd Sparrow

173   Ralph Arnold

190   Dr. Walter Ratto

Withdrew after 18 holes:

75   Jimmy Demaret (NC)

77   Olin Dutra* (NC), Bob MacDonald (NC), Bill Rhodes, Jack Tinnin

78   Robert Goldwater

79   Jack Stoddard

80   Bob Byrnes (NC), Johnny Revolta (NC), Jack Stammer (DQ), Tyrrell Garth Jr. (NC)

81   Fred Haas Sr. (NC), Eddie Held, Labron Harris (NC), Charles Lacey

82   Leland Gibson, Brad Rang, Morgan Baker

83   George Howard

84   John Manion, R.V. Van Kleeck

86   Lorin Shook

Withdrew after 9 holes:

B.Y. Chamberlain, Zell Eaton, Willie Low, Charles Shelden

Names in italics indicate amateurs.
NC - No card
WD - Withdrew
*indicates former U.S. Open champion

A WALL OF CHAMPIONS

Like any good opening hole, the first at Colonial is a feast for the eyes. A grove of trees featuring a century-old pecan down the right side serves as an immediate hint as to where not to hit the ball. There is a large expanse of sand along the outside corner of the dogleg, clearly within view and, if the tee shot is slightly pulled, within range.

In between, there is all that carefully manicured grass, luring the player out onto the grounds where a few hours of sublime torture awaits.

There is, however, something other than the landscape to see while on Colonial's first tee -- a place where Ben Hogan stood. Where Byron Nelson put a peg in the ground, as did Sam Snead and Julius Boros and Billy Casper and so many other greats of the game, then and now.

ABOVE:
Colonial's famous Wall of Champions on the first tee.
FACING PAGE:
Tom Watson celebrates his Colonial victory in 1998.

Ben Hogan tees off #1 in 1952. Note Marvin Leonard and young daughter Madelon seated in the left background looking on.

Alongside the tee box is a 20-foot long wall and on its surface is a listing of the tournament's winners in chronological order. It serves as both a history lesson and a constant memo to the newest generation that golf is, first and foremost, about tradition.

A few weeks before he won the U.S. Open for the first time, Lee Trevino made his initial appearance at Colonial. "What a thrill it was to be invited," Trevino remembers. "For a local guy, getting to play at Colonial was like getting into the Masters. And when I won there (in 1976), I knew my name was going on that Wall."

Among all the noteworthy tournaments in American golf, only the Masters has been played longer on the same piece of ground than has the event that takes place annually at Colonial

Country Club. Colonial, therefore, has a lengthy and varied list of winners, their names inscribed on what is known officially as the "Wall of Champions". In white letters and numerals on black granite, the champions and their final scores beckon the curious so that they are in danger of committing an act of slow play before they strike their very first shot.

There is Hogan's name, found on the wall in five locations covering a 13-year span during which the Fort Worth legend performed some of golf's most historic feats. Snead's name is there, the man who could hit any shot from any spot. The names of Boros and Casper are to be seen twice each. They also combined for four U.S. Open titles, a fact that touches on one of Colonial's central themes during what, with the passage of time, must be looked upon as the tournament's formative years.

Names cherished in the sport are scattered throughout. Arnold Palmer came up short in three U.S. Open playoffs, but he won a playoff at Colonial. Gene Littler, owner of one of the sport's most seemingly effortless swings, and Trevino, whose swing was not as attractive but every bit as effective, have their spots on the Wall.

Ben Crenshaw won the tournament on two occasions --13 years apart. Eleven years separated two wins by Corey Pavin, and Nick Price won his second title eight years after capturing his first. Phil Mickelson's name is there, as are those of Lanny Wadkins, Tom Weiskopf, Cary Middlecoff, Fuzzy Zoeller, Tommy Bolt, Tom Lehman, Dave Stockton, Roberto de Vicenzo, Al Geiberger and Ian Baker-Finch -- major champions all.

And then there are Jack Nicklaus and Tom Watson, whose landmark careers on the regular tour were winding down when they walked off Colonial's 18th green as a champion once more. It was almost as if they looked around to see if there was any unfinished business and realized they had not won at Colonial. So they went out and did it.

Nicklaus won 72 times on the PGA Tour and only two of those victories came after the one at Colonial in 1982. The last of Watson's 39 tour triumphs was recorded at Colonial in 1998. He was 48 at the time and during Colonial's first 60 years was the event's oldest champion.

"Colonial Country Club reflects on the history of American golf in the same way as Augusta National has," Watson said. "After so many attempts at winning the Colonial (21 such tries in the span of 24 years), my victory was made that much sweeter."

TOP:
Champions Ben Crenshaw and Lee Trevino at the annual Champions Dinner.
MIDDLE:
1965 champion Bruce Crampton accepts Leonard Trophy from Colonial President Ralph McCann.
BOTTOM:
1962 champion Arnold Palmer tries to coax a putt into the hole on #18.

ABOVE:
1982 champion Jack Nicklaus sinks a birdie putt on #16 to cement his win on Sunday.

For those familiar with golfing lore, the nationally recognized Colonial course usually conjures up an instant image. It certainly does among those who have won there. "First of all," said Bolt, "you think about Ben Hogan. That's No. 1."

"Colonial is special in my heart because it's Hogan's Alley," is the way Doug Sanders put it. "Ben had a killing instinct to win. That was his only motivation."

"The Colonial is one of the important tournaments on the tour for many reasons," according to Palmer. "One, it's longevity. Two, its historical place in the annals of the PGA Tour. And the fact that it was, in effect, the birthplace of the Hogan era."

Trevino, like all the Colonial champions, fully recognizes the link the tournament has with its five-time winner. "Golfers come and they go," he said. "Generations come and they go. And those from the younger generations tend to forget about the older generations. But if you bring up the word 'Colonial,' everybody thinks of Hogan."

As he was in the process of challenging for, and eventually winning, his first tournament in the United States, Sergio

Garcia displayed a swing that drew comparisons to that of Hogan. "To be able to win at his course, where he played almost his whole life, it's something special and it makes me feel prouder," Garcia said after donning the tartan jacket that goes to the Colonial winner.

Those who were fortunate enough to have associated with Hogan have a wealth of stories. But two of the best from Colonial winners are told by Bolt and Stockton.

Bolt became known as one of the best ball strikers of his era. And he was an established player when he arrived in Fort Worth for the 1955 tournament. But he was suffering from a problem that was limiting his opportunity for greatness. He was fighting a bad hook.

"When I got to Colonial that year I came to Ben and asked him to get me out of the hook," Bolt said. "He was the greatest player that ever lived in my book and I played with all of them."

Hogan worked with Bolt for a few days that week and the results were like magic. "You know Ben," Bolt said. "He would tell you once and if you didn't listen he wouldn't tell you again.

But later that week I saw him hiding over in the bushes watching me to make sure I had got it right.

"I had won tournaments before, but I don't know how I won them," he added. "Working with Ben changed my whole golfing career. It made me feel like a champion." Two weeks later, Bolt finished third at the U.S. Open, where Jack Fleck defeated Hogan in a playoff. Three years later, Bolt won at Colonial -- hanging on for the victory when Hogan, who was trailing by just one, duck hooked his tee shot on the final hole on his way to a double bogey. "I loved Ben," Bolt said. "But I was sure glad to see him hook that ball."

Stockton was issued an invitation in 1967 by a vote of the tournament's champions. He fulfilled their expectations by breaking the 36-hole record with rounds of 65-66. Sitting at his locker after the second round, Stockton suddenly realized Hogan was walking toward him. But Hogan strolled right by without saying a word.

Stockton stumbled to a 74 in the third round and found himself tied for the lead with Weiskopf. Following that round, Stockton again was sitting in front his locker when he heard a

voice nearby. "It was Hogan," Stockton said. "I heard him asking somebody where Mr. Stockton's locker was. And around the corner he came."

Stockton said Hogan shook his hand and then said, "I know you expected me to say something to you last night, but you didn't need anything from me. You've got your bad round out of the way and you're playing better than anybody here."

Stockton was stunned. Hogan was only three shots back, in the hunt for his sixth Colonial title. "It just blew me away," Stockton said.

The next day Weiskopf shot himself out of the tournament and Stockton won by two strokes over Charles Coody. At the age of 54, and 21 years after he won the inaugural Colonial, Hogan finished tied for third, three shots back.

Colonial's reputation as a stern test grew during the 1960s when it became known as the perfect tune-up for the U.S. Open. "It darned well played as a championship," Bolt said. As Hogan was winning at Colonial in 1946, 1947, 1952 and

ABOVE LEFT:
Sergio Garcia made the 2001 Colonial championship his first victory in America.
ABOVE RIGHT:
1961 champion Doug Sanders.

1953, he was also winning the U.S. Open in 1948, 1950, 1951 and 1953.

Middlecoff, a winner in Fort Worth in 1951, also captured the Open in 1949 and 1956. Dick Mayer finished second at Colonial to De Vicenzo in 1957 and then, a few weeks later, defeated Middlecoff in a playoff to win the Open.

Bolt was both the Colonial and Open champion in 1958 and Boros captured both tournaments in 1963. Littler finished second at Colonial in 1960 and fourth in 1961 and then won the Open in 1961. He finally won at Colonial 10 years later.

In 1962, Palmer defeated Johnny Pott in an 18-hole playoff. Finishing alone in fourth that year was a fellow who had just started his professional career. Jack Nicklaus was his name and two weeks later he defeated Palmer in a playoff to win the Open -- the first of his 18 major titles. "I apply what I do here to the U.S. Open," Nicklaus said at Colonial two years later. "The

driving is similar. You have to use the same shots here as at the Open."

Time has moved along, but the players who competed during that era shared a common experience with those who have appeared at Colonial in the 21st century. All have been recipients of hospitality of the first order. It is something the tournament's champions invariably mention. "Colonial's place in history is secure," said 1974 champion Rod Curl, "because of the people at the club and how they treat you."

"It's class," said Sanders. "Everything at Colonial is done first class. Just a bunch of congenial people who don't try to call attention to what they are doing. You go to some tournaments and everybody is a prima donna. But not at Colonial."

Littler first came to Colonial just eight years after the tournament was founded and played in the event 29 times. "It was a lot of fun to go to Fort Worth and be treated like they

treated you," he said. "Most tournaments were not into that. The people were great. It was one of the first clubs I remember that served food inside the clubhouse just for the players. That was something we all noticed."

Kenny Perry, whose career climbed to world class status after his first Colonial victory in 2003, is a walking testimonial for the manner in which players are treated at the club. "I love the history here," he said. "I love the people who run this tournament. I've always told them that I feel like I'm home. I feel like when I come to Colonial that I'm in my backyard.

"They treat the players great," he continued. "I've had members of the tournament staff come up to me and hug me and tell me how proud they are to have me here. They have a passion for the tournament and they have a passion for the people who play in it."

Nicklaus recorded five top 10 finishes in nine appearances through 1975, but then did not play at Colonial for seven years, when it conflicted with his own event. When he finally returned, he was the only player in the field not to have an over-par score and he won by three shots over Andy North.

"It was nice to be welcomed back so enthusiastically after my long absence," Nicklaus wrote to tournament chairman Rodney Johnston. "I hope you will convey my thanks to all the people involved, not only for their hard work, but also for their warm hospitality."

The fact that the same golf course has hosted a PGA Tour event for such a long period of time speaks wonders to Colonial's quality. And even though the ball goes much farther than it did in days gone by and even though the scores are lower, the layout still draws songs of praise.

"Colonial was always held in high regard by everyone who ever played it and was lucky enough to have won it," said Crenshaw, who as much as anyone of his generation has studied the history of the game and the historic courses on which it is played.

"One thing I hope the players of today will do is appreciate Colonial for what it has been," he continued. "It is a different test of golf. It is more of an Eastern sort of conservative depiction of architecture. By that, I mean it is a placement course. Length certainly has its due, but the ball has to be strategically placed. It is a wonderful course."

Littler also chimed in on that subject. "I remember how challenging the course was," he said. "I was brought up playing the kind of golf where you had to get to point 'A' before you got to point 'B.' Length is nice. But accuracy was all important. That's the way I played and that's the kind of golf course that I liked to play. That was absolutely true about Colonial, especially off the tee. You had to have good iron play, but you really had to hit your driver."

A study of the history book reveals what should be considered the course's supreme quality. Time and again, the players who

ABOVE:
Colonial's Ben Hogan statue.
FACING PAGE:
Ben Hogan's wins in the Majors are honored in this case in the Hogan Room.

have won at Colonial Country Club -- whether they were bound for the Hall of Fame or not -- were at the very peak of their careers when they did so.

Jim Colbert, for instance, had one year on the tour in which he won twice. That was in 1983 and one of those victories came at Colonial. His 15th place finish on the money list that year was the best of his career. Sanders counted his Colonial victory as one of five triumphs in 1961. He was third in earnings for his best season.

Casper led the tour in money winnings in 1968 and won six times -- the third of which came at Colonial. Jerry Heard's best year on the tour was 1972, when he finished fifth on the money list and won twice -- in Florida and Fort Worth. Almost half of Palmer's 62 victories came in a four-year stretch beginning in 1960 and his Colonial win was right in the midst of all that.

Weiskopf was a five-time winner the year he captured the Colonial title (1973). He won more money that year than in any other. Bruce Crampton had what was, up to that point, his career year in 1965. Colonial was one of three victories that season. Fulton Allem cracked the top 10 in earnings just once and that came in 1993, when he bested Greg Norman by a single shot at Colonial.

The second best year Peter Jacobsen had on tour came when he won twice in 1984 and was 10th on the money list. He defeated Payne Stewart in a playoff at Colonial that year with Watson, Tom Kite, Gil Morgan, Crenshaw and Raymond Floyd -- a Who's Who of Golf -- being among the top 10.

Homero Blancas had four career victories, one of them coming at Colonial during what was his best season on the circuit -- 1970. Dan Pohl, en route to finishing fifth on the money list and earning a spot on the Ryder Cup team, won at Colonial in 1986. It was easily his best year.

"You can't go in there with your 'B' game," Pohl said. "The course doesn't just wear you out. You don't go around it and say it is super demanding. But it calls for such a variety of golf shots. It's not just one or two things. You have to be on top of all aspects of your game. The golf course speaks for itself."

And so does the tournament. Those who have taken part, and especially those who have won, are certainly aware that Colonial is unique in its longevity, and they are unanimous in their hope that the tradition does nothing but continue.

ABOVE:
Ben Hogan's five Leonard Trophy replicas, on display in Colonial's Hogan Room.
FACING PAGE:
Two-time champion Kenny Perry.

"Colonial will always hold its own," said Mike Souchak, who edged Bolt by a shot in 1956, one year after Hogan cured Bolt of his hook. A half century later, the appreciation for the course, for the tournament and for those who watch over it has only grown.

"I remember playing my rookie year, looking at those names and thinking, 'every good player that has ever played golf has run through this place,'" said 2004 champion Steve Flesch. "Having my name on the Wall with that group of great champions is unbelievable."

And from The King comes a fitting look to the future. "It's wonderful that the tournament has remained vibrant through 60 years to celebrate an anniversary with its history and traditions intact," said Palmer, who in 1982, four months shy of his 53rd birthday, shot a 68 in the opening round of what was his final competitive appearance at the tournament. "I hope that will continue for years to come and enhance the memories of the Colonial."

The list of Colonial memories, forged by some of the game's most famous and fascinating characters, has grown to sizeable proportions and many of those memories are preserved so that they can easily be recalled.

All it takes is a stroll past the first tee.

EARLY COLONIAL

DAN JENKINS REMEMBERS

A nyone who didn't know the old Colonial golf course of 50 or 60 years ago missed spending some quality time at a truly fascinating zoo.

I say this in the most flattering sense. I say it because I miss the original layout that held a U. S. Open in 1941, and starting in 1946 ushered in an exclusive PGA Tour event that was once known as the "Masters of the Southwest" -- and lived up to it.

The Colonial course in those days was a narrow, dark, swampy, shaggy, suffocating, unforgiving river-bottom layout that made you think there couldn't be a tougher test for human-being type golfers anywhere.

ABOVE:
Colonial's front entrance in the 1940s.
FACING PAGE:
Tee shots on the original par 3 hole #13 traversed the meandering Trinity River.

Every U.S. Open before '41 had been held at a striped-tie, blueblazer, trust-fund joint. A Merion, Oakland Hills, Oakmont, or Baltusrol, to list a few. Courses that are about as close to a river-bottom as the 10th floor of a Wall Street brokerage house.

But Fort Worth's golf-loving Marvin Leonard, who incidentally may have been the nicest rich guy I ever knew, sought the help of two other nice gents, Amon Carter Sr. and Dr. Alden Coffey, and together the three of them Texas-charmed and money-whipped the U. S. Open to Cowtown.

Mr. Leonard had also brought the first bent grass greens to Colonial and the whole Southwest, and he'd put Ben Hogan on the Tour to stay. Then after the '41 Open and World War 11, the Big Deuce, he helped originate the Colonial National Invitation, and later on he would build Shady Oaks Country Club.

I don't know how any one person could have done more for golf in Fort Worth than Marvin Leonard, although somewhere along the way he might have given some thought to curing my hook.

The manicured, beautified, scrubbed-up Colonial of today is still a strong par-70 course for humans -- best in Texas -- but it's nothing like the punishing track of yesteryear, which was a strong "280" golf course, as they say (meaning 280 was the target score for 72 holes).

Ben Hogan won five Colonials and never shot better than 279, and once won with 282 and won again with 285. What did Kenny Perry shoot in 2003 and 2005? Something like 261, right? So, do you want to let Kenny Perry play Ben Hogan for your own money?

Gone are the small greens that I swear were about half the size they are now. Greens that used to sit down low instead of wearing push-up bras. And they were greens guarded by clusters of tall, overhanging trees that are also gone now -- victims of storms, wind, age, meddlesome architects, and the occasional do-good committee.

Also gone are the tight fairways that were bordered by matted rough and shadowy rows of trees. Such things made a straight tee ball far more important than length. And by the way, length had to come from talent and timing on the old lush Bermuda fairways that rarely allowed more than six feet of roll, unlike today, when the PGA Tour cuts them down to the length of a hardwood floor so its heroes can get a 95-yard roll on every hole and possibly shoot a 62 or 63.

Gone, too, are the damp, deep ditches that encroached on several fairways, making some of them even narrower. Gone are the ditches along with numerous trees that stood guard over the greens on holes like No. 5, No. 7, and No. 15. You had to go underneath them with a bump-and-run kind of thing unless your drive was center-cut perfect.

But let's take a hole-by-hole journey from the championship tees and see what one man's memory can come up with in regard to then and now:

ABOVE:
The 17th hole was, and is, a demanding short par four, though the "Big Annie" tree is now gone.

HOLE BY HOLE

NO. 1, PAR-5, 563 YARDS

Either part of my brain is missing or another tree is missing. A big one in the grove on the right. I vividly recall how out-of-bounds on the right used to be a big concern. I think the tee might have been more forward and the green sat back more. The hole played 15 yards longer in the '40s and '50s, but it was still the best chance for a birdie. Still is.

NO. 2, PAR-4, 387 YARDS

A bland design. More calm before the storm. Most players think of it as another opportunity for a birdie. It played 10 yards longer for the '41 Open. High rough forced a more acute dogleg.

NO. 3, PAR-4, 467 YARDS

Same length as in the old days but there was ugly rough on the right, and it took Sam Snead's best drive to clear the bunker on the left, which was once dotted with patches of ornery Pampas grass. There was great excitement on that day in the early '50s when George Bayer played in the Colonial for the first time and hit the third green with a driver and 7-iron. Eye popping. Forehead smoting. Of course, George was 6-5, weighed 240, and his driver looked like one of the big guns on the USS Missouri.

ABOVE:
The 7th hole navigated a gauntlet of trees.

NO. 4, PAR-3, 252 YARDS

Second peg in the "Horrible Horseshoe," the third, fourth, and fifth holes, toughest stretch on the course, the name that a young golf writer for the now-extinct Fort Worth Press -- well, me -- came up with in a moment of rare poetic brilliance. Kind of a lame effort to give Colonial its own "Amen Corner," is what it was. The hole played 30 yards shorter for the '41 Open, and the smaller green sat more to the right, closer to the fence.

NO. 5, PAR-4, 472 YARDS

Once upon a time, this hole was as tough and dangerous as any on the planet. From the tee, you couldn't go right -- there was a river over there. But you also couldn't go left -- there was a deep watery ditch over there. Lost ball. Unplayable. All sorts of adventures awaited you. Then even if you'd hit a perfect drive into the fairway, long and well-positioned, you couldn't get to the green in the air. A huge tree on the left of the green prevented it. For those who don't know the history, Marvin Leonard bought the pecan tree infested property on which to build the new fourth and fifth holes less than a year before the '41 Open. Somehow, he got them ready. The original fourth and fifth holes were short and weak and were located where you now find the practice area. The winner of the '41 Open, Craig Wood, cautiously bogied the fifth in all four rounds, making sure he didn't suffer a worse fate on a hole that's earned its reputation as an evil legend.

NO. 6, PAR-4, 394 YARDS

The only hole at Colonial with absolutely no character. No drama, unmemorable. But every great layout has one of these holes somewhere, except, of course, Pine Valley.

The original eighth hole, with prevailing winds pushing balls toward the Trinity River, may have been Colonial's toughest par three.

NO. 7, PAR-4, 432 YARDS

Narrow fairway and trees on both sides always suggested a layup tee ball; demanded some kind of run-up shot in the old days when the trees leaned over and darkened the green. A creek bed meandered along the left side, but back when I thought I could play golf I was usually in the trees on the right. Originally, it was 25 yards shorter. Great hole.

NO. 8, PAR-3, 194 YARDS

The yardage has always been about the same. Too bad you can't say the same about the river. In the early years it didn't take much of a fade or a push to land in the water -- the Trinity encroached all the way to the green. Left of the green was down a severe slope. A mere few feet right of the green was hard pan or weeds. Wonderful hole, like all of the par-threes. Ben, as in Hogan, back in the 50s, once told me that the often overlooked strength of Colonial was in the four par-three holes.

NO. 9, PAR-4, 408 YARDS

This hole -- played 65 yards shorter for the '41 Open and all of the early Colonials, and it was a much more unique hole back then. A great short hole. Drive and pitch. There was the chance for a birdie after you'd gone through that rugged stretch of the third through the eighth, but you had to deal with the water. When the green was smaller and sloped more toward the water and there was no rock wall, a shot with too much backspin could slowly crawl through the fringe and mud and down into the pond. Fun, though. The only hole on the course where most of us could generate any backspin. Couldn't get that done at Worth Hills.

NO. 10, PAR-4, 407 YARDS

Pretty much the same hole it's always been. Pinpoint the tee shot or you have to deal with the trees on both sides in order to reach the green. A friend calls it "dead man's hole -- I have to press on eleven." If the Club ever gets around to naming the holes, this one should be "Annika." In honor of her appearance and the splendid opening drive she somehow managed here, going with her 4-wood, when the whole world was watching.

NO. 11, PAR-5, 611 YARDS

Back when the hole played at 593 yards, 20 yards shorter, it was still longer because of the plush fairways. Long ago when I was privileged to be in a recreational game with Hogan and two fine golfing members, Carl Vandervoort and Reub Berry, we all had our minds boggled when Ben hit this green in two with a driver, brassie. Such a thing seldom happened. But nowadays, with the fairways firmed up for the tournament, and technology kicked in, well just about anyone can reach it in two. Tragic, is what I think about it.

NO. 12, PAR-4, 417 YARDS

Seems like the river on the right beyond the trees was more in play in days gone by, but this was only if you had a tendency to hit a falling-down slice. The hole continues to stand out in the design because it's the only one on the course that seriously invites a hook off the tee.

NO. 13, PAR-3, 171 YARDS

This was a much more sinister hole in the old days. It was 20 yards longer, for one thing, certainly uglier and scarier in what you had to carry to reach the green -- like a river and a DMZ of waste -- and anything landing 10 yards short of the green was a cinch to dribble back into the Trinity. Not to mention out of bounds on the right. A heroic par three hole.

NO. 14, PAR-4, 448 YARDS

For some reason, nobody remembers this but me; but in the '41 Open and for the first few Colonials, players would hit their drives on 14 before going to the 13th green to deal with their putts. It was a speed up play thing. Meanwhile, the 14th has never been anything but long. Innocent and long.

NO. 15, PAR-4, 428 YARDS

Another friend, Dr. Donald Matheson, as good a golfer as ever stopped a nose bleed, will argue that this was once the hardest hole on the course. I tend to agree. When there was a mass of trees up near the tee on the left, and with the mass of trees on the right down the fairway, and with bunkers and rough on the left, it was impossible to get the drive in the fairway unless you could hit a hook-fade. Then there was the smallest green on the course with the creek very much in play on the left side of it. Apart from all that, the hole used to be 25 yards longer.

NO. 16, PAR-3, 188 YARDS

Shorter than it once was, prettier and cleaner than it once was, and certainly easier than it once was. But I miss the caddies hanging out and chipping in the dirt on the side of the hill to the right, between the hole and where the tennis courts were first located.

NO. 17, PAR-4, 382 YARDS

Big Annie. Both a lovable and cussable tree down there on the right, just this side of what was once a rippling creek. Big Annie was lost in the thunderstorm of '86 when it was struck by lightning. The green used to sit further back and the hole played 25 yards longer for the '41 Open, but it still called for a layup tee shot.

NO. 18, PAR-4, 433 YARDS

Primarily because the tiny, left-sloping green has been enlarged and reshaped and the fairways and technology provide more distance today, this finishing hole was once more treacherous, even though Craig Wood birdied it to complete his U. S. Open victory, and Ben Hogan stiffed it and birdied it on his way to winning the first Colonial in '46. I'm talking about treacherous for normal people. In the bygone days if you landed your second shot anywhere left of the middle of the green, it was guaranteed to trickle down into the water.

Actually, I have to go back to George Bayer again to recall the greatest shot I ever saw hit on No. 18. George skied his drive on the tee, but the ball cleared the creek and sat in the fairway at the top of the hill. That's where George smashed a 4-wood that must have traveled well over 300 yards in the air and came down on top of the clubhouse and settled in a roof gutter. From where he was given a free drop in back of the green. It remains the longest 4-wood I've ever seen hit, and it's still the silliest free drop I've ever witnessed.

Only at old Colonial.

REMEMBERING MARVIN

A DAUGHTER REFLECTS

"**G**od must have had fun creating Daddy," mused Martha (Marty) Leonard in Colonial Country Club's living room, which features a portrait of club founder John Marvin Leonard above the fireplace and a bronze sculpture of the golf pioneer by the main staircase. Approaching the 60th staging of Colonial's enduring PGA Tour event, and the club's 70th birthday, an adoring daughter reminisced about her father, the man who started it all.

"I'm sure God enjoys making all his creations, but he definitely had a unique individual in mind when he made my father," she said. "Certainly, God blessed Daddy with a rare quality, that of vision. Not only did Daddy have vision, but he possessed the ability, determination and perseverance to make his visions become realities. Not many people are able to do that."

Such was the case with Leonard Bros., the downtown department store Marvin opened in 1918 with brother Obie, and transformed during the next half-century or so into a Texas landmark. Such was the case as well with Colonial Country Club, which Leonard

49

ABOVE:
Marvin Leonard with his namesake permanent trophy, awarded to the annual PGA Tour event's champion.

Passion was at the core of Marvin Leonard's existence, which spanned from February 10, 1895 (he was born in the East Texas town of Linden), to August 26, 1970, when he passed away at All Saints Hospital in Fort Worth.

He was passionate about his family -- his wife, Mary, and four daughters (Mary Elinor, Miranda, Martha, Madelon). He was passionate about Leonard Bros., which adhered to the principle of offering customers the best value at the lowest possible price.

He was also passionate about Fort Worth. So much that he worked feverishly to showcase the city by bringing to town in 1941 a major American sporting event -- golf's United States Open Championship. So much that two decades later, Leonard sought to forestall racial tensions in Fort Worth, and stave off the potential for demonstrations or riots, by striking down lingering vestiges of the Jim Crow era at his retail store.

Leonard possessed a generous, giving nature. Through Leonard Bros., as well as on a personal level, he contributed to community projects, education, health care, and the arts. Marvin and Mary Leonard were major supporters of their church, the Lena Pope Home, and Fort Worth Little Theater, among many others.

"Daddy was a quiet giver," Marty Leonard recalled. "He was always helping people in some way, whether it happened to be with paying bills, or with food programs at local schools, providing college funds, or helping out in a personal crisis. To this day, people occasionally come up to me and say, `Let me tell you what your father did for me, something you probably never knew anything about.' There have been so many stories through the years, but that's the way he was. Everybody loved him, and that was because Daddy loved people. He showed his love for them by the things he did, and by all the people he helped through the years."

established in 1936 on Trinity River bottomland near the Texas Christian University campus.

"Colonial is a prime example of his ability to turn visions into realities," Marty Leonard reflected. "Daddy took raw farmland and created what is recognized as one of the outstanding golf courses in the world. He didn't begin playing golf until he was in his thirties, after his doctor recommended regular exercise outdoors. Once Daddy discovered this challenging, magnetic, and often frustrating game, he was inspired to create."

Create he did. "First Daddy built Colonial, then years later he created a couple of other clubs in the area (Shady Oaks, Starr Hollow). He built these clubs primarily for the pleasure and enjoyment of others who shared his passion for the game of golf. I know how proud he would be of all the Colonial members who have carried on with his vision and who have enhanced his dream."

The entire Leonard clan: L-R Madelon, Mary Elinor, Mary, Miranda, Marvin and Marty.

In the 1930s, Marvin Leonard supplied some sorely needed cash to a struggling Fort Worth golf pro whose path to the top echelon was stymied by two obstacles: empty pockets and snap hooks.

Ben Hogan would never forget Marvin Leonard's generosity (Hogan later offered to repay the several hundred dollars Leonard had advanced; the merchant graciously refused). The two became steadfast friends, even business partners. When Hogan tamed his tee shots and went on to enjoy a celebrated career that became the stuff of golf lore, no one was more pleased than his early backer.

Marvin Leonard was down-to-earth, matter-of-fact and as genuine as cow leather. Marty Leonard describes him as analytical, detail-oriented, understated, determined and decisive. In short, he was an uncommon man with a common touch.

"Daddy had the ability to relate to people," she said. "Not just some people, but all people, regardless of their station in life. He was equally comfortable with Ben Hogan, the President of the United States, employees at his store or the waiters who served him. I believe people skills were Daddy's greatest God-given asset."

Marty Leonard was born in 1936, the same year her father swung open the doors to Colonial and welcomed in friends, neighbors and business associates, along with their families.

She was four-years-old when her father spearheaded the campaign to bring the U.S. Open to Fort Worth, seven when he awakened her in the middle of night and took her with him to inspect damages at a half-razed Colonial clubhouse. (Undismayed, Marvin Leonard promptly rebuilt, tapping his vast network of connections to secure the necessary raw materials.)

ABOVE:
Leonard Bros. Department Store was a busy place in downtown Fort Worth.

She was ten when her father and his colleagues created their own blue-chip event -- the Colonial National Invitation Tournament, or, familiarly, the NIT. She was thirteen when the great flood of 1949 engulfed the entire property, leaving maintenance workers clinging to the limbs of towering cottonwoods, praying for rescuers to arrive.

Marty Leonard possesses a deep pool of memories from the club's formative years. She pulled the levers on the slot machines, slid down the banister of the spiral staircase, wolfed down pieces of chicken her father grilled at after-church picnics that took place between the second and third holes. She annually entertained ideas about finding the "Golden Egg" during Colonial's Easter Egg Hunt on the front lawn. (Alas, she never did.)

Among Marvin Leonard's four children, Marty had the most interest in golf. She became an ardent follower of Hogan, keeping a scrapbook filled with press clippings and photographs. She pressed against the gallery ropes each May as Hogan turned the NIT into a virtual annuity, winning the trophy named after her father four times between 1946 and 1953.

"The story goes that Daddy said that if Hogan won the Leonard trophy for a fifth time, he would let him keep it," Marty noted. "Of course, Ben finally did get that fifth win, in a playoff with Fred Hawkins in 1959, but he declined to take Daddy up on his offer."

The Hawk clipped Hawkins 69-73 in the 18-hole Monday playoff and no one in the gallery pulled harder for Hogan than a certain Southern Methodist University senior who skipped classes and drove over from Dallas to spectate. By then a scratch golfer, Marty Leonard would win the Colonial Ladies' Club Championship that same year.

Schooled by professionals A.G. "Mitch" Mitchell at Rivercrest, Alwyn McCombs at Colonial, and Mel Smith, an

instructor in California (the Leonards spent many summers during Marty's teenage years in Santa Barbara), Leonard developed a serious game. Among her accomplishments were a victory in the California junior girls and becoming a finalist at the Women's Southern Amateur.

On three separate occasions Leonard reached the finals of the Texas Women's Amateur, only to finish runner-up to Mary Ann Rathmell. One of those tournaments took place at Colonial Country Club. "Can you imagine what that was like to have the tournament played here, on the course my Daddy built?" she said. "That was something special for me and for our family."

Marvin Leonard always supported Marty's athletic endeavors -- be they golf, tennis, or football. "I played football in elementary school, the only girl on the team at North Hi Mount," she recalled. "Our games were on Saturday mornings, and on his way down to the Store, Daddy would stop by and watch me play. He loved to tell the story about being at a game

and hearing a boy on the opposing team yell out `hit her. And hit her hard.' He thought that was hilarious. I guess it meant that I was holding my own."

In 1969, Marty Leonard accepted an invitation from United States Golf Association Executive Director Joseph Dey to serve on the USGA's Women's Committee. Leonard's 18-year tenure culminated with her chairing the committee in 1986-87. By then, thanks to the efforts of many Colonial members, especially Paul Cato Jr., the club had been awarded the 1991 U.S. Women's Open.

Under the hot skies of a Texas summer, a half-century after her father brought the U.S. Open to Colonial, Marty Leonard watched rising star Meg Mallon out-duel Pat Bradley to win her second major championship within three weeks.

Like father, like daughter. The Leonards, Colonial and national golf championships had come full circle.

OFFICIAL
SOUVENIR PROGRAM
PRICE 50 CENTS

WEAR YOUR TAG, WHERE IT CAN BE SEEN!

Please

This is the players competition. Treat them as you would like to be treated if you were a player.
Treat the course as if it were your own.
Be silent and motionless when a player takes his stance and throughout his stroke.
Give the player plenty of room. The bigger the are, the more people can see.
PHOTOGRAPHY IS PROHIBITED UNTIL AFTER A PLAYER COMPLETELY FINISHES A STROKE. THIS IS VERY IMPORTANT FOR FAIR PLAY. IT IS PREFERABLE THAT AMATEURS ENTIRELY REFRAIN FROM PHOTOGRAPHY.

PAIRINGS AND STARTING TIME
SATURDAY, MAY 18TH, 1946

		Caddy No.		Caddy No.		Caddy No.
	*Royal Hogan	30			*Wilford Wehrle	29
A. M.	*Reynolds Smith	21	Charles Akey	31		
11:30	*Bob Cochran	32	Fred Haas, Jr.	13	Dick Metz	15
11:40	E. J. Harrison	25			Harold McSpaden	7
11:50		4	Elsworth Vines	27	Ed Dudley	16
P. M.	Ben Hogan	19	Vic Ghezzi	2	Lawson Little	20
12:00	Tony Penna	8	Jimmy Thomson	26	Jimmy Hines	1
12:10	Jimmy Demaret	3	Lloyd Mangrum	10	Harry Todd	33
12:20	Byron Nelson	9	Geo. Schneiter	18	Johnny Bulla	
12:30	Herman Keiser	11	Bob Hamilton	1		
12:40	Herman Barron		Henry Picard	5		
12:50	Sam Snead	6				
1:00						

FRIDAY'S TOTALS
36 Holes

Sam Snead	140	Bob Hamilton	144	Henry Picard	145	Jimmy Demaret	148
Herman Keiser	141	Tony Penna	144	Harold McSpaden	145	Jimmy Thomson	151
Geo. Schneiter	141	Byron Nelson	144	Ben Hogan	146	*Royal Hogan	153
Harry Todd	142	Dick Metz	144	Lloyd Mangrum	146	Ed Dudley	157
Herman Barron	143	E. J. Harrison	144	Fred Haas, Jr.	147	*Reynolds Smith	158
Johnny Bulla	143	Vic Ghezzi	145	*Wilford Wehrle	148	*Bob Cochran	159
Jimmy Hines	143	Elsworth Vines	145	Lawson Little	148	Charles Akey	164

*Designates Amateur

FIRST ANNUAL
COLONIAL NATIONAL INVITATION
GOLF TOURNAMENT

May 16, 17, 18, 19
1946

COLONIAL COUNTRY CLUB
FORT WORTH, TEXAS

54

THE 1940s

PRESTIGIOUS TOURNAMENT BEGINS WITH LEONARD AND HOGAN LEADING THE WAY

Colonial's successful 1941 U.S. Open was the impetus for creating its 60-year-old annual tournament, but no one originally expected to wait until 1946. Planning commenced in the summer of '41 for an inaugural event the very next year. On August 19, the Fort Worth Star-Telegram reported on Colonial's preliminary plans for a May 1942 tournament. Then the Japanese bombed Pearl Harbor and put that plan on the shelf. Even the "majors" suspended play for several years.

But Colonial didn't miss a beat after the conclusion of WWII. On May 29, 1945, just three weeks after V-E Day, the club announced formal plans for a 1946 golf tournament second to none. "The U.S. Open here was a big success, so Mr. Leonard called Max Highfill and me about starting a Colonial tournament," remembered charter member Johnny Ballard, the Club's second president. "It was to be strictly invitation for a limited field. No matter how good a golfer you were, we would invite only the type person we wanted as our guest."

ABOVE:
Marvin Leonard and Ben Hogan made Colonial famous together.
FACING PAGE:
The first tournament's souvenir program and daily pairings sheet.

ABOVE:
Hometown favorites Byron Nelson and Ben Hogan helped attract big crowds to the National Invitation.
LEFT:
Texan Lloyd Mangrum was another Colonial favorite.

The world's best golfers came to Fort Worth for Marvin Leonard's inaugural showcase. The elite 29-man field featured 25 pros and four top amateurs. Among the field were Toney Penna, Sam Snead, Lloyd Mangrum, Harold McSpaden, Jimmy Demaret, Vic Ghezzi, Lawson Little and newly-crowned Masters champion Herman Keiser. They joined favorite sons Ben Hogan and Byron Nelson of Fort Worth. "It is our purpose to have an event that will be unique and outstanding," explained Tournament Chairman Max Highfill. "We want to have a field any member of which can win without surprise." Colonial made it a carte blanche visit for the contestants. There were no entry fees. Transportation and caddies were furnished, and unlimited signing privileges were extended in the clubhouse. Such hospitality was unheard of in those days. Outside the clubhouse, officials committed to the finest spectator services and tournament amenities. This included signal corps walkie-talkies and telephone artillery communications, used to send up-to-date scores into the main scoreboard from several key holes throughout the course.

Combining the tournament's debut with the fact that Texans Demaret, Hogan, Mangrum, and Nelson were among the nation's best, the excitement in Fort Worth reached a fever pitch. Furthermore, the $15,000 purse was one of the biggest in all of golf -- even bigger than the Masters. Hogan had won five events late in 1945 after getting out of the Army Air Corps, including a PGA tournament record score of 261 in Portland. Coming into the '46 Colonial, he had placed first or second in 10 of 13 events from January to May, and was the Tour's leading money winner.

"Ben Hogan wants to win the Colonial Invitation more than anything else in the world," warned '41 Open champ Craid Wood. "And when you're in that frame of mind and have the golf game that Ben has, you are hard to beat."

Penna and Fred Haas stroked the first shots off #1 tee on May 16 at 11:30 am. The wiry little Penna fired a 69 that briefly took the lead until soft-spoken George Schneiter's 67 captured first-round honors and broke Hogan's mark of 68 from the '41 Open. Schneiter's round was keyed by five straight threes on the front nine, from holes #3-7. "Those are positively the best greens in the South," Penna remarked. "Anyone who can't putt on them just can't putt. Period."

After two rounds, the smooth, "Slammin' Sam" Snead held a one-shot lead at even par. Hometown favorite Hogan lay five shots back, but a nifty third-round 69 clawed within three of Dallasite Harry Todd, two of Snead, and one of Schneiter. Two of Hogan's Saturday approach shots hit the pin. Still, Hogan thought he may be too far back. "Needed 67," he said, claiming that he couldn't play finer from tee to green, but that putts just wouldn't drop.

Best of Luck
Harry Todd

Hogan then captivated the city and the event by birdieing the first two holes Sunday and charging from behind for a thrilling one-stroke victory and a $3,000 first-place check. Still one back of Todd when making the turn Sunday, Hogan attacked and grabbed three birdies in a row, beginning at #11. The winning shot was a putt on #13 that hung on the lip before dropping. But it wasn't really over till the 18th, where Fort Worth Star Telegram writer Amos Melton said Hogan "gave the gallery a touch of heart failure," by rolling his 40-foot birdie putt by the hole a good four feet. The par putt dropped for a one-stroke victory. Hogan's incredible final-round 65 stood as the course record for 24 years.

Marvin Leonard and Fort Worth could not have been more thrilled. Tireless Fort Worth promoter and Honorary Tournament Chairman Amon Carter claimed, while giving Todd the second place check, that it was the first time he had ever given a Dallas man money. Hogan told the crowd that because of Marvin Leonard, he'd rather win the first Colonial than even the U.S. Open.

Despite heart-breaking losses at the Masters and U.S. Open that year, Hogan collected 13 titles and his first major championship -- the PGA. His year's winnings were a Tour record -- $43,212. Ironically, his cross-town rival Byron Nelson, who had lit the Tour up just one year earlier with 18 wins, retired from full-time golf.

With the first National Invitation Tournament a huge success, the event was off and running. "The players thought it was the best course they played each year, even better than the Open," recalled Colonial's Ballard, himself a competitor in the 1922 U.S. Amateur at Brookline. Hogan won the 1947 championship, too, battling Toney Penna down to the wire for a one-shot victory. The 36-hole Sunday battle, due to a Friday rainout, included stars Lawson Little and South African Bobby Locke. The straight-hitting, smooth-putting Locke was the tournament's first foreign player, and he was an immediate hit with the Fort Worth gallery. Hogan led after the first round, and held the lead well into Sunday morning's third round. However he hit his approach into the lake at #18 for double bogey, dropping him into a tie with Penna with one round to go. Locke and Little were one shot back. The two leaders remained tied through seven holes, then Penna bogeyed #8 and Hogan birdied. Another Hogan birdie on #12 gave him a three-shot cushion, and the rest was a formality.

This era became the heyday of Hogan's emergence on Tour. In the 3 1/2 years between his discharge from the Army Air Corps (1945) and his infamous auto accident in 1949, Hogan won 37 tournaments. Hogan probably would have also won the 1948 NIT for a Fort Worth hat trick if not for the grueling match-play PGA Championship. That event immediately preceded Colonial's 1948 affair, and did not end until Tuesday, when Hogan won the finals after playing a total of 212 holes (nearly 12 rounds).

Colonial officials intentionally set up the course to promote low scoring in 1948, and that is exactly what they got. The young tournament had also gained enough acclaim that the Mutual Broadcast System picked up some of the action for hundreds of radio stations in its national network. Hogan was exhausted, for sure, after beating Mike Turnesa in the finals 7-6 on Tuesday in a 30-hole match. En route to his second PGA title he had knocked off Jock Hutchison Jr. Johnny Palmer, Gene Sarazen, Chick Harbert and pal Jimmy Demaret. If there was any course on which Hogan didn't need to practice, it would be hometown Colonial. But there he was, after catching a morning train from St. Louis, out for a last-minute practice round Wednesday afternoon. He admitted to other players that he was "dog-tired," but told reporters the PGA marathon had done nothing but get him into shape.

In the first round, burly blond Clayton Heafner, a late invitee to the event, used three 30-foot putts to spark a leading 67. The North Carolinan was certainly enjoying his first trip to Colonial, as he then dropped two 68s on the field. "This is the way all golf tournaments should be run," Heafner stated early on. "I'd rather finish last here and get to take part than be up in the money at some tournaments." In Saturday's third round,

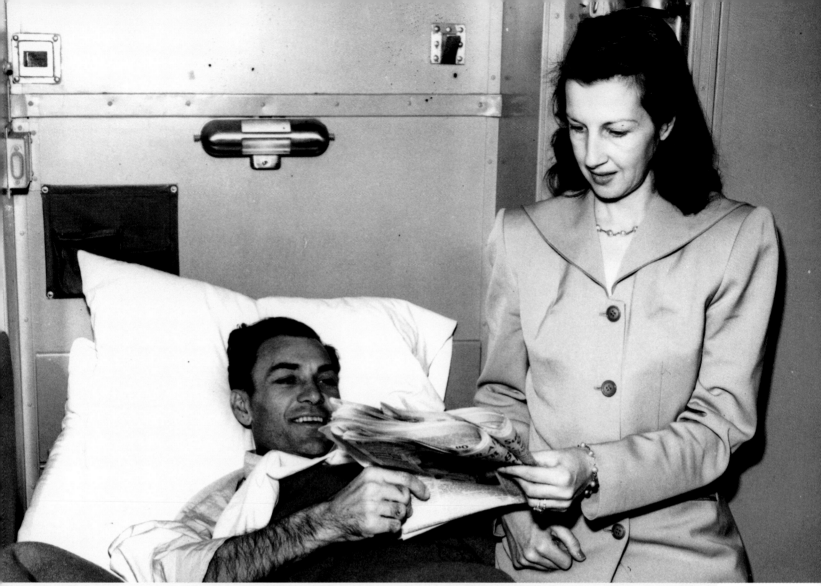

ABOVE:
Ben and Valerie Hogan read newspaper articles about their terrible auto accident.

Hogan found the magic for another incredible 65, and thus climbed his way to second place. But Heafner's hot putter was unfazed, and he concluded his four-day roll with a closing 69, blistering the course for a winning record of 272, eight-under-par, and a six-shot victory. Hogan tied for second place with the popular Skip Alexander.

Heafner was the first Colonial champion to lead wire to wire, and the first to record four sub-par rounds in the process. His 72-hole record stood for 27 years. "I always had enough lead after the first day to relax and shoot my best," he claimed later. Flamboyant Jimmy Demaret had such fun at the event that he hung around for the awards ceremony and serenaded the crowd with "How Lucky You Are."

Hogan nonetheless barnstormed to another fantastic year, winning the money title, the Vardon Trophy, and the first ever PGA Player of the Year award. Included in his 10 wins was his first U.S. Open victory -- at Riviera. In November 1,500 of Fort Worth's finest attended an invitation-only reception at Colonial Country Club to honor the "King of Golf," Ben Hogan, and his wife Valerie.

Then came the cursed year of 1949.

After winning two of the year's first four events, Hogan and Valerie, headed home from the Phoenix Open (where he had finished second). On the foggy morning of February 1, they were east-bound on Highway 80 near Van Horn in far west Texas. A west-bound Greyhound bus, behind schedule, attempted to pass a truck on a small bridge and smashed the Hogans head-on. Ben's last-second lunge in front of Valerie saved both of their lives, but he still

suffered a fractured pelvis, broken collarbone, fractured and crushed left leg, a fractured rib and an injured left eye. Then days later, with Hogan seemingly "out of the woods," dangerous blood clots almost killed him, requiring dramatic, life-saving surgery and resulting in great physical pain throughout his life. His remarkable comeback from those life-threatening injuries became one of the greatest stories in all of sports history.

Three months later on Sunday, May 15, LaGrave Field -- home of the beloved Fort Worth Cats pro baseball team -- burned to the ground just north of downtown. The next day, a five-inch deluge flooded the Trinity River and much of the city. A handful of people died and thousands were homeless. The National Invitation loomed just two weeks away, and the golf course was 10 feet under water. Some course workers, clinging

to treetops, had to be rescued in boats. Colonial officials, all their maintenance equipment washed away, vowed to clean up the course and stage the tournament on schedule. After four days, water service was restored to most of the city. But the following Wednesday, May 25, more rain fell, with more flooding. It was just too much.

"We're canceling the tournament because the city has been struck by tragedy and we feel that this is no time to hold a golf tournament," declared Marvin Leonard after meetings on Thursday. Club members became involved in volunteer relief efforts all over town; so the course, and the tournament, would have to wait.

J. Y. BALLARD, PRESIDENT
S. SCOTT TEEL, SEC'Y.-TREAS.

VICE PRESIDENTS
E. G. PARKER
LACY BOGGESS

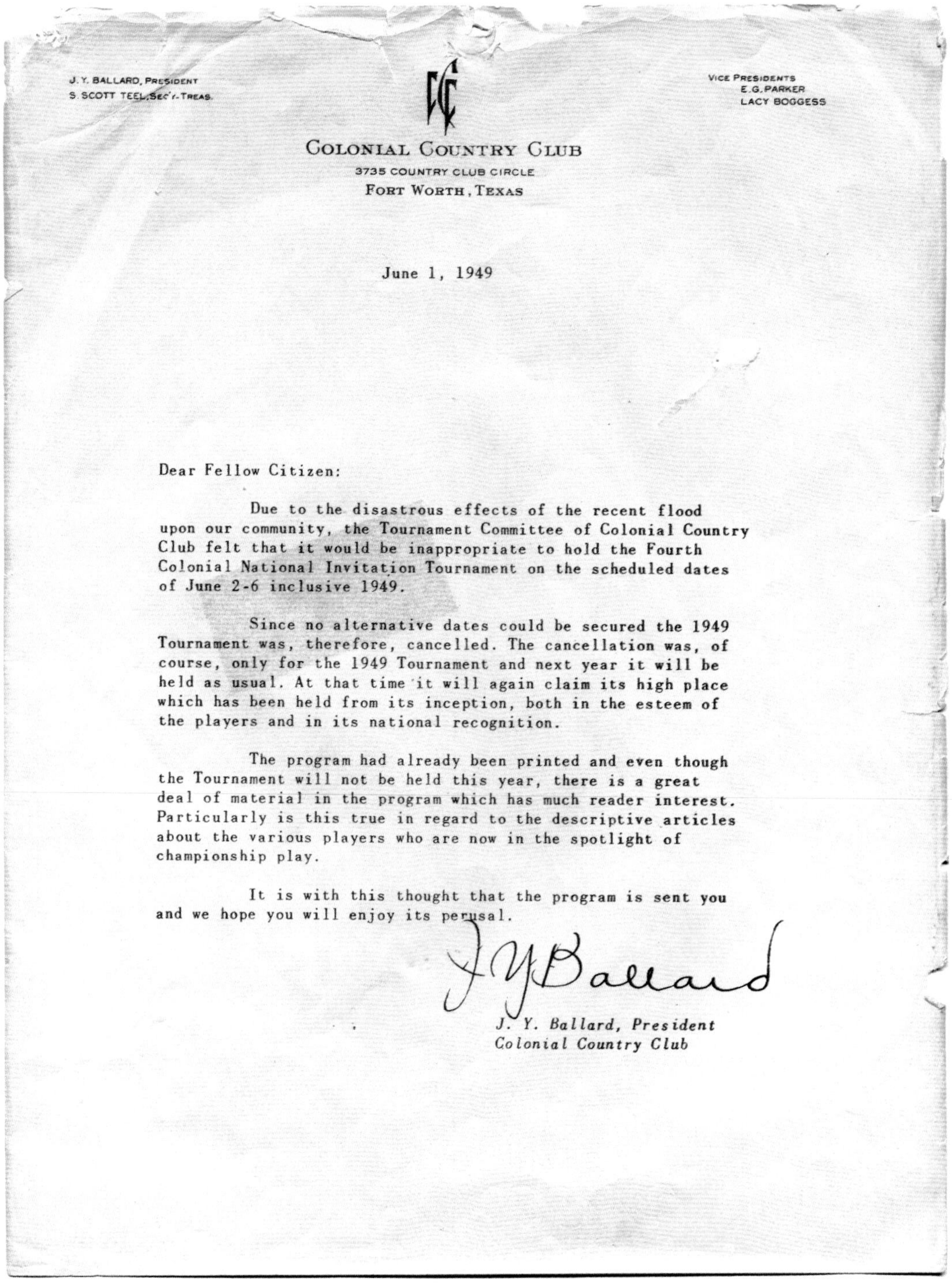

COLONIAL COUNTRY CLUB
3735 COUNTRY CLUB CIRCLE
FORT WORTH, TEXAS

June 1, 1949

Dear Fellow Citizen:

Due to the disastrous effects of the recent flood upon our community, the Tournament Committee of Colonial Country Club felt that it would be inappropriate to hold the Fourth Colonial National Invitation Tournament on the scheduled dates of June 2-6 inclusive 1949.

Since no alternative dates could be secured the 1949 Tournament was, therefore, cancelled. The cancellation was, of course, only for the 1949 Tournament and next year it will be held as usual. At that time it will again claim its high place which has been held from its inception, both in the esteem of the players and in its national recognition.

The program had already been printed and even though the Tournament will not be held this year, there is a great deal of material in the program which has much reader interest. Particularly is this true in regard to the descriptive articles about the various players who are now in the spotlight of championship play.

It is with this thought that the program is sent you and we hope you will enjoy its perusal.

J. Y. Ballard

J. Y. Ballard, President
Colonial Country Club

In hindsight, it seems oddly fitting that the tournament went unplayed that year. Without Ben Hogan, the 1949 NIT just couldn't have been the same. Colonial without Hogan? No way. Was it fate? Or just a freak flood?

The golf tour went on without Colonial. Sam Snead captured the money title that year, winning the Masters and the PGA Championship, along with the Vardon Trophy and PGA Player of the Year honors.

As the decade came to an end, on December 10, 1949, a battling and courageous Hogan stepped onto the first tee at Colonial and quietly played his first 18-hole round in 11 months. Things were looking up.

ABOVE:
Colonial President Johnny Ballard's letter to Fort Worth citizens after canceling the 1949 tournament.

1940s

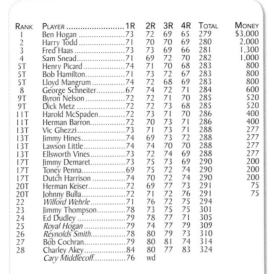

1946
May 16-19

RANK	PLAYER	1R	2R	3R	4R	TOTAL	MONEY
1	Ben Hogan	73	72	69	65	279	$3,000
2	Harry Todd	71	70	70	69	280	2,000
3	Fred Haas	73	69	66	73	281	1,300
4	Sam Snead	71	69	72	70	282	1,000
5T	Henry Picard	74	71	70	68	283	800
5T	Bob Hamilton	71	73	72	67	283	800
5T	Lloyd Mangrum	74	72	68	69	283	800
8	George Schneiter	67	74	72	71	284	600
9T	Byron Nelson	72	72	71	70	285	520
9T	Dick Metz	72	72	73	68	285	520
11T	Harold McSpaden	72	73	71	70	286	400
11T	Herman Barron	72	70	73	71	286	400
13T	Vic Ghezzi	73	71	73	71	288	277
13T	Jimmy Hines	74	69	73	72	288	277
13T	Lawson Little	74	74	70	70	288	277
13T	Ellsworth Vines	73	72	74	69	288	277
17T	Jimmy Demaret	73	75	73	69	290	200
17T	Toney Penna	69	75	72	74	290	200
17T	Dutch Harrison	74	70	72	74	290	200
20T	Herman Keiser	72	69	77	73	291	75
20T	Johnny Bulla	72	71	72	76	291	75
22	*Wilford Wehrle*	71	76	72	75	294	
23	Jimmy Thompson	78	73	75	75	301	
24	Ed Dudley	79	78	77	71	305	
25	*Royal Hogan*	79	74	77	79	309	
26	*Reynolds Smith*	78	80	79	73	310	
27	Bob Cochran	79	80	81	74	314	
28	Charley Akey	84	80	77	83	324	
	Cary Middlecoff	76	wd				

1947
May 15-18

RANK	PLAYER	1R	2R	3R	4R	TOTAL	MONEY
1	Ben Hogan	68	72	70	69	279	$3,000
2	Toney Penna	70	70	70	70	280	2,000
3T	Bobby Locke	72	72	67	72	283	1,100
3T	Fred Haas	71	73	70	69	283	1,100
3T	Johnny Palmer	70	69	74	70	283	1,100
6T	Vic Ghezzi	71	68	72	73	284	700
6T	Chick Harbert	74	70	68	72	284	700
6T	Cary Middlecoff	75	70	69	70	284	700
9T	Jimmy Demaret	76	73	70	66	285	562
9T	Lawson Little	69	72	70	74	285	562
11	Dick Metz	77	69	69	72	287	525
12T	Lloyd Mangrum	71	73	72	72	288	466
12T	Lew Worsham	76	70	70	72	288	466
12T	Henry Picard	72	71	69	76	288	466
15T	Johnny Bulla	72	69	75	73	289	350
15T	George Schoux	75	75	70	69	289	350
17T	Ky Laffoon	75	73	69	73	290	225
17T	George Fazio	71	77	70	72	290	225
17T	Ellsworth Vines	72	70	73	75	290	225
20	Harry Todd	74	73	74	71	292	175
21	Herman Keiser	75	72	72	76	295	
22	Herman Barron	74	71	76	75	296	
23	George Schneiter	72	73	77	78	300	
24	*Wilford Wehrle*	77	73	77	75	302	
25	*Royal Hogan*	74	77	76	76	303	
26	*Bob Willits*	78	76	77	75	306	
27	Bobby Morris	80	79	78	79	316	

1948
May 27-30

RANK	PLAYER	1R	2R	3R	4R	TOTAL	MONEY
1	Clayton Heafner	67	68	68	69	272	$3,000
2T	Ben Hogan	71	70	65	72	278	1,700
2T	Skip Alexander	71	68	69	70	278	1,700
4T	Lloyd Mangrum	70	68	72	70	280	950
4T	Herman Keiser	68	74	68	70	280	950
6	Byron Nelson	70	69	73	71	283	800
7T	Bobby Locke	70	68	73	73	284	650
7T	Johnny Bulla	70	71	72	70	284	650
9	Jimmy Demaret	70	71	70	76	287	575
10T	Ed Oliver	73	72	72	71	288	525
10T	Johnny Palmer	69	73	70	76	288	525
10T	Toney Penna	68	72	75	73	288	525
13T	Lawson Little	74	72	71	72	289	426
13T	Dick Metz	72	69	74	74	289	426
13T	Chandler Harper	68	74	75	72	289	426
16T	George Schoux	68	75	75	72	290	265
16T	Cary Middlecoff	70	73	69	78	290	265
16T	Ellsworth Vines	73	72	71	74	290	265
19	Vic Ghezzi	73	73	72	73	291	200
20T	*Charles Coe*	75	74	70	73	292	
20T	Bob Hamilton	71	70	80	71	292	43
20T	Henry Picard	75	71	74	72	292	43
20T	Ky Laffoon	73	74	72	73	292	43
20T	George Fazio	74	73	72	73	292	43
25T	Jim Ferrier	72	77	74	70	293	
25T	Dutch Harrison	78	70	68	77	293	
27T	George Schneiter	75	72	71	76	294	
27T	Ed Furgol	75	72	71	76	294	
29	Al Smith	73	71	75	76	295	
30	Harry Todd	73	74	74	76	297	
31	*Wilford Wehrle*	78	71	74	77	300	
32	*Tommy Barnes*	77	71	76	78	302	

Names in italics designate amateurs.

THE 1950s

INTO THE NATIONAL SPOTLIGHT
FOR COLONIAL AND HOGAN

As Colonial's young tournament entered the 1950s it was quickly rising to the top of national prominence for professional golf events. The 1950 event was eagerly awaited if for no other reason than the 1949 tourney had been canceled. But most important, Hogan was back.

Excitement built steadily as the event approached. Jimmy Demaret had just become the first three-time winner of the Masters. Sam Snead, who reportedly disliked the galleries at Colonial for their bias toward Hogan, was the Tour's leading money winner. He had already won four tournaments that year, beating Hogan in the famous LA Open playoff for one of them. Hogan then whipped his rival by 10 shots at Snead's home Greenbrier tournament. Yes, folks relished the idea of a Snead-Hogan duel at Colonial. Tournament officials hired the public relations firm of Witherspoon & Ridings to promote the event, the beginning of a long relationship. More than 1,000 clubhouse tickets sold out at $15, so Colonial introduced a $7.50 "Grounds Season" ticket. Individual daily tickets cost $1.80 for rounds 1 and 2, and $2.50 for rounds 3 and 4. Twice as many fans showed up than any previous year, approaching just under an estimated 10,000 in attendance for the final round.

ABOVE:
Ben Hogan congratulates Sam Snead on his 1950 victory.
FACING PAGE:
Spectators surround the first tee as Ben Hogan warms up.

Unfortunately, they never got the duel they hoped for. Snead eagled the first hole on the first day and never looked back. Finishing the third round with two closing birdies, Snead staked a five-shot lead that put a choke-hold on the tournament. Leading start to finish, Snead eventually won by three shots, and Hogan never got within four of the winning total of 3-under 277. Snead's game was so flawless that one writer remarked, "Snead missed a belt loop when he put his pants on for the first round. It was the only mistake he made." Snead had exacted his revenge for Hogan winning in Greenbrier.

The Virginian went on to claim 10 victories that year and lead the Tour in everything. But still it was Hogan's dramatic, uplifting playoff win at the U.S. Open in Merion that June that captivated the world. It was his only major title that year, but it won him PGA Player of the Year honors, something that forever stuck in the craw of Snead.

TOP:
Colonial made history in 1950 by introducing the first scoreboard system with telephone service from all 18 greens.
BOTTOM LEFT:
Jimmy Demaret sings at the 1950 awards ceremony.
BOTTOM RIGHT:
Ben Hogan won back-to-back titles in 1952 and 1953.

ABOVE:
Marvin Leonard congratulates 1951 champion Cary Middlecoff.

Colonial made history in 1950 by introducing the first scoreboard system with telephone service from all 18 greens. Local WBAP-TV broadcast weekend action into area homes, the first time any golf tournament action had ever been transmitted direct to Fort Worth viewers (the U.S. Open wasn't televised until 1954.) Seventeen radio stations broadcast the tournament throughout the Texas State Network for one hour each day, with local station KFJZ adding a second hour for Fort Worth listeners. Nationally, the Mutual Broadcast System aired some of Saturday's action on their 400-station radio network. After Saturday's round, the committee presented Snead with a birthday cake on #18 while Jimmy Demaret led the crowd in "Happy Birthday." Demaret, making a habit of this, had such a good time that after Sunday's award presentations, he closed the proceedings by singing "Some Enchanted Evening." At that presentation Colonial introduced the beautiful, silver, five-foot

tall Leonard Trophy -- the permanent trophy for displaying all champions' names. The trophy had been built to debut at the 1949 event, but had to wait because of the flood canceling the tournament that year. Showing Leonard's vision, the trophy base contained room for 100 years of winners.

In 1951, Colonial had a decision to make. The tournament had lost money each year so far, and a special Board meeting was called for March 5. The previous year, the event lost $346.55 against $35,793.02 in total expenses, the closest it had ever coming to breaking even. Officials projected that sales revenue could be increased in 1951. "It was nip and tuck," recalled Board member Lacy Boggess, "but the result was a unanimous vote to continue the tournament." Whew. Forty-two players comprised the field in 1951. Lead-in festivities that Spring included the debut of Hollywood's movie about Hogan's dramatic life story, "Follow the Sun," at three Fort Worth theaters.

Hogan threatened to win again as he led the first two rounds, but the former dentist Cary Middlecoff wrestled the event away from the hometown master on Saturday. Hogan shot himself out of the tournament that day with a 74. Texan Jack Burke Jr. closed with a 67 to get within a stroke on Sunday. Middlecoff, who had appeared in the 1946 event as an amateur, won with a 2-over-par total on Colonial's layout, which some were now calling the toughest par 70 in the world. Middlecoff himself commented that, "If I had to play this course every day for a living, I'd go back to pulling teeth."

For Colonial, more good news was that for the first time in five years, the tournament finally made money. Having reached that milestone, Chairman Highfill turned the reins over to Vice Chairman S.M. "Bing" Bingham.

In 1952, Burke came to town as the year's hottest player, with four victories already in hand. The purse was raised to $20,000, matching the Masters. But it was Fort Worth's Raymond Gafford who threatened to steal Hogan's local bragging rights, holding a three-shot lead after two rounds. Top amateur Bill Campbell found himself paired with Hogan and Demaret in the second round, and he was completely intimidated. After spraying balls for several holes, including hitting a spectator off the first tee, he was beside himself. Hogan came over to Campbell on the fourth hole, put his arm around his shoulder and told him, "You have just as much right to be out here as we do. So settle down. Take your time. And remember we're with you." Campbell settled down, shot even par over the last two rounds, and won low amateur honors.

Rain had postponed the second round to Saturday and set up a 36-hole finale for the second time in tournament history. Playing with Hogan and Doug Ford, Gafford held a remarkable five-shot lead at the midday 54-hole break. Then going four-over-par on holes 4, 5, and 6 in the final 18, Gafford let Hogan back in it. Hogan birdied holes 7 and 9 for a one-shot lead at the turn, and Gafford collapsed with four straight bogeys. Hogan claimed his third Colonial title. It was the only 72-hole event he played in that year besides the Masters and U.S. Open.

Colonial's famous plaid jacket, with Royal Stewart tartan cloth imported for Scotland, was introduced this year. Bingham noted that the jackets would allow officials to "shine with the same brilliance as our field." The tournament also introduced the tradition of making a first-round "feature threesome" of Hogan, the defending champion and the defending low amateur. (This required modification in '53 and '54 since Hogan was the defending champ! The reigning runner-up played in this case.) The first such pairing featured Hogan with Cary Middlecoff and Charles Coe.

ABOVE:
Amon Carter shakes hands with 1951 runner-up Jack Burke Jr. as Dr. Alden Coffey looks on.

The following Spring, Colonial almost lost its second tournament in five years. Just one month before the 1953 event, a devastating fire roared through the clubhouse. Proud officials, however, declared that "the course is still there," so the tournament would be held even "if the clubhouse was a tent."

Defending champ Hogan entered having won two of three events that Spring, including a stunning Masters victory in record fashion. Despite windy conditions, Tommy Bolt set the course on fire with 12 one-putts for a first round of 67. The average score for the field that day was 75.32. But more wind sent the club-throwing Bolt to an 81 on Friday, and conditions were so tough that Jimmy Demaret picked up after a front nine 43 -- the first player ever to withdraw from Colonial without a physical injury. He was 17-over par at the time. But reigning Masters champ Hogan held tough, and on Sunday, still in severe wind, he fired a masterful 67 to win his fourth NIT by five shots. He carded one eagle and three birdies, versus only two bogeys.

Accepting his second place check, '51 Colonial champ Cary Middlecoff remarked, "Maybe one of these days Ben will be too old to play in this tournament and the rest of us will have a chance." Local sports writers started calling the Colonial tournament the "Hogan Benefit."

Only 10 sub-par and six even-par rounds were recorded during the windy 1953 event. And 13 of the rounds were in the 80s. Nearly 40 percent of the field totaled 300 or higher for the four rounds and only six golfers managed to shoot under 290.

Hogan then finished the most incredible year of his career. His fabulous wins in the 1953 U.S. and British Opens helped earn him the famous Hickok Belt as Professional Athlete of the Year, a New York City ticker tape parade, and icon status in all of sports. He was the toast of the world, as well as Fort Worth, where Colonial made him a lifetime honorary member.

In 1953, Colonial began the tradition of allowing champions to vote on two invitations to up-and-coming players who had yet to qualify for the event. Hogan, Heafner, Snead, and Middlecoff selected Milton Marusic and Fred Wampler to be the first such honorees.

TOP:
1955 champion Chandler Harper accepts the trophy from Marvin Leonard.
MIDDLE:
1956 champion Mike Souchak receives the winner's check from Marvin Leonard.
BOTTOM:
Arnold Palmer and Gary Player made their Colonial debut in the 1950s.

72

Officials started another tradition that year -- having Fort Worth native son Byron Nelson hit the first ball of the tournament each year. Nelson regrettably never won Colonial in his semi-retirement, but the 1954 event marked his best finish, a tie for third. Australian star Peter Thomson took control of the '54 tournament early. Hogan was only three back after 36 holes, but had to withdraw with the flu. Nelson tied for the 54-hole lead, and much talk centered around a potential playoff, as nine players stalked within two shots of the lead. But Johnny Palmer's 69 claimed the title by two strokes on Sunday. Just five weeks removed from a car accident, the short-hitting Palmer went the entire tournament without a three-putt. He hit his approach shot stiff on the 71st hole to seal the win over Fred Haas.

Sensational amateur Harvie Ward's third place tie was the best finish ever by an amateur in the event; and he followed it up by winning the U.S. Amateur Championship two years in a row. 18-year-old Rex Baxter Jr., the USGA Junior Champion, became the youngest player ever to compete at Colonial. With a $25,00 purse, ticket prices had grown to $10 for a week-long ticket, or $5 for one day on the weekend.

In 1955, Chandler Harper destroyed the field for an eight-stroke victory. The course played much tougher for the rest of the field -- Harper finished four under par and the second place finisher, Dow Finsterwald, was four over par. Harper was the third Colonial champ to lead wire-to-wire, and his four-under-par 276 score stood untouched for 10 years. His record for an 8-shot margin of victory still stands today.

Finishing in last place that year, in his first appearance at Colonial, was young Arnold Palmer. He was the reigning U.S. Amateur champion, who had just turned professional. Also debuting in 1955 was a beautiful new red-brick Colonial clubhouse, which featured a sparkling Hogan Trophy Room to forever celebrate the hometown legend's accomplishments.

ABOVE:
1954 champion Johnny Palmer with this winner's check.

Earlier that year, an aspiring young pro from Davenport, Iowa, wrote Ben Hogan about obtaining a set of his company's new clubs. Hogan invited him to send in his club specs and then drop by the Fort Worth plant in the Spring if he were to earn an invitation to Colonial. Interestingly, many weeks later that player received a coveted Champions' Choice invitation to the NIT, along with Dow Finsterwald. He dutifully reported to the Hogan Co. on Monday of tournament week, where Hogan himself greeted him. Hogan refused to take a penny for the new set of clubs, took a great deal of interest in the player's progress, and offered support and encouragement.

That young player was Jack Fleck, who instantly felt that his new clubs and the meeting with Hogan would transform his life. He finished a quiet 24th that week. Several weeks later, the unknown Fleck stunned the golfing world by winning the U.S. Open Championship. He beat Ben Hogan in an 18-hole playoff.

1956 was a soggy year for the tournament, with pick-and-clean conditions prevailing in the first two rounds. Two-time British Open champ Peter Thomson and Dow Finsterwald wrestled with the lead for two days. Then former Duke football star Mike Souchak and Tommy "Thunder" Bolt took over the battle on the weekend. Mike Souchak slogged in a champion, edging Bolt by one shot. Trailing by two on the 18th, Bolt almost holed out his approach shot for eagle and a tie. At age

1957 champion Roberto De Vicenzo putts out for the victory at #18.

28, Souchak was the youngest Colonial champ to date, and also the first former Champions' Choice to win the event. The most talked-about item of the event was giant George Bayer's wayward four-wood approach to the 18th green during the first round. It ended up on the roof of Colonial's shiny new three-story clubhouse! Talk about an unplayable lie (he made bogey with a free drop).

Golf Digest reported in a feature article in '56 that Colonial's event had reached the "same class of the U.S. Open and Masters." Indeed, the magazine referred to Colonial as being "One of Golf's Big Four" -- along with the Masters, U.S. Open, and PGA Championship. It was this year that Colonial first roped all 18 holes from tee to green, as crowds were becoming too big to continue the practice of allowing spectators to walk down fairways behind the players.

Rain soaked Colonial again in 1957, requiring a 36-hole Sunday for the third time in 10 years, keeping the field bunched up throughout. All 48 players invited showed up, and it was heralded the "finest field in golf," as it included champions of 35 of the last 36 PGA tournaments. Still, only eight sub-par rounds were fired during the tournament -- a record that may last forever. Young Ken Venturi made his first Colonial appearance (tie for 14th), and a young Gary Player waited around as an alternate, but didn't get in.

Argentine star Roberto De Vicenzo claimed he didn't even know he was in the hunt until after he finished. Overtaking 16 players on Sunday, De Vicenzo unknowingly took the lead with only four holes to play. Still, Dick Mayer had a chance until he bogeyed #17 to lose by shot. Thus, De Vicenzo became Colonial's first foreign champion. Mayer went on to win the U.S. Open a month later, and PGA Player of the Year honors.

In 1958, rain doused Colonial yet again, but 28-year-old Masters champion Arnold Palmer fired a first-round 65 under pick-and-clean conditions to claim the early lead. The wet conditions produced this strange quote from Byron Nelson after the first round: "The course is too wet to be muddy, and,

somehow, it's the driest wet I've ever seen." Lift-and-clean conditions prevailed the entire tournament. There were almost as many contestants as spectators in the early rounds. Tony Lema broke his putter on the twelfth hole Friday, but made 27-foot and 48-foot putts with his driver!

A calmer, gentler Bolt took the 36-hole lead and finally claimed the Colonial championship, holding off Ken Venturi and Hogan to win by one shot. "I'm the new Bolt," he claimed. "I'm tired of throwing things." No one believed him, but he went on to win the U.S. Open a month later. Big weekend crowds and sunshine helped keep the tournament in the black, as the event staved off more talk of cancellation after the third straight year

COLONIAL COUNTRY CLUB'S
13th annual
NATIONAL INVITATION
GOLF TOURNAMENT

April 30 – May 4, 1958
Fort Worth, Texas

of rain. Gary Player got in as an alternate this year, and tied for 22nd place. It was the first of 17 appearances at Colonial for the future Hall of Famer from South Africa. "This is my idea of what a golf course should be," Player said of Colonial. "I don't know of a finer course anywhere. This course has everything."

To close out the decade in 1959, record crowds embraced the tournament each day, and Ben Hogan set a new course record on Wednesday with a practice round 63. Lionel Hebert, the 1957 PGA champion, appeared to be off and running toward victory with a record-tying six-under-par lead after two rounds. 46-year-old Hogan lurked two shots behind.

—by Heck

Golf's Most Exclusiv

Extremely windy conditions controlled play Saturday. Only Arnold Palmer and Cary Middlecoff broke par, shooting 69. Hogan ballooned to a 77, his worst competitive round ever at Colonial. Hebert shot 78, but both were still in the hunt. A steady 72 on Sunday tied Hogan with good friend Fred Hawkins, setting up Colonial's first playoff. The huge gallery on #18 gasped in shock as Hogan missed a three-footer for the outright win.

The windy, 18-hole duel on Monday saw Hawkins lead Hogan by one after three holes. On the par-3 fourth hole, Hawkins bogeyed and Hogan birdied. That gave Hogan a lead he never relinquished, winning his fifth Colonial title by four shots. Hogan did it with his company's own clubs -- his only career victory for which he could say that. "It was the finest golf I ever shot under those conditions," Hogan claimed. To complete the product endorsement, Hawkins was playing with a new set of Hogan clubs himself. It was standard procedure in the day of 18-hole playoffs that the golfers got a piece of the Monday gate. Hogan and Hawkins thus pocketed an extra $549.94 each. It was an emotional, popular win and Marvin Leonard gifted the fabulous Leonard Trophy to Hogan in honor of the achievement. Fittingly, it was the final victory of Hogan's career. This, too, most assuredly was fate.

The wildly successful tournament put Colonial in a great position for capitalizing on the coming professional golf boom. The Arnold Palmer era was about to explode onto the national sports scene.

1950s

1950
May 25-28

Rank	Player	1R	2R	3R	4R	Total	Money
1	Sam Snead	66	72	66	73	277	$3,000
2	Skip Alexander	66	74	70	70	280	2,000
3T	Dutch Harrison	69	73	68	72	282	1,200
3T	Ben Hogan	71	73	68	70	282	1,200
5T	Ed Oliver	68	71	70	74	283	850
5T	Cary Middlecoff	72	69	71	71	283	850
7T	Johnny Palmer	70	75	71	70	286	625
7T	Henry Picard	70	76	68	72	286	625
7T	Lloyd Mangrum	73	69	74	70	286	625
10T	Pete Cooper	74	72	72	70	288	525
10T	Norman Von Nida	72	72	70	74	288	525
10T	Toney Penna	74	73	70	71	288	525
10T	*Charles Coe*	74	72	69	73	288	
14	Jimmy Demaret	69	75	73	72	289	475
15	Jim Ferrier	76	73	73	68	290	425
16	Lawson Little	75	75	69	72	291	375
17	Chandler Harper	71	71	76	74	292	325
18T	Dave Douglas	75	75	70	73	293	225
18T	Harry Todd	70	76	71	76	293	225
18T	Marty Furgol	78	67	75	73	293	225
21T	Glenn Teal	75	73	72	74	294	87
21T	Buck White	72	75	71	76	294	87
23T	Joe Kirkwood	72	71	76	76	295	
23T	Paul O'Leary	75	75	76	69	295	
25	Ky Lafoon	74	78	71	73	296	
26	Dick Metz	73	79	71	74	297	
27T	Henry Ransom	71	76	77	73	298	
27T	Al Smith	80	73	74	71	298	
27T	Byron Nelson	74	72	76	76	298	
30	Bill Nary	74	79	72	74	299	
31	Raymond Gafford	72	74	78	76	300	
32T	Fred Haas Jr.	76	72	75	78	301	
32T	George Schneiter	76	76	73	76	301	
32T	Ed Furgol	74	78	70	79	301	
35	Clayton Heafner	74	77	72	81	304	

1951
May 24-27

Rank	Player	1R	2R	3R	4R	Total	Money
1	Cary Middlecoff	69	71	69	73	282	$3,000
2	Jack Burke, Jr.	75	71	70	67	283	2,000
3	Lloyd Mangrum	74	69	71	70	284	1,400
4T	Byron Nelson	71	71	70	73	285	900
4T	Ben Hogan	68	71	74	72	285	900
4T	Ed Oliver	75	67	68	75	285	900
7	Earl Stewart, Jr.	75	72	71	68	286	700
8	Julius Boros	71	71	76	69	287	600
9T	Al Brosch	77	72	67	72	288	550
9T	Johnny Palmer	71	70	75	72	288	550
9T	Clayton Heafner	74	68	75	71	288	550
12T	Henry Ransom	75	71	71	72	289	467
12T	Jerry Barber	72	75	69	73	289	467
12T	Jim Ferrier	72	71	74	72	289	467
15T	Raymond Gafford	73	76	69	72	290	350
15T	Tommy Bolt	70	72	73	75	290	350
17T	Bob Toski	77	69	72	73	291	237
17T	Toney Penna	69	73	76	73	291	237
19T	Fred Haas	72	73	75	72	292	75
19T	Jimmy Demaret	72	75	76	69	292	75
19T	Robert Riegel	72	73	76	71	292	75
19T	Ed Furgol	74	75	72	71	292	75
19T	Sam Snead	71	71	76	74	292	75
24T	Dutch Harrison	71	72	74	76	293	
24T	Bill Nary	69	77	77	70	293	
26T	Dave Douglas	78	70	74	73	295	
26T	Doug Ford	72	75	76	72	295	
28T	Fred Hawkins	75	74	71	76	296	
28T	Chandler Harper	75	75	74	72	296	
30	Jimmy Clark	80	76	71	71	298	
31T	Joe Kirkwood, Jr.	76	69	78	77	300	
31T	Harry Todd	73	71	80	76	300	
33	Ky Lafoon	77	70	79	75	301	
34	Marty Furgol	74	75	75	78	302	
35T	Jack Shields	79	77	73	74	303	
35T	Dick Metz	76	74	78	75	303	
37	George Schneiter	75	78	75	76	304	
38	Glen Teal	77	77	74	77	305	
39	Dick Mayer	79	77	73	80	309	
40	Lawson Little	78	77	79	76	310	
41	Charles Klein	82	76	76	78	312	
42	*Juan Segura*	86	78	75	81	320	

1955
May 5-8

Rank	Player	1R	2R	3R	4R	Total	Money
1	Chandler Harper	69	65	70	72	276	$5,000
2	Dow Finsterwald	72	69	69	74	284	3,000
3	Ed Oliver	71	71	72	72	286	2,000
4T	Julius Boros	72	69	75	71	287	1,430
4T	Antonio Cerda	74	67	71	75	287	1,430
4T	Fred Hawkins	74	72	71	70	287	1,430
4T	Cary Middlecoff	74	71	70	72	287	1,430
4T	Harry Todd	73	70	69	75	287	1,430
9T	Ted Kroll	73	70	74	71	288	950
9T	Earl Stewart, Jr.	76	73	69	70	288	950
11	Ben Hogan	72	69	75	72	288	800
12T	Jack Burke, Jr.	73	69	76	72	290	593
12T	Byron Nelson	72	71	73	74	290	593
12T	Peter Thomson	73	75	72	70	290	593
12T	Wally Ulrich	75	73	73	69	290	593
16T	Gene Littler	77	71	70	73	291	425
16T	Johnny Palmer	70	74	72	75	291	425
18	Ed Furgol	73	74	75	72	292	350
19	Billy Maxwell	74	72	72	75	293	300
20	Bo Wininger	75	72	76	71	294	275
21T	Johnny Bulla	75	73	72	75	295	225
21T	Fred Haas	74	72	75	74	295	225
21T	Art Wall, Jr.	73	73	72	77	295	225
24T	Jack Fleck	70	72	75	79	296	108
24T	Doug Ford	77	69	75	75	296	108
24T	F. (Bud) Holscher	75	75	73	73	296	108
27T	George Bayer	73	72	74	78	297	
27T	Leo Biagetti	71	77	74	75	297	
29T	Eric Monti	75	74	73	76	298	
29T	Ernie Vossler	75	78	68	77	298	
31	Dick Mayer	74	80	73	72	299	
32	Doug Higgins	77	73	81	69	300	
33T	Skip Alexander	76	71	75	79	301	
33T	Stan Leonard	77	74	75	75	301	
35T	Jerry Barber	72	76	80	74	302	
35T	Gardner Dickinson	77	72	76	77	302	
37T	Al Besselink	77	76	76	74	303	
37T	*Charles Coe*	76	79	74	74	303	
37T	Fred Wampler	73	72	81	77	303	
40	Raymond Gafford	77	75	74	78	304	
41	Mike Souchak	75	76	74	81	306	
42	Jack Harden	74	78	75	83	310	
43	Arnold Palmer	81	79	80	72	312	
	Tommy Bolt	71	72	78	(41)	wd	
	Jimmy Clark	75	71	78	(32)	wd	
	Bob Rosburg	80	71	(40)		wd	
	Marty Furgol	78	wd				

1956
May 3-6

Rank	Player	1R	2R	3R	4R	Total	Money
1	Mike Souchak	74	72	65	69	280	$5,000
2	Tommy Bolt	70	72	68	71	281	3,000
3	Gardner Dickinson	73	71	67	74	285	2,000
4T	George Bayer	73	72	71	70	286	1,700
4T	Stan Leonard	72	74	69	71	286	1,700
6T	Jimmy Demaret	75	73	69	70	287	1,187
6T	Ben Hogan	70	72	73	72	287	1,187
6T	Bo Wininger	72	70	70	75	287	1,187
6T	Peter Thomson	69	72	73	73	287	1,187
10T	Paul Harney	69	74	72	73	288	850
10T	Dow Finsterwald	69	72	72	75	288	850
12	Fred Hawkins	76	70	73	70	289	700
13	Gene Littler	73	71	73	73	290	625
14T	Billy Maxwell	76	71	76	68	291	475
14T	Dick Mayer	73	78	73	67	291	475
14T	*Joe Conrad*	78	73	71	69	291	
14T	Roberto De Vicenzo	72	74	74	71	291	475
14T	Doug Ford	74	70	75	72	291	475
19	*Hillman Robbins, Jr.*	73	74	72	73	292	
20T	Lloyd Mangrum	75	72	74	72	293	308
20T	Bob Rosburg	73	76	71	73	293	308
20T	Jack Burke, Jr.	72	71	75	75	293	308
23T	Johnny Palmer	73	76	72	73	294	212
23T	Wally Ulrich	74	72	76	72	294	212
23T	Frank Stranahan	75	69	77	73	294	212
23T	Al Balding	78	72	71	73	294	212
27T	Billy Casper	75	73	75	72	295	50
27T	Fred Haas	74	74	72	75	295	50
27T	Ted Kroll	73	74	74	74	295	50
30T	Chandler Harper	76	75	71	74	296	
30T	Arnold Palmer	73	71	76	76	296	
30T	Cary Middlecoff	73	75	71	77	296	
33T	Lionel Hebert	78	75	72	72	297	
33T	Art Wall, Jr.	74	74	76	73	297	
35T	Bill Mawhinney	77	77	73	72	299	
35T	Jerry Barber	76	73	74	76	299	
35T	Gordon Brydson	72	77	74	76	299	
35T	Murray Tucker	81	75	73	70	299	
39	F. (Bud) Holscher	73	72	80	75	300	
40	Walker Inman, Jr.	77	71	76	77	301	
41T	Earl Stewart, Jr.	73	77	79	73	302	
41T	Byron Nelson	70	76	74	82	302	
43T	Jay Hebert	75	77	77	74	303	
43T	Bill Kerr	75	74	80	74	303	
43T	Harry Todd	73	76	81	73	303	
46T	Mike Fetchick	79	74	77	74	304	
46T	Don Fairfield	74	76	77	77	304	
46T	Doug Higgins	74	74	76	77	304	
49	Max Evans	78	73	75	79	305	
50T	*Ed Hopkins*	79	78	73	80	310	
50T	Jack Kay	80	76	77	77	310	
52	Don January	81	80	74	77	312	
	Ernie Vossler	76	76	74	81	dq	
	Jack Fleck	76	76	78		dq	

1952
May 22-25

Rank	Player	1R	2R	3R	4R	Total	Money
1	Ben Hogan	74	67	71	67	279	$4,000
2	Lloyd Mangrum	72	69	70	72	283	2,700
3	Tommy Bolt	70	73	75	67	285	1,875
4T	Raymond Gafford	68	69	69	80	286	1,200
4T	Doug Ford	69	72	74	71	286	1,200
6	Cary Middlecoff	72	68	74	73	287	900
7	Byron Nelson	74	71	72	71	288	850
8T	Jack Burke, Jr.	78	68	69	74	289	750
8T	Jerry Barber	71	73	73	72	289	750
8T	Jimmy Demaret	73	73	73	70	289	750
11T	Jimmy Clark	74	72	77	68	291	650
11T	*Wm. C. Campbell*	74	77	71	69	291	
13T	Henry Ransom	73	74	71	74	292	575
13T	Harry Todd	75	73	74	70	292	575
15T	Charles Klein	73	75	70	75	293	475
15T	Al Besselink	72	75	76	70	293	475
17T	Dick Mayer	74	74	73	74	295	350
17T	Roberto De Vicenzo	77	74	73	71	295	350
17T	*Joe Conrad*	68	76	74	77	295	
17T	O'Neal White	74	73	76	72	295	350
21T	*Charles Coe*	73	73	71	79	296	
21T	Fred Haas	72	71	77	76	296	237
21T	Johnny Palmer	73	71	77	75	296	237
24T	Bob Toski	72	76	76	73	297	187
24T	Julius Boros	75	74	74	74	297	187
26T	Dick Metz	76	74	76	72	298	93
26T	Jack Shields	75	74	75	74	298	93
26T	Bill Nary	73	76	75	74	298	93
26T	Bob Hamilton	73	76	76	73	298	93
30	John Barnum	76	72	74	77	299	
31T	Fred Hawkins	70	80	76	74	300	
31T	Joe Kirkwood, Jr.	76	75	76	73	300	
31T	Dutch Harrison	73	80	74	73	300	
34T	Shelley Mayfield	75	77	72	77	301	
34T	Earl Stewart, Jr.	76	73	75	77	301	
36	Ky Laffoon	80	75	75	74	304	
37	George Schneiter	79	75	79	73	306	
38	Al Zimmerman	81	72	77	78	308	
39	Skip Alexander	79	81	75	75	310	
40	Jimmy Thompson	72	80	80	79	311	
41	Bob Duden	77	79	81	75	312	
42	*L. M. Crannell, Jr.*	77	80	81	79	317	

1953
May 21-24

Rank	Player	1R	2R	3R	4R	Total	Money
1	Ben Hogan	73	71	71	67	282	$5,000
2T	Doug Ford	73	71	72	71	287	2,500
2T	Cary Middlecoff	72	73	73	69	287	2,500
4T	Ted Kroll	72	72	72	73	289	1,600
4T	Jerry Barber	74	69	72	74	289	1,600
4T	Lloyd Mangrum	71	76	71	71	289	1,600
7	Harry Todd	74	70	74	72	290	1,250
8T	Dutch Harrison	73	74	74	70	291	1,000
8T	Skip Alexander	79	68	70	74	291	1,000
8T	Clayton Heafner	74	66	75	76	291	1,000
11T	Bill Nary	74	73	69	76	292	708
11T	Marty Furgol	75	73	71	73	292	708
11T	Wally Ulrich	74	72	73	73	292	708
14T	Bo Wininger	77	72	75	69	293	475
14T	Jack Burke, Jr.	75	73	70	75	293	475
14T	Buck White	72	73	71	77	293	475
14T	Jim Ferrier	75	70	72	76	293	475
18	Byron Nelson	74	73	73	74	294	350
19T	Al Besselink	73	71	74	78	296	288
19T	Fred Hawkins	71	77	74	74	296	288
21T	Bob Toski	74	73	75	75	297	225
21T	Skee Riegel	78	73	69	77	297	225
21T	Peter Thomson	72	72	75	78	297	225
24	Johnny Palmer	76	72	71	79	298	175
25T	Fred Haas	77	74	72	76	299	50
25T	Chandler Harper	71	73	78	77	299	50
25T	Ed Oliver	74	73	73	79	299	50
28	Shelley Mayfield	77	72	70	81	300	
29T	Fred Wampler	77	72	79	73	301	
29T	Tony Holguin	73	75	75	78	301	
31T	*Joe Conrad*	84	76	69	73	302	
31T	Raymond Gafford	75	76	74	77	302	
33	*Don Cherry*	78	78	73	76	305	
34T	Dick Mayer	79	73	78	76	306	
34T	Dick Metz	76	71	78	81	306	
36T	*Charles Coe*	74	75	80	78	307	
36T	Jack Harden	81	77	73	76	307	
36T	Jimmy Gauntt	81	72	76	78	307	
39T	*Billy Erfurth*	74	74	80	80	308	
39T	Milon Marusic	76	77	76	79	308	
41T	Jack Shields	78	78	76	77	308	
41T	Art Wall, Jr.	80	75	77	77	309	
43	Earl Stewart, Jr.	74	79	79	78	310	
44	Jimmy Clark	80	78	79	77	314	
	Tommy Bolt	67	81	72	dq		
	Ansel Snow	80	79	74	(42)	wd	
	Johnny Bulla	80	77	wd			
	Jimmy Demaret	79	(43)	wd			

1954
May 27-30

Rank	Player	1R	2R	3R	4R	Total	Money
1	Johnny Palmer	70	72	69	69	280	$5,000
2	Fred Haas	74	72	68	68	282	3,000
3T	*Harvie Ward, Jr.*	70	70	71	72	283	
3T	Byron Nelson	67	74	69	73	283	2,000
5T	Gardner Dickinson	72	74	66	72	284	1,700
5T	Ed Furgol	70	73	69	72	284	1,700
7	Jack Burke, Jr.	74	72	68	72	286	1,400
8T	Peter Thomson	66	71	77	73	287	1,175
8T	Dutch Harrison	71	70	69	77	287	1,175
10T	Cary Middlecoff	75	74	67	72	288	950
10T	Lloyd Mangrum	73	69	69	77	288	950
12T	Earl Stewart, Jr.	80	70	67	72	289	708
12T	Bo Wininger	72	72	71	74	289	708
12T	Gene Littler	72	74	69	74	289	708
15T	Shelley Mayfield	78	71	72	69	290	475
15T	Walter Burkemo	73	72	72	73	290	475
15T	Fred Hawkins	70	73	69	78	290	475
15T	Mike Souchak	72	67	72	79	290	475
19T	Dick Metz	76	72	72	71	291	325
19T	Billy Maxwell	73	70	72	76	291	325
21T	Leo Biagetti	74	74	74	70	292	263
21T	Bob Rosburg	75	76	69	72	292	263
23T	Marty Furgol	74	75	69	75	293	225
23T	*Ernie Vossler*	72	73	72	76	293	
25	Bob Toski	72	75	72	75	294	200
26T	Jerry Barber	74	69	75	77	295	163
26T	Al Besselink	74	71	78	72	295	163
28T	Bob Inman	72	79	73	73	297	
28T	*Don Cherry*	75	74	72	76	297	
28T	Harry Todd	77	75	73	72	297	
28T	Art Wall, Jr.	75	74	72	76	297	
32	Tommy Bolt	75	73	75	75	298	
33T	Wally Ulrich	77	73	73	76	299	
33T	Raymond Gafford	76	69	73	81	299	
35T	O'Neal White	73	78	73	76	300	
35T	*Charles Coe*	75	72	78	75	300	
37T	Skip Alexander	74	76	72	79	301	
37T	Jimmy Clark	72	74	78	77	301	
39	Doug Ford	77	76	77	72	302	
40	Fred Wampler	73	76	77	77	303	
41	Bud Holscher	71	81	78	75	305	
42	Dick Mayer	78	78	75	75	306	
43	Pete Fleming	78	72	78	80	308	
44	*Rex Baxter Jr.*	78	76	74	81	309	
45	Bill Nary	77	79	77	77	310	
	Ben Hogan	69	71	wd			
	Chandler Harper	78	wd				

1957
May 2-5

Rank	Player	1R	2R	3R	4R	Total	Money
1	Roberto De Vicenzo	72	74	68	70	284	$5,000
2	Dick Mayer	71	72	67	75	285	3,000
3	Ed Furgol	73	70	71	72	286	2,000
4T	Mike Souchak	70	73	72	72	287	1,800
4T	*Harvie Ward, Jr.*	70	73	71	73	287	
6	Doug Ford	73	72	73	70	288	1,600
7	Jimmy Demaret	74	73	70	72	289	1,400
8T	Gene Littler	68	74	73	75	290	1,116
8T	Bob Rosburg	69	76	73	72	290	1,116
8T	Peter Thomson	72	74	76	68	290	1,116
11T	Paul Harney	73	71	77	70	291	800
11T	Ben Hogan	70	75	73	73	291	800
11T	Art Wall, Jr.	68	72	75	76	291	800
14T	Dutch Harrison	71	72	72	77	292	531
14T	Jay Hebert	73	75	73	71	292	531
14T	Stan Leonard	73	78	67	74	292	531
14T	Ken Venturi	73	71	73	75	292	531
18T	Tommy Bolt	72	76	73	72	293	315
18T	Joe Conrad	72	73	74	74	293	315
18T	Billy Maxwell	69	75	74	75	293	315
18T	Dick Metz	70	77	70	76	293	315
18T	Doug Sanders	72	74	77	70	293	315
23T	Al Balding	73	79	71	71	294	200
23T	George Bayer	72	77	71	74	294	200
23T	Lloyd Mangrum	72	74	76	72	294	200
26	Mike Fetchick	74	73	74	74	295	150
27T	Jack Burke, Jr.	73	74	72	77	296	
27T	Billy Casper	72	76	74	74	296	
27T	Freddie Haas	70	75	77	74	296	
27T	Cary Middlecoff	78	74	70	74	296	
27T	Byron Nelson	77	76	73	70	296	
27T	Bill Trombley	74	74	74	74	296	
33T	Julius Boros	79	75	72	72	298	
33T	Pete Cooper	73	76	74	75	298	
33T	Arnold Palmer	70	74	75	79	298	
33T	Ernie Vossler	75	76	73	74	298	
37	Frank Stranahan	73	77	73	76	299	
38	Johnny Palmer	74	76	74	76	300	
39T	Doug Higgins	77	76	73	75	301	
39T	Don Whitt	74	77	77	73	301	
41T	Don January	74	74	75	79	302	
41T	Fred Hawkins	73	75	77	77	302	
43	Frank (Bud) Holscher	73	78	74	78	303	
44	Gardner Dickinson	75	77	77	75	304	
45	Bo Wininger	73	80	78	77	308	
46	Bob Toski	74	81	78	79	312	
	Chandler Harper	75	(58)	wd			
	Jack Fleck	71	(45)	wd			

1958
May 1-4

Rank	Player	1R	2R	3R	4R	Total	Money
1	Tommy Bolt	68	70	70	74	282	$5,000
2	Ken Venturi	72	73	69	69	283	3,000
3T	Gardner Dickinson	69	74	72	69	284	1,900
3T	Ted Kroll	74	72	68	70	284	1,900
5T	Don January	73	72	71	69	285	1,417
5T	Lloyd Mangrum	68	73	70	74	285	1,417
5T	Ben Hogan	73	69	70	73	285	1,417
8	Dow Finsterwald	72	73	70	71	286	1,100
9T	Stan Leonard	68	72	72	75	287	950
9T	Ed Oliver	70	73	70	74	287	950
11	Fred Hawkins	72	69	73	74	288	800
12T	Billy Casper	75	75	69	70	289	663
12T	Arnold Palmer	65	77	73	74	289	663
14T	Al Besselink	73	74	71	72	290	525
14T	Roberto De Vicenzo	73	78	68	71	290	525
16T	Billy Maxwell	72	73	75	71	291	425
16T	Julius Boros	75	73	70	73	291	425
18T	George Bayer	76	73	74	69	292	308
18T	Bob Goalby	71	74	74	73	292	308
18T	Cary Middlecoff	71	73	71	77	292	308
21	Howie Johnson	75	75	70	73	293	250
22T	Gary Player	73	73	76	72	294	150
22T	Lionel Hebert	74	72	74	74	294	150
22T	Bill Johnston	75	72	74	73	294	150
22T	Paul Harney	69	73	77	75	294	150
22T	Gene Littler	70	73	73	78	294	150
27T	Bo Wininger	76	74	75	70	295	
27T	Jay Hebert	69	75	76	75	295	
27T	Tom Nieporte	77	73	70	75	295	
27T	Al Balding	73	72	74	76	295	
31T	Frank Stranahan	72	76	73	75	296	
31T	Ernie Vossler	72	76	72	76	296	
31T	Byron Nelson	69	76	72	79	296	
34T	Mike Souchak	74	81	72	70	297	
34T	Fred Haas	74	73	76	74	297	
36T	J. C. Goosie	73	79	73	73	298	
36T	Tony Lema	74	73	77	74	298	
38	Johnny Palmer	70	78	75	76	299	
39	Jack Fleck	71	74	76	79	300	
40T	Joe Conrad	72	82	74	73	301	
40T	Earl Stewart, Jr.	75	78	74	74	301	
40T	Dave Ragan	73	76	75	77	301	
43T	Dick Metz	77	81	71	73	302	
43T	*Rex Baxter, Jr.*	73	80	74	75	302	
45T	*Hillman Robbins, Jr.*	75	79	80	73	307	
45T	Dick Mayer	77	77	73	80	307	
	Bob Rosburg	76	(29)	wd			
	Chandler Harper	83	(39)	wd			

1959
April 30-May 3

Rank	Player	1R	2R	3R	4R	Total	Money
1	Ben Hogan	69	67	77	72	285*	$5,000
2	Fred Hawkins	72	69	73	71	285*	3,000
3T	Billy Maxwell	74	71	72	69	286	1,900
3T	Tommy Jacobs	70	70	73	73	286	1,900
5T	Lionel Hebert	67	67	78	75	287	1,500
5T	Ted Kroll	68	71	71	77	287	1,500
7T	Dow Finsterwald	70	73	76	69	288	1,117
7T	Ernie Vossler	73	70	73	72	288	1,117
7T	Bo Wininger	73	69	73	73	288	1,117
10	Peter Thomson	75	72	72	70	289	900
11T	H. R. (Bert) Weaver	73	75	73	69	290	604
11T	Fred Haas	71	74	73	72	290	604
11T	Gary Player	74	71	74	71	290	604
11T	Gardner Dickinson	70	71	75	74	290	604
11T	Jim Ferree	70	69	77	74	290	604
11T	Don January	72	68	75	75	290	604
17T	George Bayer	71	74	74	71	291	331
17T	Stan Leonard	75	72	71	73	291	331
17T	Jay Hebert	71	72	76	72	291	331
17T	Arnold Palmer	73	74	69	75	291	331
21T	Joe Campbell	77	74	72	69	292	213
21T	Gene Littler	71	77	73	71	292	213
21T	John McMullin	73	75	71	73	292	213
21T	Lloyd Mangrum	74	70	74	74	292	213
25	Byron Nelson	76	69	76	72	293	150
26T	Marty Furgol	76	72	74	73	295	100
26T	Bill Collins	73	74	75	73	295	100
26T	Johnny Palmer	75	74	73	74	295	100
29	Mike Souchak	69	78	81	68	296	100
30	Cary Middlecoff	75	77	69	76	297	100
31T	Tommy Bolt	72	76	77	73	298	100
31T	Ed Oliver	73	73	78	73	298	100
33T	Tom Nieporte	74	76	75	75	300	100
33T	Dick Mayer	75	73	73	79	300	100
33T	Bill Johnston	69	75	73	83	300	100
36T	Roberto De Vicenzo	80	73	77	71	301	100
36T	Howie Johnson	76	73	81	71	301	100
36T	Bruce Crampton	74	76	79	72	301	100
36T	Wes Ellis, Jr.	75	74	79	73	301	100
36T	Jack Burke, Jr.	69	79	73	80	301	100
41	Ken Venturi	76	72	79	75	302	100
42T	Johnny Pott	79	75	75	74	303	100
42T	Earl Stewart, Jr.	76	70	77	80	303	100
44	Pete Cooper	75	77	78	75	305	100
45T	Frank Stranahan	79	75	73	79	306	100
45T	Julius Boros	77	76	75	78	306	100
47T	Ed Furgol	70	77	81	73	311	100
47T	Bob Goalby	77	80	78	76	311	100

*In playoff: Ben Hogan 69; Fred Hawkins 73.

Names in italics designate amateurs.

FREE OFFICIAL PROGRAM

$60,000 EIGHTEENTH ANNUAL

COLONIAL NATIONAL INVITATION

GOLF TOURNAMENT

COLONIAL COUNTRY CLUB • FORT WORTH, TEXAS

FRIDAY, MAY 10, 1963

HOW THEY STAND AT 18		
1	Doug Sanders	67
2	Bill Collins	68
3T	Jerry Barber	69
3T	Bob Rosburg	69
5T	Bruce Crampton	71
5T	Gardner Dickinson	71
5T	Phil Rodgers	71
5T	Tony Lema	71
5T	Jack Nicklaus	71
5T	Julius Boros	71
10T	Jerry Edwards	72
10T	Al Johnston	72
10T	Dan Sikes	72
10T	Bob Wininger	72
10T	Tommy Bolt	72
10T	Cary Middlecoff	72
10T	Jack Fleck	72
10T	Bert Weaver	72
10T	Earl Stewart, Jr.	72
20T	Ted Kroll	73
20T	Gary Player	73
20T	Jerry Pittman	73
20T	Dick Mayer	73
20T	Bobby Nichols	73
25T	Gene Littler	74
25T	Jack Burke	74
25T	Raymond Floyd	74
25T	Gay Brewer, Jr.	74
25T	Arnold Palmer	74
25T	Fred Hawkins	74
25T	Kel Nagle	74
25T	Stan Leonard	74
33T	Ernie Vossler	75
33T	Jacky Cupit	75
33T	Dave Ragan	75
33T	Mike Souchak	75
33T	Al Balding	75
33T	Joe Campbell	75
39T	Byron Nelson	76
39T	Homero Blancas*	76
39T	Fred Marti*	76
39T	Jay Hebert	76
39T	Jim Ferree	76
44T	Doug Ford	77
44T	Billy Maxwell	77
44T	Bob Goalby	77
44T	Johnny Pott	77
44T	Jerry Steelsmith	77
44T	Dow Finsterwald	77
51T	Charles Coody*	78
51T	Lionel Hebert	78
51T	Al Geiberger	78
51T	Art Wall, Jr.	78
51T	George Bayer	78
56T	Labron Harris, Jr.*	79
56T	Miller Barber	79
56T	Dutch Harrison	79
56T	Rex Baxter, Jr.	79
60T	Dave Hill	80
60T	Don Massengale	80
62T	Tommy Aaron	81
62T	Bob Charles	81
62T	Tommy Jacobs	81
65	Don Fairfield	84

* indicates amateurs.

THE 1960s

A TURBULENT, EXCITING TIME FOR GOLF AND COLONIAL

Professional golf exloded in the 1960s, with television and fans jumping on for a ride that hasn't slowed down yet. Colonial's first event of the decade featured great weather and a different leader every day. The purse jumped to $30,000. A lanky young Californian named Al Geiberger received a Champions' Choice invitation. Arnold Palmer was well on his way to PGA Player of the Year, having won his second Masters and four other events early in the season.

Defending champ Ben Hogan kicked things off with an opening 69, joining 13 other top players at par or better. "This is quite an education," claimed Geiberger after two competitive rounds. "I've played five rounds here and it's never the same. I think you'd have to play it 100 times to learn it thoroughly."

ABOVE:
Julius Boros won at Colonial twice in the 1960s; pictured here with Colonial President George Hill.

ABOVE:
Colonial President George Hill (left) and Tournament Chairman Bing Bingham (right) flank the top players in 1961. L-R Champion Doug Sanders, runner-up Kel Nagle, third place finisher Billy Casper, and low amateurs Deane Beman and Charles Coe. In the early days, the awards ceremony included the top three finishers and low amateurs. But only the champion got to keep the jacket.

On Sunday, sweet-swinging Julius Boros, Australian Kel Nagle, Gene Littler and Ted Kroll all had a shot at the title with two holes to play. Each player birdied the 17th hole, giving Boros a one-shot lead. Nagle's dramatic 50-foot birdie putt to tie on #18 circled the cup and refused to drop. Boros, the 1952 U.S. Open champion, two-putted for par and the win. Palmer was in the hunt after two rounds, but tied for 22nd place.

The 1961 tournament set high benchmarks for Colonial. The event sold more than $100,000 in tickets and saw 50,000 people march through the turnstiles, both records. The purse rose to $40,000. The tournament staged its first pro-am, as well as a nursery for the players' children -- now a Tour staple. (a pro-am playing spot could be secured with a $150 ticket purchase and $35 entry fee). "World Amateur" champion Jack Nicklaus made his first appearance at Colonial, joined by British Amateur champ Charles Coe and U. S. Amateur champ Deane Beman.

ABOVE:
Arnold Palmer was hot in 1962, as his Colonial win went along with several victories that year.

Kel Nagle, paired with Hogan during the first round, carded the tournament's first ace in history, on No. 13. After the cheering subsided, a stone-faced Hogan deadpanned, "Good shot," and then smiled. That popular story has been retold many times over the years. Arnold Palmer, Gene Littler, Mike Souchak, Nagle, and Billy Casper all fought for the lead with Doug Sanders. Nagle finished second once again, though, as Sanders captured the title by one shot, Casper took third. Coe and Beman tied for low amateur honors, besting the young Nicklaus by four shots.

In 1962 Arnold Palmer took the Tour by storm. After winning three out of four tournaments, and two in a row, he wanted to take off a week - which happened to be Colonial week. Tournament Chairman Bing Bingham hopped on a plane to Las Vegas and persuaded Palmer to honor his prior commitment to the Colonial event. Palmer agreed, proceeded to win the Vegas Tournament of Champions that weekend, and took two days off before flying into Fort Worth late Wednesday. He then dueled with Gary Player for four exciting rounds as they traded the lead (Palmer had recently beaten Player and Dow Finsterwald in a Masters playoff). On Saturday, Australian Bruce Crampton joined the fray and stood on the 18th tee with a chance to tie Hogan's course record of 65 with a par. He knocked his second shot into the lake for a double bogey, but still tied Player for second place with one round to go.

Sunday's round was incredible. Playing together, Palmer and Player struggled mightily, shooting 76 and 78, respectively. Crampton stood on the 18th tee with a chance to win, but knocked it into the water again, and lost by a shot. A 69 by Johnny Pott tied Palmer for first place, so an 18-hole playoff Monday determined the winner - Palmer. Shooting the identical playoff scores as Hogan and Hawkins three years earlier, 69-73, Palmer wrestled the title from Pott. It was his third win in a row, and he finally got his week off. Crampton got a lake named after him. Nicklaus placed fourth in his first professional run at Colonial, and then won the U.S. Open Championship a month later.

1963 was a stormy year, and a turning point in the future of Colonial and professional golf. The Tour and its players were gaining collective strength and demanding more control over events. They had fought with the PGA of America for autonomy in the 1950s, and this was the next step. A spat between Colonial officials and player Don January grew into a full-blown PGA feud. Just one week prior to the tournament, the event's field was an unknown, and its future was in jeopardy. Once again, Bingham came to the rescue. Pride was swallowed, fences were mended and the tournament was a big success. Colonial would no longer be an entirely independent event, but its future as a prestigious invitational tournament was secure.

The purse was raised to $60,000, and the field grew to 66 players -- the most ever.

The 1963 field featured the new "Big Three" -- Palmer, Nicklaus and Player. Nicklaus had just become the youngest player to win the Masters. Player was the reigning PGA champion. 1961 Colonial champ Doug Sanders grabbed the first round lead, then 1960 winner Julius Boros took it. Player charged from the pack on Sunday with a 67, but could not catch Boros, who became the first man besides Hogan to win more than one Colonial championship. Ironically, it was the first NIT missed by Hogan, who was recovering from shoulder surgery.

ABOVE:
Pete Brown, a tournament winner earlier in the year, was the first black to compete at Colonial, in 1964.
TOP:
Bruce Crampton took the championship in 1965.
MIDDLE:
Gary Player accepts congratulations from Colonial President Ralph McCann for his runner-up finish in 1963.
BOTTOM:
Jack Nicklaus made his Colonial debut in 1961, as an amateur; pictured here in 1962 after turning professional.

ABOVE:
Bruce Devlin captured the championship in 1966.

ABOVE RIGHT:
Young Dave Stockton shocked everyone by winning in 1967 as a Champions' Choice.

Boros' 279 was the first under-par win in eight years. Nicklaus finished third, behind Player. Boros won his second U.S. Open championship a month later. Also in 1963, a 20-year-old Raymond Floyd made his first Colonial appearance, and TCU's Charles Coody captured low amateur honors.

National television embraced the National Invitation in 1964, as ABC broadcast the event Saturday and Sunday. Twelve-year Tournament Chairman Bing Bingham stepped aside for Frank Rogers, and Colonial began a new practice of having three-year tours of duty for its chairmen. The purse jumped to $75,000, and a Grounds Badge now cost $12.50 for the week. Tommy Bolt boasted about his new pair of $12,000 gold golf shoes, but wouldn't wear them because "Fort Worth just isn't ready for those shoes yet."

Pete Brown, the first black golfer to compete in the NIT, earned an invitation by winning a tournament earlier in the year.

Gary Player led after one round, but lost his touch after rain canceled Friday play. 1959 U.S. Open champion Billy Casper stormed into the lead in a 36-hole Saturday, and dusted the field on Sunday to win by four. The turning point came on the treacherous eighth hole, where Gene Littler knocked his tee shot in the hazard for bogey, while Casper trickled in a 12-foot putt for birdie. An early TV finish at 4 pm saved the day, because rain poured at 4:30.

Nicklaus didn't finish in the top five as he had the previous two years, but still sang Colonial's praises. "Colonial and Las Vegas (Tournament of Champions) are probably pretty close together as the fifth best tournament," he commented. "Colonial carries a lot more prestige than any regular tour tournament. Actually, it's better than the British Open -- but you know the prestige angle isn't the same."

FREE SOUVENIR PROGRAM

TWENTIETH ANNUAL

COLONIAL COUNTRY CLUB

COLONIAL NATIONAL INVITATION

20TH

$100,000 GOLF TOURNAMENT
MAY 6·9, 1965
PRO·AM MAY 5

SUNDAY, MAY 9, 1965

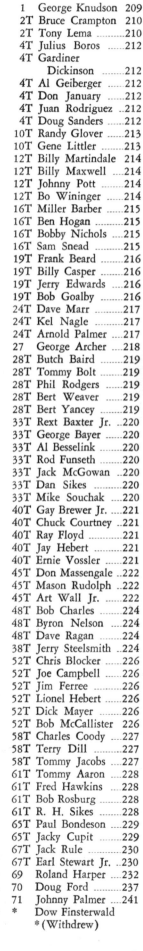

Bruce Crampton exorcised his watery devil in 1965 and captured the Colonial title. But another watery devil - rain - left its mark. The final round was canceled Sunday and Monday. Canadian George Knudson, who led all the early rounds, claimed after Monday's rain-out that he was the only man in history to lead a golf tournament for five days and still not win. Finally, on Tuesday, the players battled it out. Don January, Tony Lema, and Gardner Dickinson all briefly grabbed the lead. But Crampton shot a spectacular four-under-par on the last six holes to claim a three-shot win. Knudson's undoing was a double-bogey on #10. "Crampton played that back nine like I've never seen it played before," he marveled. As Crampton stood in #18 fairway with a two-shot lead, he contemplated laying up to take the dreaded lake out of range. "But it was vitally important to me that I win

like a true champion, worthy of carrying the NIT crown," he said later. So he bravely knocked a six iron on the green and two-putted for top share of the record $100,000 purse.

Trivia buffs should know that the 1965 Colonial NIT featured the Tour's first use of the "waiting-for the-ball-to-drop" rule. This rule was created after an incident in the 1964 Phoenix Open with Don January. Tommy Bolt waited two minutes on Colonial's 14th green Friday for his ball the drop off the lip and into the hole, and was penalized. Even the great Sam Snead showed up for the tournament, finishing 15th in his last Colonial appearance. Also this year, a national poll of media pronounced 52-year-old Ben Hogan as the "Greatest Professional Golfer of All Time," and he was honored with a Thursday night dinner and a post-play ceremony at Colonial on Saturday.

In 1966, the foreign players picked up where they left off in 1965. Australians Bruce Devlin and Peter Thomson led the first round in perfect weather, with New Zealander Bob Charles. Devlin, having practiced with Ben Hogan the week before, nearly ran away with the event. A 75 on Sunday kept it interesting, though, and Arkansas' R.H. Sikes missed a 20-foot birdie putt to tie on #18. Devlin would be Colonial's last foreign winner for 23 years. In the broadcast booth for national TV that year was none other than Byron Nelson, who made his last appearance in Colonial's tournament field.

In 1967, an unknown 25-year-old, Champions' Choice invitee named Dave Stockton stunned himself and the golf world. He fired an opening round, record-tying 65, and then backed it up with a 66 to set a new 36-hole record. Tom Weiskopf tied him on Saturday and then birdied the first two holes on Sunday. But two quick double-bogeys took him out of contention, and Stockton out-battled Charles Coody and 54-year-old Ben Hogan for the title.

"I've probably shocked a lot of people," Stockton said. "I know I've shocked myself."

Billy Casper and Gary Player made the 1968 Colonial their own personal duel, and found themselves tied with a four-shot lead on the field with 18 holes to play. A mighty wind attacked on Sunday, and only two players broke par. Casper's 68 included a double bogey, but won by five shots. He joined Julius Boros as a two-time Colonial champion.

1969 brought significant changes to the course from the Trinity River levee project, especially holes #7, 8, and 13 -- the flood of '49 would never happen again. 100 players competed for a purse of $125,000. Another stellar field battled it out, with Nicklaus, Player, Crampton and January the leaders going into Sunday. But a lanky 41-year-old veteran on the verge of retirement shot a terrific 66 to beat Player by a shot. He was

Gardner Dickinson, and he credited the victory to a 1 1/2 hour lesson on Saturday from friend Ben Hogan, who was unable to play that year.

Colonial saw its one millionth fan pass through the gates in this decade's final year, and it marked the first time the field was large enough to necessitate a cut after 36 holes. That first cut fell at seven over par. Just around the corner were the wild and crazy 1970s. Times, they were a changin'.

ABOVE:
Gardner Dickinson (left) closed out the decade by winning the 1969 tournament; pictured here with Colonial President Jack Melcher.

1960
May 12-15

Rank	Player	1R	2R	3R	4R	Total	Money
1	Julius Boros	70	71	69	70	280	$5,000
2T	Gene Littler	69	70	70	72	281	2,500
2T	Kel Nagle	69	68	72	72	281	2,500
4	Ted Kroll	75	69	69	69	282	1,700
5T	Mike Souchak	74	69	71	70	284	1,400
5T	Ken Venturi	69	74	72	69	284	1,400
5T	Jerry Barber	68	72	73	71	284	1,400
8	Ben Hogan	69	72	75	69	285	1,200
9T	Tommy Bolt	71	77	71	67	286	1,050
9T	Jay Hebert	72	75	70	69	286	1,050
11T	Gary Player	72	72	70	73	287	845
11T	Doug Sanders	69	70	76	72	287	845
11T	Don January	69	74	70	74	287	845
14T	Ernie Vossler	72	73	74	69	288	498
14T	Jack Burke, Jr.	73	70	77	68	288	498
14T	Stan Leonard	74	73	71	70	288	498
14T	Mason Rudolph	70	72	76	70	288	498
14T	Johnny Palmer	69	76	72	71	288	498
14T	Doug Ford	70	72	76	70	288	498
14T	Bert Weaver	73	73	71	71	288	498
14T	Dow Finsterwald	72	73	71	72	288	498
22T	Al Geiberger	74	71	73	71	289	243
22T	Tommy Jacobs	75	72	71	71	289	243
22T	Fred Haas	75	75	68	71	289	243
22T	Billy Maxwell	67	76	73	73	289	243
22T	Bill Collins	70	73	74	72	289	243
22T	Arnold Palmer	71	70	73	75	289	243
28T	Tom Nieporte	71	77	72	70	290	150
28T	Dan Fairfield	72	73	72	73	290	150
30T	Billy Casper	70	74	77	70	291	110
30T	Dick Knight	74	71	74	72	291	110
32T	Bo Winninger	71	72	78	71	292	100
32T	Dave Marr	73	74	71	74	292	100
34T	Chandler Harper	73	76	71	73	293	100
34T	Paul Harney	72	77	71	73	293	100
34T	Joe Jimenez	76	69	74	74	293	100
37T	Byron Nelson	72	75	74	73	294	100
37T	Bob Rosburg	73	70	74	77	294	100
39T	Don Whitt	73	73	76	73	295	100
39T	Fred Hawkins	74	71	78	72	295	100
41T	Roberto De Vicenzo	75	76	74	72	297	100
41T	Lloyd Mangrum	73	75	77	72	297	100
41T	George Bayer	74	77	70	76	297	100
44T	Peter Thomson	78	70	78	72	298	100
44T	Ed Oliver	73	71	79	75	298	100
46T	Earl Stewart, Jr.	77	75	76	72	300	100
46T	Jack Fleck	74	73	77	76	300	100
48T	Joe Campbell	75	74	78	74	301	100
48T	Dave Ragan	78	72	76	75	301	100
50T	Jim Ferree	75	75	79	74	303	100
50T	Pete Cooper	75	80	77	71	303	100
52	Lionel Hebert	77	77	76	74	304	100
53	Frank Stranahan	75	75	76	81	307	100
	Cary Middlecoff	75	78	wd			100

1961
May 11-14

Rank	Player	1R	2R	3R	4R	Total	Money
1	Doug Sanders	69	75	67	70	281	$7,000
2	Kel Nagle	65	76	74	67	282	3,500
3	Billy Casper	69	72	69	73	283	2,500
4T	Don Whitt	71	74	69	70	284	1,900
4T	Gene Littler	72	70	67	75	284	1,900
6	Arnold Palmer	68	73	69	76	286	1,700
7T	Doug Ford	71	71	75	70	287	1,550
7T	Stan Leonard	72	72	68	75	287	1,550
9T	Gary Player	74	75	71	68	288	1,158
9T	Gardner Dickinson	71	73	68	76	288	1,158
9T	Ted Kroll	74	75	70	69	288	1,158
9T	Jack Burke, Jr.	71	73	73	71	288	1,158
9T	Paul Harney	73	73	71	71	288	1,158
9T	Jay Hebert	71	76	69	72	288	1,158
15T	Al Geiberger	73	73	75	68	289	875
15T	Mike Souchak	69	70	73	77	289	875
17T	Jacky Cupit	71	77	73	69	290	775
17T	Bill Collins	75	73	72	70	290	775
19T	Dow Finsterwald	73	73	74	71	291	550
19T	Don January	74	74	73	70	291	550
19T	Bob Goalby	70	76	71	74	291	550
19T	Johnny Pott	73	73	71	74	291	550
19T	Ben Hogan	68	75	72	76	291	550
19T	Ernie Vossler	71	71	73	76	291	550
19T	Howie Johnson	73	73	71	74	291	550
26T	*Charles Coe*	76	76	70	71	293	
26T	*Deane Beman*	68	79	74	72	293	
28T	Bob Rosburg	73	74	75	72	294	315
28T	Tommy Bolt	72	78	73	71	294	315
28T	Roberto De Vicenzo	71	76	72	75	294	315
28T	George Bayer	76	74	70	74	294	315
32T	Peter Thomson	75	76	74	70	295	225
32T	Lionel Hebert	72	78	74	71	295	225
32T	Gay Brewer	71	80	71	73	295	225
35T	Jerry Barber	76	72	75	73	296	152
35T	Don Fairfield	75	74	74	73	296	152
35T	Art Wall, Jr.	75	70	73	78	296	152
38	*Jack Nicklaus*	75	74	76	72	297	
39T	Dave Ragan	72	77	73	76	298	103
39T	Ken Venturi	71	74	76	77	298	103
39T	Tom Nieporte	71	74	76	77	298	103
39T	Dick Mayer	73	77	69	79	298	103
43	Byron Nelson	74	78	69	78	299	100
44T	Cary Middlecoff	79	72	75	74	300	100
44T	Jim Ferree	77	76	74	73	300	100
44T	Billy Maxwell	72	75	79	74	300	100
44T	Dave Marr	80	75	71	74	300	100
48T	Johnny Palmer	76	78	74	74	302	100
48T	Jack Fleck	74	77	76	75	302	100
50T	Fred Hawkins	75	80	78	70	303	100
50T	Dave Hill	77	73	77	76	303	100
52	Julius Boros	78	75	76	75	304	100
53	Mason Rudolph	75	79	73	79	306	100
54	Butch Baird	76	78	76	77	307	100
55	Lloyd Mangrum	76	77	81	74	308	100
	Pete Cooper	76	76	70	(56) wd		100
	Bill Johnston	(37)	wd				

results

1962
May 10-14

Rank	Player	1R	2R	3R	4R	Total	Money
1	Arnold Palmer	67	72	66	76	281*	$7,000
2	Johnny Pott	69	70	73	69	281*	3,500
3	Bruce Crampton	71	70	67	74	282	2,500
4	Jack Nicklaus	69	71	74	69	283	2,000
5T	Jim Ferree	71	73	71	69	284	1,750
5T	Gay Brewer	70	75	67	72	284	1,750
7T	Bo Wininger	68	73	72	71	285	1,550
7T	Doug Ford	68	72	69	76	285	1,550
9T	Doug Sanders	71	71	72	72	286	1,350
9T	Gary Player	68	70	70	78	286	1,350
11	Bill Casper	71	72	73	71	287	1,200
12T	Jack Burke, Jr.	72	73	71	72	288	1,017
12T	Don January	70	75	70	73	288	1,017
12T	Billy Maxwell	75	71	69	73	288	1,017
15T	Ben Hogan	72	71	71	75	289	875
15T	Kel Nagle	72	71	71	75	289	875
17T	Earl Stewart	72	72	74	72	290	750
17T	Byron Nelson	73	70	74	73	290	750
17T	Phil Rodgers	70	73	73	74	290	750
20T	Fred Hawkins	70	77	72	72	291	600
20T	Al Geiberger	74	74	71	72	291	600
20T	Julius Boros	74	74	70	73	291	600
23T	Jay Hebert	70	72	75	75	292	427
23T	Jim Ferrier	70	74	73	75	292	427
23T	Dow Finsterwald	70	75	71	76	292	427
23T	Dave Ragan	72	72	73	75	292	427
27	George Bayer	73	74	74	72	293	325
28T	Gene Littler	70	75	76	73	294	262
28T	Bill Collins	69	73	77	75	294	262
28T	Tommy Jacobs	69	75	73	77	294	262
28T	Ernie Vossler	72	74	71	77	294	262
32	Bob Goalby	73	75	72	75	295	200
33T	Tommy Aaron	74	72	76	74	296	141
33T	Ted Kroll	73	73	75	75	296	141
33T	Jacky Cupit	69	78	72	77	296	141
33T	Joe Campbell	71	73	74	78	296	141
37T	Dave Hill	72	74	78	73	297	100
37T	Dave Marr	72	76	74	75	297	100
39T	Eric Monti	73	74	73	78	298	100
39T	Cary Middlecoff	75	73	72	78	298	100
41T	Mason Rudolph	76	73	78	72	299	100
41T	Bob McCallister	70	75	79	75	299	100
41T	Lionel Hebert	73	79	70	77	299	100
44T	George Knudson	74	78	76	73	301	100
44T	Jerry Barber	72	75	76	78	301	100
44T	Don Massengale	76	73	73	79	301	100
47T	Paul Bondeson	73	75	77	77	302	100
47T	Bobby Nichols	75	76	74	77	302	100
47T	Lloyd Mangrum	71	74	75	82	302	100
50	Jerry Steelsmith	72	73	78	80	303	100
51T	Frank Boynton	74	79	76	75	304	100
51T	Tommy Bolt	72	79	76	77	304	100
53	Paul Harney	75	79	74	77	305	100
54	Gardner Dickinson	79	74	70	83	306	100
	Bob Rosburg	80	81	wd			
	Don Fairfield	83	wd				
	Mike Souchak	dq					
	Ken Venturi	dq					

*In 18-hole playoff: Palmer 69; Pott 73.

1963
May 9-12

Rank	Player	1R	2R	3R	4R	Total	Money
1	Julius Boros	71	66	71	71	279	$12,000
2	Gary Player	73	72	67	71	283	6,000
3	Jack Nicklaus	71	69	74	70	284	3,500
4T	Doug Sanders	67	72	72	75	286	2,800
4T	Tony Lema	71	69	73	73	286	2,800
6T	Jerry Edwards	72	70	75	70	287	2,200
6T	Gene Littler	74	71	69	73	287	2,200
8T	Gardner Dickinson	71	75	76	66	288	1,850
8T	Jack Burke, Jr.	74	67	78	69	288	1,850
10T	Jack Fleck	72	71	74	72	289	1,550
10T	Phil Rodgers	71	71	74	73	289	1,550
10T	Bruce Crampton	71	69	74	75	289	1,550
10T	Bobby Nichols	73	67	74	75	289	1,550
14	Bob Rosburg	69	74	71	76	290	1,300
15T	Jay Hebert	76	71	70	74	291	1,150
15T	Dave Ragan	75	72	74	70	291	1,150
17T	Billy Maxwell	77	76	69	70	292	900
17T	Jacky Cupit	75	74	73	70	292	900
17T	Dow Finsterwald	77	70	72	73	292	900
17T	Bert Weaver	72	75	72	73	292	900
17T	Bill Collins	68	76	73	75	292	900
22T	Jerry Pittman	73	73	76	71	293	725
22T	Al Johnston	72	72	76	73	293	725
24T	Al Geiberger	78	70	74	72	294	525
24T	Miller Barber	79	69	75	71	294	525
24T	Dutch Harrison	79	73	71	71	294	525
24T	Dick Mayer	73	71	76	74	294	525
24T	Mike Souchak	75	74	71	74	294	525
24T	Bo Wininger	72	76	71	75	294	525
30T	Doug Ford	77	78	68	72	295	322
30T	Jim Ferree	76	73	73	73	295	322
30T	Dan Sikes	72	75	74	74	295	322
30T	Kel Nagle	74	75	71	75	295	322
34T	Gay Brewer	74	72	76	74	296	250
34T	Bob Goalby	77	77	67	75	296	250
36T	Charles Coody	78	73	74	72	297	
36T	George Bayer	78	70	75	74	297	220
36T	*Kermit Zarley, Jr.*	78	76	69	74	297	
36T	Ted Kroll	73	75	72	77	297	220
36T	Stan Leonard	74	73	72	78	297	220
41T	Jerry Steelsmith	77	75	75	71	298	195
41T	*Labron Harris, Jr.*	79	75	71	73	298	
41T	Art Wall, Jr.	78	71	71	78	298	195
44T	*Fred Marti*	76	75	76	72	299	
44T	Arnold Palmer	74	75	75	75	299	170
44T	Fred Hawkins	74	75	73	77	299	170
44T	Earl Stewart, Jr.	72	74	75	78	299	170
48T	Al Balding	75	71	81	73	300	150
48T	Byron Nelson	76	77	73	74	300	150
48T	Bob Charles	81	71	75	73	300	150
48T	Jerry Barber	69	75	81	75	300	150
48T	Johnny Pott	77	73	76	74	300	150
53	Cary Middlecoff	72	76	79	74	301	150
54T	Ray Floyd	74	75	78	75	302	150
54T	Lionel Hebert	78	72	73	79	302	150
56T	Joe Campbell	75	76	77	75	303	150
56T	Tommy Bolt	72	76	75	80	303	150
58	Ernie Vossler	75	76	78	76	305	150
59T	Dave Hill	80	75	77	74	306	150
59T	*Homero Blancas*	76	76	76	78	306	
59T	Don Fairfield	84	74	71	77	306	150
62T	Rex Baxter, Jr.	79	78	73	77	307	150
62T	Tommy Aaron	81	73	71	82	307	150
64T	Don Massengale	80	81	73	76	310	150
64T	Tommy Jacobs	81	77	72	80	310	150
	Don January	dq					

1964
May 7-10

Rank	Player	1R	2R	3R	4R	Total	Money
1	Billy Casper	72	67	70	70	279	$14,000
2	Tommy Jacobs	69	71	74	69	283	7,000
3	Gene Littler	71	71	68	75	285	4,000
4T	Ben Hogan	72	72	71	72	287	3,160
4T	Dow Finsterwald	74	69	74	70	287	3,160
4T	Gay Brewer	70	73	72	72	287	3,160
4T	Arnold Palmer	75	71	69	72	287	3,160
4T	Gary Player	68	73	72	72	287	3,160
9	Kel Nagle	71	76	68	73	288	2,500
10T	Dave Marr	76	71	72	70	289	2,175
10T	Mason Rudolph	72	72	71	74	289	2,175
12T	Ray Floyd	70	77	74	69	290	1,620
12T	Lionel Hebert	73	73	72	72	290	1,620
12T	Pete Brown	76	70	71	73	290	1,620
12T	Jack Rule, Jr.	74	66	78	72	290	1,620
12T	Doug Sanders	73	70	73	74	290	1,620
17T	Tony Lema	78	71	71	71	291	1,150
17T	Dan Sikes	71	74	74	72	291	1,150
17T	Billy Maxwell	71	70	74	76	291	1,150
17T	George Knudson	74	70	70	77	291	1,150
21T	Phil Rodgers	76	75	71	70	292	775
21T	Jack Nicklaus	76	72	71	73	292	775
21T	Bob Charles	77	71	69	75	292	775
21T	Jerry Edwards	70	74	73	75	292	775
21T	Miller Barber	77	68	71	76	292	775
21T	Art Wall	71	72	71	78	292	775
27T	Bob Rosburg	72	71	76	74	293	525
27T	Julius Boros	77	72	70	74	293	525
27T	Al Besselink	70	77	69	77	293	525
27T	Frank Beard	74	71	72	76	293	525
31T	Harold Kneece	79	74	72	69	294	387
31T	Dutch Harrison	74	72	75	73	294	387
31T	Gardner Dickinson	72	77	71	74	294	387
31T	Jacky Cupit	73	75	71	75	294	387
35	Bob Goalby	80	70	72	73	295	325
36T	Ken Venturi	74	76	73	73	296	262
36T	Bruce Devlin	74	74	74	74	296	262
36T	Earl Stewart, Jr.	73	72	75	76	296	262
36T	Al Geiberger	71	70	77	78	296	262
40T	Don Fairfield	76	75	73	73	297	220
40T	Mike Souchak	73	74	74	76	297	220
42T	Ramon Sota	82	70	75	71	298	195
42T	Bill Collins	76	69	77	76	298	195
42T	Fred Hawkins	72	74	75	77	298	195
45T	Johnny Pott	73	76	73	77	299	175
45T	Al Balding, Jr.	74	75	75	75	299	175
45T	Jay Hebert	76	75	70	78	299	175
48T	Bo Wininger	76	71	78	75	300	162
48T	Bobby Nichols	80	74	68	78	300	162
50T	Cary Middlecoff	76	75	74	76	301	155
50T	Chuck Courtney	74	72	78	77	301	155
50T	Don January	71	76	77	77	301	155
50T	Rex Baxter, Jr.	75	74	72	80	301	155
54T	Tommy Bolt	78	73	74	77	302	155
54T	Jim Ferrier	77	76	74	75	302	155
56T	Jack Burke, Jr.	76	76	76	75	303	155
56T	Bruce Crampton	75	75	78	75	303	155
56T	Dave Ragan	77	79	73	74	303	155
59T	Shelly Mayfield	75	75	77	77	304	155
59T	Jerry Steelsmith	80	75	73	76	304	155
61T	Doug Ford	72	80	74	79	305	155
61T	Charles Coody	77	77	74	77	305	155
63	George Bayer	71	76	77	82	306	155
64T	Ernie Vossler	73	78	75	82	308	155
64T	Rod Funseth	81	80	73	74	308	155
66	Jim Ferree	76	79	75	79	309	155
67	Dave Hill	79	78	76	83	316	155
68	Roland Harper	85	81	82	79	327	155
69	Johnny Palmer	87	81	82	81	331	155
	Tommy Aaron	77	75	wd			
	Jimmy Demaret	78	wd				
	Chi Chi Rodriguez	75	wd				

*Names in italics designate amateurs.

1960s

1965
May 6-11

Rank	Player	1R	2R	3R	4R	Total	Money
1	Bruce Crampton	71	68	71	66	276	$20,000
2	George Knudson	68	71	70	70	279	11,500
3T	Gardner Dickinson	72	69	71	68	280	5,100
3T	Don January	72	72	68	68	280	5,100
3T	Tony Lema	71	69	70	70	280	5,100
3T	Chi Chi Rodriguez	70	73	69	68	280	5,100
7	Julius Boros	72	68	72	69	281	3,400
8T	Gene Littler	69	71	73	69	282	2,850
8T	Doug Sanders	70	72	70	70	282	2,850
10T	Ben Hogan	69	71	75	69	284	2,233
10T	Billy Martindale	72	72	70	70	284	2,233
10T	Bobby Nichols	73	71	71	69	284	2,233
13T	Al Geiberger	71	74	67	73	285	1,850
13T	Johnny Pott	69	75	70	71	285	1,850
15T	Jerry Edwards	71	71	74	70	286	1,650
15T	Sam Snead	71	72	72	71	286	1,650
17T	Randy Glover	74	70	69	74	287	1,300
17T	Bob Goalby	72	71	73	71	287	1,300
17T	Billy Maxwell	71	73	70	73	287	1,300
17T	Kel Nagle	75	71	71	70	287	1,300
17T	Arnold Palmer	73	74	70	70	287	1,300
22T	Frank Beard	70	73	73	72	288	894
22T	Tommy Bolt	69	78	72	69	288	894
22T	Billy Casper	70	73	73	72	288	894
22T	Bert Yancey	72	71	76	69	288	894
26T	George Archer	75	73	70	71	289	775
26T	Rex Baxter Jr.	72	74	74	69	289	775
26T	Bert Weaver	72	70	77	70	289	775
29	Bo Wininger	71	70	73	76	290	725
30T	Butch Baird	70	77	72	72	291	663
30T	Miller Barber	71	71	73	76	291	663
30T	Dave Marr	72	70	75	74	291	663
30T	Art Wall Jr.	73	75	74	69	291	663
34T	Jack McGowan	74	77	69	72	292	588
34T	Dan Sikes	75	70	75	72	292	588
36T	Chuck Courtney	74	76	71	72	293	538
36T	Mike Souchak	69	75	76	73	293	538
38T	Al Besselink	74	69	77	74	294	454
38T	Dave Ragan	74	76	74	70	294	454
38T	Phil Rodgers	74	71	74	75	294	454
38T	Mason Rudolph	74	75	73	72	294	454
42T	George Bayer	71	77	72	75	295	303
42T	Gay Brewer	72	72	77	74	295	303
42T	Jim Ferree	75	76	75	69	295	303
42T	Jay Hebert	71	70	80	74	295	303
46T	Bob Charles	72	77	75	72	296	200
46T	Rod Funseth	75	70	75	76	296	200
46T	Lionel Hebert	76	76	74	70	296	200
46T	Dick Mayer	77	76	73	70	296	200
46T	Bob McCallister	79	72	75	70	296	200
46T	Jerry Steelsmith	73	74	77	72	296	200
46T	Ernie Vossler	73	74	74	75	296	200
53	Don Massengale	76	75	71	76	298	150
54T	Joe Campbell	76	73	77	73	299	150
54T	Chris Blocker	74	78	74	73	299	150
56T	Charles Coody	75	77	75	73	300	150
56T	Jacky Cupit	74	79	76	71	300	150
58	Byron Nelson	78	72	74	78	302	150
59	Earl Stewart Jr.	73	80	77	74	304	150
60	Terry Dill	76	73	78	78	305	150
61	Roland Harper	76	83	73	77	309	150
	Tommy Aaron	75	75	78	wd		150
	Paul Bondeson	73	76	80	dq		150
	Ray Floyd	76	74	71	dq		150
	Doug Ford	81	80	76	wd		150
	Fred Hawkins	71	76	81	wd		150
	Tommy Jacobs	80	74	73	wd		150
	Johnny Palmer	78	80	83	wd		150
	Bob Rosburg	80	76	72	wd		150
	Jack Rule	76	80	74	wd		150
	R. H. Sikes	74	80	74	wd		150
	Dow Finsterwald	74	80	wd			—

1966
May 19-22

Rank	Player	1R	2R	3R	4R	Total	Money
1	Bruce Devlin	67	68	70	75	280	$22,000
2	R. H. Sikes	76	67	67	71	281	12,540
3T	Al Geiberger	70	69	72	71	282	6,765
3T	Tony Lema	71	71	69	71	282	6,765
5T	Ben Hogan	72	72	71	69	284	4,455
5T	Jack McGowan	73	69	68	74	284	4,455
7T	Gardner Dickinson	74	72	70	69	285	2,887
7T	Don January	69	73	70	73	285	2,887
7T	Gene Littler	69	69	70	77	285	2,887
7T	Johnny Pott	70	72	71	72	285	2,887
7T	Peter Thomson	68	72	71	74	285	2,887
7T	Bo Wininger	72	72	71	70	285	2,887
13T	George Archer	72	69	73	72	286	1,760
13T	Randy Glover	70	76	71	69	286	1,760
13T	Harold Henning	70	75	71	70	286	1,760
13T	Gary Player	70	74	72	70	286	1,760
13T	Phil Rodgers	74	73	72	67	286	1,760
13T	Chi Chi Rodriguez	72	76	67	71	286	1,760
13T	Tom Weiskopf	74	68	75	69	286	1,760
20T	Frank Beard	71	73	70	74	288	1,111
20T	Gay Brewer	75	67	68	78	288	1,111
20T	Babe Hiskey	73	73	71	71	288	1,111
20T	Earl Stewart, Jr.	73	71	74	70	288	1,111
20T	Bert Weaver	69	71	73	75	288	1,111
25T	Billy Casper	71	71	73	74	289	838
25T	Bob Goalby	74	70	71	74	289	838
25T	Jay Hebert	75	72	72	70	289	838
25T	George Knudson	72	71	74	72	289	838
25T	Dan Sikes	69	72	76	72	289	838
25T	Mike Souchak	74	71	72	72	289	838
31T	Miller Barber	70	73	72	75	290	701
31T	Julius Boros	73	75	71	71	290	701
31T	Charles Coody	71	73	73	73	290	701
31T	Don Massengale	73	73	69	75	290	701
35T	Raymond Floyd	75	70	71	75	291	605
35T	Ed Furgol	73	70	73	75	291	605
35T	Rocky Thompson	75	75	66	75	291	605
38T	Joe Campbell	72	72	72	76	292	536
38T	Chuck Courtney	72	72	74	74	292	536
40T	Bob Verwey	75	74	75	69	293	462
40T	Bert Yancey	73	78	69	73	293	462
42T	Lionel Hebert	72	73	71	78	294	352
42T	Dave Marr	71	75	76	72	294	352
42T	Ken Venturi	75	74	72	73	294	352
45T	Homero Blancas	76	74	75	70	295	258
45T	Bob Charles	68	74	76	77	295	258
45T	Rod Funseth	74	74	74	73	295	258
45T	Art Wall, Jr.	72	73	73	77	295	258
49T	Tommy Aaron	73	78	71	74	296	205
49T	Butch Baird	74	73	74	75	296	205
49T	Kel Nagle	74	73	73	76	296	205
52T	Bruce Crampton	74	79	69	75	297	165
52T	Jacky Cupit	74	79	70	74	297	165
52T	Dave Ragan	76	71	77	73	297	165
52T	Jack Rule, Jr.	73	74	77	73	297	165
56T	George Bayer	73	76	74	76	299	165
56T	Terry Dill	73	74	75	77	299	165
56T	Jack Montgomery	73	75	75	76	299	165
56T	Charles Sifford	76	77	69	77	299	165
60	Jerry Edwards	77	76	73	74	300	165
61T	Jim Ferree	73	73	83	72	301	165
61T	Ernie Vossler	76	78	72	75	301	165
63T	Dick Crawford	73	73	76	83	305	165
63T	Dow Finsterwald	75	80	76	74	305	165
65	Billy Martindale	80	76	78	72	306	165
66	Al Besselink	76	80	71	82	308	165
67	Johnny Palmer	76	76	81	79	312	165
68T	Tommy Bolt	75	70	71	(36)	wd	
68T	Doug Sanders	70	71	74	(42)	wd	
70	Mason Rudolph	74	70	73	wd		
71	Billy Maxwell	71	72	wd			
72	Byron Nelson	75	wd				

1967
May 18-21

Rank	Player	1R	2R	3R	4R	Total	Money
1	Dave Stockton	65	66	74	73	278	$23,000
2	Charles Coody	74	67	70	69	280	13,800
3T	Ben Hogan	67	72	67	73	281	7,187
3T	George Archer	72	68	68	72	281	7,187
5	Gene Littler	71	73	68	71	283	4,945
6T	Gardner Dickinson	71	67	72	73	284	4,140
6T	Arnold Palmer	73	73	67	71	284	4,140
8T	Frank Beard	72	71	68	74	285	3,258
8T	Jack Nicklaus	72	71	72	70	285	3,258
8T	Dan Sikes	70	72	71	72	285	3,258
11T	Bob Charles	72	71	71	72	286	2,369
11T	Bob Goalby	75	68	72	71	286	2,369
11T	Tom Weiskopf	70	65	70	81	286	2,369
11T	Homero Blancas	72	66	73	75	286	2,369
11T	Chi Chi Rodriguez	71	71	72	72	286	2,369
16T	Harold Henning	73	69	71	74	287	1,782
16T	Julius Boros	71	72	71	73	287	1,782
16T	Mason Rudolph	67	76	73	71	287	1,782
16T	Randy Glover	73	71	73	70	287	1,782
20T	Earl Stewart, Jr.	75	67	73	73	288	1,380
20T	Gay Brewer	68	73	71	76	288	1,380
20T	Johnny Pott	73	68	74	73	288	1,380
23T	Bruce Crampton	72	71	71	75	289	933
23T	Deane Beman	71	68	76	74	289	933
23T	Bobby Nichols	67	72	73	77	289	933
23T	Joe Campbell	74	71	71	73	289	933
27T	Miller Barber	73	72	71	74	290	765
27T	Billy Maxwell	71	72	75	72	290	765
27T	Billy Martindale	77	71	70	72	290	765
30T	Don January	74	71	69	77	291	650
30T	Charles Sifford	73	70	72	76	291	650
30T	Dave Hill	70	73	73	75	291	650
30T	Kel Nagle	73	70	73	75	291	650
30T	Al Geiberger	77	69	73	72	291	650
35T	Tommy Aaron	71	69	74	78	292	520
35T	Tommy Bolt	72	74	70	76	292	520
35T	Rocky Thompson	71	68	76	77	292	520
35T	Art Wall	75	70	73	74	292	520
39T	Ken Venturi	73	74	72	74	293	395
39T	Kermit Zarley	70	73	73	77	293	395
39T	Ernie Vossler	73	71	73	76	293	395
39T	Dudley Wysong	71	71	79	72	293	395
43T	Ray Floyd	76	75	70	73	294	241
43T	Bruce Devlin	72	75	70	77	294	241
43T	Ken Still	74	73	72	75	294	241
46T	R. H. Sikes	79	70	71	75	295	150
46T	George Knudson	78	69	70	78	295	150
46T	Paul Bondeson	74	71	75	75	295	150
49T	Phil Rodgers	73	74	75	74	296	150
49T	Tom Nieporte	73	74	75	74	296	150
51	Jerry Edwards	73	73	75	76	297	150
52T	Jay Hebert	76	75	74	73	298	150
52T	Terry Dill	77	73	70	78	298	150
52T	Billy Casper	75	72	75	76	298	150
52T	Lionel Hebert	72	75	75	76	298	150
52T	Doug Sanders	73	76	74	75	298	150
52T	Dave Ragan	78	70	80	70	298	150
58T	Ted Makalena	78	73	75	74	300	150
58T	Dave Marr	74	75	78	73	300	150
60	Doug Ford	79	70	76	77	302	150
61T	Jack Burke, Jr.	79	75	73	76	303	150
61T	Bert Yancey	74	75	77	77	303	150
61T	Lou Graham	75	71	76	81	303	150
61T	Jay Dolan	75	73	78	77	303	150
65T	Jacky Cupit	70	73	75	78	306	150
65T	John Schlee	75	80	75	76	306	150
67	Rod Funseth	79	71	76	81	307	150
68	Dow Finsterwald	73	78	77	80	308	150
69T	Dale Douglass	77	75	75	84	311	150
69T	Mike Souchak	80	76	80	75	311	150
71	Bo Wininger	81	73	79	79	312	150
72	Don Massengale	79	77	78	81	315	150

Rank	Player	1R	2R	3R	4R	Total	Money
1	Billy Casper	68	71	68	68	275	$25,000
2	Gene Littler	71	72	69	68	280	15,000
3	Tommy Aaron	69	74	68	70	281	9,375
4T	Lee Trevino	71	71	70	71	283	5,812
4T	Gary Player	70	68	69	76	283	5,812
6T	Harold Henning	71	73	70	71	285	4,291
6T	Julius Boros	73	71	70	71	285	4,291
6T	Earl Stewart	69	73	69	74	285	4,291
9T	Dudley Wysong	72	73	70	71	286	3,375
9T	Tommy Bolt	70	72	73	71	286	3,375
11	George Knudson	75	70	72	70	287	3,000
12	Bob Goalby	75	70	72	72	288	2,750
13T	George Archer	74	72	72	71	289	2,225
13T	Terry Dill	70	75	73	71	289	2,225
13T	Ken Still	69	71	74	75	289	2,225
13T	Jack Montgomery	69	77	68	75	289	2,225
13T	Dave Stockton	70	72	71	76	289	2,225
13T	Gardner Dickinson	71	73	70	75	289	2,225
19T	Johnny Pott	71	70	76	73	290	1,550
19T	Kel Nagle	69	77	69	75	290	1,550
19T	Tony Jacklin	72	73	69	76	290	1,550
22	Rocky Thompson	77	73	71	70	291	1,250
23T	Don January	73	75	71	73	292	975
23T	Bob Lunn	72	81	68	71	292	975
23T	Homero Blancas	76	77	67	72	292	975
23T	R. H. Sikes	72	74	70	76	292	975
23T	Steve Spray	72	74	69	77	292	975
28T	Chuck Courtney	74	73	72	74	293	800
28T	Phil Rodgers	74	75	67	77	293	800
30T	Chris Blocker	74	76	72	72	294	683
30T	Lionel Hebert	71	72	77	74	294	683
30T	Billy Maxwell	76	73	68	77	294	683
33T	Jay Hebert	77	73	72	73	295	587
33T	Tommy Jacobs	79	73	70	73	295	587
33T	John Lotz	72	77	72	74	295	587
33T	Kermit Zarley	72	74	72	77	295	587
37T	Bob Verwey	75	75	73	73	296	487
37T	Miller Barber	72	77	73	74	296	487
37T	Bob Charles	70	74	77	75	296	487
37T	Bruce Devlin	75	71	72	78	296	487
41T	Laurie Hammer	75	72	74	76	297	412
41T	Marty Fleckman	68	76	75	78	297	412
43T	Charles Coody	78	73	73	74	298	350
43T	Doug Sanders	77	72	73	76	298	350
43T	Dick Crawford	74	77	71	76	298	350
46T	Steve Reid	74	77	72	76	299	287
46T	Frank Beard	72	78	70	79	299	287
48T	Don Cherry	78	72	74	76	300	215
48T	Bobby Nichols	74	81	72	73	300	215
48T	Jack McGowan	77	73	73	77	300	215
48T	Gay Brewer	73	75	75	77	300	215
48T	Bert Yancey	75	75	70	80	300	215
53T	Charles Sifford	78	76	71	76	301	200
53T	Roland Harper	75	72	77	77	301	200
53T	Steve Oppermann	74	75	73	79	301	200
53T	Jerry Edwards	74	77	72	79	301	200
53T	Deane Beman	78	74	72	77	301	200
58	Don Massengale	75	75	77	75	302	175
59T	Ray Floyd	76	75	77	75	303	166
59T	Jim Colbert	74	75	76	78	303	166
59T	Ernie Vossler	73	80	70	80	303	166
62T	Dewitt Weaver	74	81	76	73	304	150
62T	Bob Dickson	76	78	75	75	304	150
62T	John Schlee	72	80	73	79	304	150
65T	Rex Baxter	74	77	81	74	306	150
65T	Ross Collins	76	78	73	79	306	150
67T	Dow Finsterwald	78	79	76	74	307	150
67T	Billy Martindale	73	78	79	77	307	150
67T	Jacky Cupit	76	81	77	73	307	150
67T	Bobby Cole	77	80	73	77	307	150
71	Bruce Crampton	78	81	75		—	
72	Raymond Gafford	79	80			—	
73	Dan Sikes	77	wd				

Rank	Player	1R	2R	3R	4R	Total	Money
1	Gardner Dickinson	71	68	73	66	278	$25,000
2	Gary Player	70	72	69	68	279	14,300
3	Don January	71	70	70	69	280	8,850
4T	Bob Charles	69	72	73	68	282	5,487
4T	Jack Nicklaus	68	70	73	71	282	5,487
6T	George Knudson	74	72	71	66	283	3,890
6T	Bob Lunn	72	71	73	67	283	3,890
6T	Dave Hill	74	69	72	68	283	3,890
6T	Bruce Crampton	70	69	69	75	283	3,890
10	Frank Beard	73	68	76	67	284	3,125
11T	Larry Mowry	71	74	71	69	285	2,625
11T	Johnny Pott	74	71	71	69	285	2,625
11T	Chuck Courtney	66	74	72	73	285	2,625
14T	Dick Crawford	68	74	75	69	286	1,937
14T	Tom Shaw	70	74	73	69	286	1,937
14T	Bruce Devlin	72	69	75	70	286	1,937
14T	Charles Coody	70	69	75	72	286	1,937
14T	Bert Yancey	71	65	77	73	286	1,937
14T	Billy Maxwell	68	70	70	78	286	1,937
20T	Tommy Aaron	75	69	73	70	287	1,325
20T	Bob Dickson	77	69	71	70	287	1,325
20T	Chi Chi Rodriguez	73	72	71	71	287	1,325
20T	Fred Marti	71	70	73	73	287	1,325
24T	Art Wall	70	73	74	71	288	986
24T	Miller Barber	69	74	74	71	288	986
24T	Jack McGowan	73	73	71	71	288	986
24T	B. R. McLendon	73	72	71	72	288	986
24T	Dave Stockton	69	72	73	74	288	986
24T	Jack Montgomery	70	68	75	75	288	986
30T	Deane Beman	70	72	77	70	289	756
30T	Tommy Jacobs	74	71	74	70	289	756
30T	Rod Funseth	71	72	75	71	289	756
30T	Lee Elder	72	74	71	72	289	756
30T	Phil Rodgers	75	69	72	73	289	756
30T	Jacky Cupit	72	69	74	74	289	756
30T	Dale Douglass	71	71	73	74	289	756
37T	Arnold Palmer	73	68	80	69	290	574
37T	Larry Hinson	75	72	74	69	290	574
37T	Don Bies	70	70	80	70	290	574
37T	Frank Boynton	70	71	75	74	290	574
37T	Tommy Bolt	71	72	72	75	290	574
37T	Howie Johnson	74	71	70	75	290	574
43T	Earl Stewart Jr	72	74	73	72	291	397
43T	Bob Smith	71	74	74	72	291	397
43T	Gay Brewer	72	71	75	73	291	397
43T	Charles Sifford	73	69	75	74	291	397
47T	Lou Graham	73	71	77	71	292	258
47T	Dick Lotz	75	72	73	72	292	258
47T	Julius Boros	72	72	74	74	292	258
47T	Bert Greene	76	68	74	74	292	258
47T	Grier Jones	74	72	72	74	292	258
47T	Gene Littler	73	68	75	76	292	258
53T	Tony Jacklin	69	73	81	70	293	200
53T	John Lotz	72	73	75	73	293	200
53T	Ernie Vossler	74	69	75	75	293	200
53T	Bobby Cole	71	71	75	76	293	200
53T	Mason Rudolph	74	70	73	76	293	200
53T	Doug Sanders	71	72	73	77	293	200
53T	Bob Stanton	72	72	72	77	293	200
60T	Dudley Wysong	71	75	76	72	294	200
60T	Harold Henning	74	71	78	71	294	200
60T	George Archer	73	74	72	75	294	200
60T	Ken Still	75	69	74	76	294	200
64T	Mike Hill	75	72	75	73	295	200
64T	Homero Blancas	72	71	78	74	295	200
66T	Kermit Zarley	74	73	75	74	296	200
66T	Orville Moody	71	74	70	81	296	200
68T	R. H. Sikes	72	69	82	74	297	200
68T	Billy Casper	71	74	76	76	297	200
68T	Tom Weiskopf	71	76	68	82	297	200
71T	Jim Colbert	71	72	82	73	298	200
71T	Labron Harris Jr.	72	72	76	75	298	200
71T	Bobby Mitchell	74	71	76	77	298	200
71T	Jerry Edwards	74	71	73	80	298	200
75	Al Balding	75	71	80	75	301	200
76	Ray Floyd	72	73	81	x		

DID NOT MAKE CUT

148	Dean Refram, Doug Ford, Bob Goalby, Rocky Thompson, Chris Blocker, Ron Cerrudo, Marty Fleckman, Steve Spray
149	Terry Dill
150	Bob Verwey, Jay Hebert, Randy Glover, Bob Murphy, Kel Nagle, John Jacobs, Dave Marr
151	John Schlee
152	Roland Harper, Bob McCallister, Lionel Hebert
154	Don Massengale
157	Rives McBee
77-wd	Billy Martindale
wd	Bunky Henry

THE 1970s

A WILD-EYED DECADE FOR FASHION AND GOLF

The 1970s brought hip-huggers and hot pants into the forefront of "fashion" at Colonial's annual Spring showcase. Thankfully, some great golf made up for those outlandish days.

The first tournament of the decade featured a determined Ben Hogan fighting a bad left knee to compete after two years of inactivity. Former NCAA champion Hale Irwin showed up on a Champions' Choice invitation, and promptly tied for fifth place. Gary Player and Lee Trevino fired 66s in the first round, but it was the 57-year-old Hogan's incredible 69 that drew all the attention. By Saturday, Homero Blancas and Trevino were dueling it out. Dale Douglass fired a record 63, using just 25 putts. The battle continued down to the wire Sunday. Trevino had the lead late, but made two costly bogeys. Blancas birdied 16 to take the lead, but bogeyed 18 to open the door. Trevino's 18-foot putt to tie missed on the last hole, and Gene Littler's 10-footer to tie lipped out. Blancas won by a shot, with the second-lowest winning score ever -- 273. He was only the second champ to score four sub-par rounds at Colonial.

ABOVE:
Homero Blancas started the decade with his 1970 victory; pictured with Colonial President Jack Melcher.
FACING PAGE:
Former PGA Tour Commissioner Joe Dey gives Al Geiberger the 1975 Tournament Players Championship trophy.

1979 Colonial National Invitation

An excited Trevino, who ended up leading the Tour money list that year, exclaimed, "Bring on the champagne! You've never had a Mexican winner and runner-up!" Hogan made the cut and finished the event, but it was his last National Invitation. His 21-year Colonial record included five wins and 15 top10 finishes, with his 1970 swan song representing the only time he finished out of the event's top 20.

Sadly, Colonial lost its visionary founder, Marvin Leonard later that summer. He was 75.

In 1971 windy conditions produced an exciting race to the finish, along with the highest winning score on Tour that year. Defending champion Blancas took the first round lead. After three rounds, 51-year-old two-time winner Julius Boros led 1967 champ Dave Stockton by one stroke. Boros held the lead Sunday with nine holes to play, but the steady Gene Littler played incredibly well in a tough wind Sunday. Hitting 14 greens, he took the lead with birdies on 15 and 16. Having finished second at Colonial three times, Littler shot 69 and finally broke through with a well-deserved victory. His total of 283 was the highest winning score at Colonial since 1959, another windy year.

Gary Player, who finished seventh, commented that "This is one of the three hardest courses in the world when the wind blows like this. It's every bit as hard as Carnoustie and Heritage (Hilton Head)."

University of Texas star Ben Crenshaw made the first of three consecutive amateur appearances, and beat 65 pros with a 289, finishing tied for 24th place.

Perfect weather bathed spectators and players in 1972, and former champs Dave Stockton and Bruce Crampton went after the tournament lead early. Then 25-year-old Jerry Heard joined the party in the second round, and promptly set a 54-hole scoring record of eight under par. A double-bogey on the 71st hole cost him the lead, but a bogey on 18 by Fred Marti gave Heard two putts to win. His lag putt birdie fell in the hole.

Another Longhorn, Tom Kite, joined teammate Crenshaw in the field, and began his incredible record streak of 29 consecutive cuts made in the tournament. Both amateurs finished in the top 25. This year marked the only time in Colonial history that the defending champion could not play. Gene Littler was diagnosed with cancer of the lymph nodes several months earlier.

The 1973 NIT included the triumphant return of a healthy Littler, who finished 18th. The tournament eventually turned into a battle between Tom Weiskopf and Bruce Crampton, finishing with a fierce Sunday shootout. Crampton led for three days, but Weiskopf caught him after 13 holes in the final round. Playing in different groups, the players volleyed the lead back and forth the rest of the way. Weiskopf's group finished first, with him posting a 69, but he still needed help. Crampton stood on the 18th tee with a one-shot lead, then succumbed to the ghosts of 1962, when his debacle on #18 gave the title to Arnold Palmer. Crampton hooked his tee shot behind a tree, slashed across the fairway and then found himself in a greenside bunker needing to get up and down for a tie. His sand wedge, however, had been damaged on his second shot, forcing him to use a pitching wedge. His heart-breaking double-bogey placed him second.

Weiskopf went on to claim several more championships and honors that year, his best ever, including the British Open. The newspaper quoted one player during the week as naming Colonial "the premier girl-watching stop on Tour. And whatever's second is way, way back."

In 1974, Colonial helped introduce a new PGA Tour experiment. The NIT was one of three "Designated" tournaments, at which all top players were required to compete. A full field of 150 professionals replaced the normal invitation-only assembly, and a record purse of $250,000 awaited them. The CBS network broadcast Colonial's event for the first time, beginning a longtime relationship that survives today.

Hale Irwin grabbed the early lead with a remarkable opening 65. A young, 5'5" Wintu Indian named Rod Curl joined the hunt in round two, along with Californian Chuck Courtney. Defending champion Tom Weiskopf joined the fray Saturday. Curl grabbed the lead on the front nine Sunday, but found himself tied with Courtney and Nicklaus after 14 holes, setting up a great showdown in the windy conditions. Curl birdied #16, Courtney bogied #16, and then the Golden Bear bogeyed #17 to cost him the tournament. Curl's caddy was the same one who helped young Dave Stockton to the Colonial winner's circle in 1967.

More special things came to Colonial in 1975, as the PGA Tour asked Fort Worth to host its fledgling Tournament Players Championship - in August. The event was in only its second year, and several years away from reaching its eventual permanent home at TPC Sawgrass in 1982. Jack Nicklaus, coming off his fourth Masters win and his fourth PGA title, entered as the event's defending champion. Yes, it was hot, but the golf course did quite well and the full summer rough was awesome. "You could lose small children out there (in the rough)," Nicklaus observed. 1966 PGA Champion Al Geiberger, who committed to play at the last minute, put on a virtual clinic. Nicklaus found himself one shot behind Geiberger's 66 after round one, and that was as close as he got. Jim Colbert battled to one under par through 16 holes. He then carded 6 - 9 on the last two holes and withdrew, vowing never to return to Colonial.

Dave Stockton chased Geiberger with a Friday 64, aided by a course-record 30 on the front nine. That broke Ben Hogan's 28 year-old mark of 31. Stockton stayed within three after 54 holes, and his front nine 32 on Sunday actually took the lead. Geiberger recovered from his front side 36 to hang tough on the back nine. When Stockton made two bogeys coming home, Geiberger pounced with a birdie on #15, winning by three shots with a new 72-hole Colonial record of 10-under-par. That broke Clayton Heafner's 27-year-old record of 272. Geiberger became the third winner to fire four sub-par rounds, the sixth champ to lead wire-to-wire, and the fourth Champions' Choice to eventually claim a Colonial title. Instead of the Leonard Trophy, however, he received the Tour's Joe Dey Trophy, in honor of the former commissioner.

A state of normalcy returned in 1976, with an invitational format of 102 players and a May date. Stockton picked up where he left off nine months earlier, grabbing a share of the early lead with Hubert Green. Then local favorite and now

five-time major winner Lee Trevino took over, grabbing the tournament lead Friday with a back nine record of 29. Ten under par and still leading after three rounds, Trevino admitted he wanted to win his first Texas tournament "real bad." He survived a wind-induced Sunday 73 for a one-shot win, thanks to a birdie on #16.

"This course is one where you can shoot 73 on the final day like I did and still win," Trevino explained. "It's the toughest golf course in the world when the wind is blowing. Personally, I like the wind." Ending a 15-month victory drought, the home-state triumph was especially sweet for Trevino.

In 1977, Tom Kite said Colonial was playing as easy as he'd ever seen it. No wind, little rough. His school chum Ben Crenshaw agreed, carding 11 one-putts for a first-round 65. Californian John Schroeder fired a 65 Friday for a four-shot lead, while Crenshaw struggled in the wind. Schroeder led by as much as five on the back nine Saturday, but Crenshaw reeled him in over the last seven holes and trailed by only one with the last round to go. Schroeder staked another five shot lead over up-and-down Crenshaw Sunday, but couldn't finish him off. The blond Texan scrambled and charged to a four-under back nine, capturing the lead finally with a birdie on #17. Schroeder's 35-foot putt to tie missed by an inch, and Crenshaw's testy 8-footer for par secured a one-shot victory.

TOP:
Tom Weiskopf was playing his best golf when he won at Colonial in 1973.
MIDDLE:
Jerry Heard captured the 1972 Colonial title; pictured with Colonial President Jim Fuller.
BOTTOM:
1971 champion Gene Littler checks his scorecard.

"I was lucky -- lucky on the back nine today and lucky all week," Crenshaw reflected. "Also, I didn't give up, and I think that won for me. Something seemed to take me by the hand through this wilderness out there." Third place Tom Watson, who lost by only two shots, probably still remembers the quintuple-bogey nine he took at the ninth hole on Friday. Still, he won five events (including two majors) and led the Tour's money list for the first time in his career. A new Colonial tradition began this year - that of awarding the winner a beautiful gold champion's ring, topped with a one -- carat diamond.

George Burns got the 1978 event off to a memorable start by recording Colonial's first double-eagle two on the par five first hole in the first round. A writer remarked that the historic feat was witnessed "by 20 people, 3 squirrels and 2 sparrows." Steve Melnyk grabbed the lead with a first round 65. After two windy days, a hot Lee Trevino caught up and led by one. On Sunday, Trevino used three back-nine birdies to finish off a 66 and a four-shot win. His 12-under-par 268 set a new record. His first place finish made him the first man to collect $100,000 at Colonial in a career, as well as the fourth man to claim more than one Colonial title.

Hard-luck Tom Watson became the first man in Colonial history to fire four sub-par rounds and not win the tournament. He placed fourth.

In 1979, the flat-bellies took a whipping from Tour veterans. Amateur Payne Stewart played as the Southwest Conference champion. Bruce Lietzke and Lee Trevino opened with 66s,

and Tom Watson made a weekend charge, but 41-year-old Geiberger blistered the course for a 64 Saturday, and a four-shot lead. Jim Colbert -- yes, he returned after the '75 debacle -- also shot 64 in the third round. 48-year-old Gene Littler and 49-year-old Don January joined the battle Sunday, and fell in behind Geiberger to lock up all the win-place-show categories. Geiberger now had a National Invitation title to go with his 1975 TPC win. Littler could have won his second Colonial title if not for a double-bogey on #17. In his 29 Colonial appearances from 1954-1983, the great Littler placed second four times, third once and fourth once, in addition to his 1971 victory. No one except Ben Hogan has had more top 10 finishes at Colonial.

TOP :
Al Geiberger won again at Colonial in 1979; pictured with wife Lynn.
ABOVE:
Ben Hogan and Lee Trevino at the annual Champions Dinner.

1970s

1970
May 14-17

Rank	Player	1R	2R	3R	4R	Total	Money
1	Homero Blancas	69	68	69	67	273	$25,000
2T	Lee Trevino	66	70	69	69	274	11,575
2T	Gene Littler	69	72	66	67	274	11,575
4	Kel Nagle	70	71	69	68	278	5,850
5T	Hale Irwin	73	68	69	69	279	4,812
5T	Bob Charles	69	70	72	68	279	4,812
7T	Tom Shaw	68	73	69	70	280	3,842
7T	Dick Lotz	69	72	71	68	280	3,842
9T	Bob E. Smith	67	69	73	72	281	3,125
9T	Lionel Hebert	70	70	71	70	281	3,125
9T	Howie Johnson	76	71	66	68	281	3,125
12T	Dale Douglass	75	72	63	72	282	2,275
12T	Bert Yancey	69	76	67	70	282	2,275
12T	Gary Player	66	74	72	70	282	2,275
12T	Grier Jones	72	73	68	69	282	2,275
12T	Dave Stockton	69	72	72	69	282	2,275
17T	Larry Ziegler	69	71	68	75	283	1,456
17T	Roberto De Vicenzo	70	66	74	73	283	1,456
17T	Jack Nicklaus	71	70	69	73	283	1,456
17T	Gibby Gilbert	70	72	69	72	283	1,456
17T	Rod Funseth	73	66	72	72	283	1,456
17T	Larry Hinson	71	75	66	71	283	1,456
17T	Bobby Nichols	69	71	72	71	283	1,456
17T	Julius Boros	69	73	71	70	283	1,456
25T	Tom Weiskopf	70	74	69	71	284	982
25T	Bobby Mitchell	70	71	74	69	284	982
25T	George Archer	74	71	70	69	284	982
25T	Billy Maxwell	73	73	73	65	284	982
29T	Bob Lunn	70	71	70	74	285	815
29T	Frank Beard	67	72	72	74	285	815
29T	Al Geiberger	74	70	69	72	285	815
29T	Terry Wilcox	68	73	74	70	285	815
29T	Tommy Aaron	70	73	74	68	285	815
34	Chuck Courtney	69	76	73	68	286	725
35T	Joel Goldstrand	71	69	73	74	287	602
35T	Miller Barber	69	68	76	74	287	602
35T	Kermit Zarley	70	75	69	73	287	602
35T	Bob Murphy	71	72	71	73	287	602
35T	Jack McGowan	71	74	71	71	287	602
35T	Bob Verwey	69	75	72	71	287	602
35T	Bert Greene	72	69	75	71	287	602
35T	Gay Brewer	67	76	76	68	287	602
43T	Ron Cerrudo	71	71	71	75	288	355
43T	Lou Graham	71	71	72	74	288	355
43T	Orville Moody	72	74	69	73	288	355
43T	Bunky Henry	74	69	73	72	288	355
43T	R. H. Sikes	67	75	74	72	288	355
43T	Johnny Pott	67	77	73	71	288	355
43T	Bruce Devlin	68	76	74	70	288	355
50T	Jim Colbert	71	73	73	72	289	211
50T	Lee Elder	69	73	72	75	289	211
50T	Bruce Crampton	72	72	70	75	289	211
53T	Art Wall, Jr.	69	69	79	73	290	192
53T	Chris Blocker	73	73	71	73	290	192
53T	Don Bies	72	71	71	76	290	192
56T	Ben Hogan	69	77	73	72	291	192
56T	Bobby Cole	73	69	76	73	291	192
56T	John Schroeder	72	75	71	73	291	192
59	Dave Hill	72	71	71	78	292	192
60T	Charles Coody	73	72	78	70	293	192
60T	Doug Sanders	70	72	76	75	293	192
62T	Terry Dill	71	72	79	72	294	192
62T	Dave Marr	72	71	76	75	294	192
62T	Bob Stanton	71	74	74	75	294	192
62T	Ken Still	71	76	72	75	294	192
62T	Pete Brown	69	78	71	76	294	192
67T	Bob Goalby	73	73	78	71	295	192
67T	Ernie Vossler	74	72	75	74	295	192
67T	Rives McBee	70	71	73	81	295	192
70	Bill Garrett	74	73	73	77	297	192
71T	Chi Chi Rodriguez	71	73	77	77	298	192
71T	Rocky Thompson	73	72	71	82	298	192
73T	George Knudson	73	74	77	75	299	192
73T	DeWitt Weaver	73	73	77	76	299	192
75	Gardner Dickinson	73	73	80	75	301	192
76	Jim Wiechers	68	74	80	80	302	192

DID NOT MAKE CUT

148 Deane Beman, Tommy Bolt, Peter Townsend, Charles Sifford
149 Mason Rudolph, Jack Montgomery, Dudley Wysong, Phil Rodgers, Steve Reid,
150 Ray Floyd, Don January, Don Massengale, Dick Crawford, Bob Dickson, Earl Stewart Jr.
152 Jacky Cupit, Fred Marti
153 Bobby Greenwood
154 Chandler Harper, Steve Spray
155 Mike Souchak, Johnny Palmer
dQ Harold Henning

1971
May 20-23

Rank	Player	1R	2R	3R	4R	Total	Money
1	Gene Littler	72	68	74	69	283	$25,000
2	Bert Yancey	69	73	72	70	284	14,300
3T	Orville Moody	71	73	72	69	285	6,081
3T	George Knudson	67	69	76	73	285	6,081
3T	Fred Marti	68	72	71	74	285	6,081
3T	Julius Boros	71	71	67	76	285	6,081
7T	Gary Player	73	70	74	69	286	3,412
7T	Jerry McGee	71	68	75	72	286	3,412
7T	Bob Rosburg	75	66	73	72	286	3,412
7T	Bert Greene	68	74	72	72	286	3,412
7T	Homero Blancas	67	73	71	75	286	3,412
12T	Hubert Green	73	74	73	67	287	1,950
12T	Tom Shaw	73	68	78	68	287	1,950
12T	Kermit Zarley	73	73	70	71	287	1,950
12T	Wilf Homenuik	70	74	71	72	287	1,950
12T	John Schlee	70	75	70	72	287	1,950
12T	Dou Sanders	72	69	73	73	287	1,950
12T	Lee Trevino	70	68	75	74	287	1,950
12T	Phil Rodgers	71	71	71	74	287	1,950
12T	John Mahaffey	71	72	70	74	287	1,950
12T	Dave Stockton	69	70	71	77	287	1,950
22T	Chi Chi Rodriguez	70	74	72	72	288	1,213
22T	Jack Montgomery	68	69	75	76	288	1,213
24T	Charles Coody	74	72	74	69	289	877
24T	Lee Elder	70	73	76	70	289	877
24T	Randy Wolff	75	69	75	70	289	877
24T	Rocky Thompson	72	74	72	71	289	877
24T	Jim Wiechers	70	71	76	72	289	877
24T	Miller Barber	74	72	72	71	289	877
24T	Bob Lunn	73	68	75	73	289	877
24T	Bruce Crampton	72	71	73	73	289	877
24T	Tommy Aaron	70	78	68	73	289	877
24T	Tom Weiskopf	71	72	72	74	289	877
24T	Frank Beard	71	70	74	74	289	877
24T	*Ben Crenshaw*	69	72	73	75	289	
24T	Ron Cerrudo	70	70	73	76	289	877
37T	Larry Ziegler	71	70	70	79	290	554
37T	Bud Allin	74	70	76	70	290	554
37T	Jerry Heard	69	75	75	71	290	554
37T	Lionel Hebert	72	74	73	71	290	554
37T	Labron Harris	74	70	73	73	290	554
37T	Bruce Devlin	73	72	72	73	290	554
37T	Ken Still	70	75	71	74	290	554
37T	Dick Lotz	73	70	72	75	290	554
37T	Mike Hill	73	73	69	75	290	554
46T	Dick Rhyan	74	74	74	69	291	313
46T	Bob E. Smith	71	75	74	71	291	313
46T	Dale Douglass	71	76	73	71	291	313
46T	Chuck Courtney	69	73	74	75	291	313
46T	Bob Dickson	72	72	71	76	291	313
46T	DeWitt Weaver	70	74	71	76	291	313
52T	Larry Wood	73	71	75	73	292	192
52T	Dick Crawford	74	71	73	74	292	192
52T	Jim Jamieson	74	74	70	74	292	192
52T	Gardner Dickinson	72	70	74	76	292	192
52T	Rod Funseth	72	72	71	77	292	192
57T	Larry Hinson	75	73	73	72	293	192
57T	George Archer	73	72	75	73	293	192
57T	Al Geiberger	70	75	73	75	293	192
60T	Hal Underwood	77	68	76	73	294	192
60T	Jack Lewis	74	73	73	74	294	192
60T	Gay Brewer	74	71	74	75	294	192
60T	Ted Hayes	70	72	76	76	294	192
60T	Billy Casper	73	75	71	75	294	192
65T	Billy Maxwell	75	73	77	70	295	192
65T	Deane Beman	75	70	77	73	295	192
65T	J. C. Snead	73	75	73	74	295	192
68T	John Schroeder	72	72	76	76	296	192
68T	Bob Charles	76	72	72	76	296	192
70T	Ray Pace	75	71	77	74	297	192
70T	Babe Hiskey	73	73	77	74	297	192
70T	Lou Graham	73	70	77	77	297	192
73	Bob Goalby	73	74	77	74	298	192
74	Don Cherry	75	73	77	74	299	192
75	Ray Floyd	74	74	78	75	301	192
76T	Terry Dill	73	74	75	81	303	192
76T	Bobby Mitchell	70	75	75	83	303	192

DID NOT MAKE CUT

149 Bill Garrett, Hale Irwin, Don Bies, Bob Murphy
150 Chris Blocker, Art Wall, R. H. Sikes, Dave Eichelberger, Johnny Miller, Don January
151 Bob Menne, Hugh Royer
152 Steve Reid, Ed Sneed
153 Grier Jones
154 Ernie Vossler
155 Bob Stone, Roland Harper, Howie Johnson
156 Jacky Cupit
78-wd César Sanudo
77-dq Dave Hill
wd Gibby Gilbert

1972
May 11-14

Rank	Player	1R	2R	3R	4R	Total	Money
1	Jerry Heard	69	66	67	73	275	$25,000
2	Fred Marti	66	70	69	72	277	14,300
3	Dave Stockton	67	68	71	72	278	8,850
4	Phil Rodgers	68	69	68	74	279	5,850
5	Bob Murphy	74	67	70	69	280	5,125
6	Bert Greene	67	73	69	72	281	4,500
7T	Bobby Nichols	71	69	68	74	282	3,687
7T	Bruce Crampton	66	74	71	71	282	3,687
7T	George Johnson	73	71	68	70	282	3,687
10T	Lee Elder	69	67	72	75	283	2,650
10T	Ray Floyd	71	72	67	73	283	2,650
10T	Mason Rudolph	72	71	68	72	283	2,650
10T	Don Bies	76	68	68	71	283	2,650
10T	Bruce Devlin	72	68	72	71	283	2,650
15T	Julius Boros	72	70	65	77	284	2,125
15T	*Ben Crenshaw*	71	72	69	72	284	
17T	Deane Beman	67	74	69	75	285	1,750
17T	Johnny Miller	69	72	70	74	285	1,750
17T	Chi Chi Rodriguez	70	73	70	72	285	1,750
17T	Homero Blancas	77	67	70	71	285	1,750
17T	Lou Graham	71	70	74	70	285	1,750
22T	George Knudson	71	72	68	75	286	1,267
22T	*Tom Kite*	70	73	70	73	286	
22T	Jerry McGee	68	76	70	72	286	1,267
22T	Art Wall	74	71	74	67	286	1,267
26T	Al Geiberger	71	72	70	74	287	1,006
26T	Bert Yancey	72	72	70	73	287	1,006
26T	John Mahaffey	72	70	72	73	287	1,006
26T	Charles Coody	69	73	74	71	287	1,006
26T	Ralph Johnston	70	70	68	79	287	1,006
31T	Bobby Mitchell	68	73	71	76	288	815
31T	Don January	72	69	71	76	288	815
31T	Lee Trevino	73	71	69	75	288	815
31T	Larry Wood	70	74	69	75	288	815
31T	Charles Sifford	72	72	73	71	288	815
36T	Leonard Thompson	67	72	73	77	289	675
36T	Dave Marr	68	71	74	76	289	675
36T	Bob Goalby	73	71	72	73	289	675
36T	Miller Barber	69	74	72	74	289	675
36T	Babe Hiskey	72	70	75	72	289	675
41T	Ken Still	70	71	73	76	290	581
41T	Hubert Green	73	73	71	73	290	581
43T	Hale Irwin	71	72	74	74	291	469
43T	Rod Funseth	72	73	73	73	291	469
43T	Steve Melnyk	72	74	73	72	291	469
43T	Larry Ziegler	77	68	74	72	291	469
47T	Gibby Gilbert	75	69	71	77	292	350
47T	Lanny Wadkins	72	73	74	73	292	350
47T	Roy Pace	73	72	75	72	292	350
50T	Ted Hayes	74	71	70	78	293	288
50T	Larry Hinson	72	74	73	74	293	288
52T	Chris Blocker	70	73	74	77	294	250
52T	Bob Stone	75	70	73	76	294	250
52T	R. H. Sikes	71	73	74	76	294	250
52T	Chuck Courtney	74	72	73	75	294	250
52T	Wilf Homenuik	71	73	75	75	294	250
52T	Kermit Zarley	70	76	75	73	294	250
52T	Mike Hill	73	72	76	73	294	250
52T	John Jacobs	72	72	77	73	294	250
60T	J. C. Snead	71	72	74	78	295	250
60T	Jack Montgomery	72	74	72	77	295	250
60T	Tom Weiskopf	76	68	74	77	295	250
60T	Billy Maxwell	68	75	75	77	295	250
60T	Chuck Thorpe	72	74	73	76	295	250
60T	Pete Brown	74	72	74	75	295	250
66	Don Iverson	75	70	74	77	296	250
67	Lionel Hebert	72	74	75	76	297	250
68T	John Lister	76	69	75	81	301	250
68T	Marty Fleckman	70	76	75	80	301	250
70	DeWitt Weaver	71	74	83	74	302	250

DID NOT MAKE CUT

147 Bill Garrett, Bob Charles, Bunky Henry, Bob Lunn, Bob Rosburg, Tom Shaw
148 George Archer, Labron Harris Jr, Ron Cerrudo
149 Gay Brewer, Dale Douglass, David Graham, Terry Dill, Grier Jones, Bob Dickson, Bob E. Smith, Herb Hooper
150 Don Cherry, John Schroeder, Dave Eichelberger, Doug Sanders Randy Wolff
151 Cesar Sanudo, Bud Allin
152 John Schlee, Ernie Vossler
153 Jim Jamieson, B.R. McLendon
155 Orville Moody
157 Jack Lewis
75-wd Bob Shaw
74-dq Tommy Bolt

1973
May 10-13

Rank	Player	1R	2R	3R	4R	Total	Money
1	Tom Weiskopf	69	68	70	69	276	$30,000
2T	Bruce Crampton	66	69	69	73	277	13,875
2T	Jerry Heard	69	69	71	68	277	13,875
4	Lee Elder	70	68	69	71	278	7,050
5	Julius Boros	69	72	70	69	280	6,150
6T	Kermit Zarley	71	70	71	69	281	5,100
6T	Hale Irwin	70	69	72	70	281	5,100
8T	Mason Rudolph	73	69	67	73	282	4,075
8T	John Mahaffey	73	70	69	70	282	4,075
8T	Leonard Thompson	74	67	71	70	282	4,075
11	Jim Wiechers	72	73	70	68	283	3,450
12T	Labron Harris, Jr	70	72	70	72	284	2,900
12T	Charles Coody	70	72	72	70	284	2,900
12T	Bert Greene	72	71	72	69	284	2,900
15T	Lou Graham	72	66	71	76	285	2,400
15T	Bob Dickson	72	73	68	72	285	2,400
15T	Charles Sifford	71	71	72	71	285	2,400
18T	*Ben Crenshaw*	75	71	73	67	286	
18T	Ken Still	68	71	73	74	286	1,875
18T	Ray Royd	74	72	73	67	286	1,875
18T	Gene Littler	71	68	76	71	286	1,875
18T	Phil Rodgers	69	74	73	70	286	1,875
23	Deane Beman	70	70	78	69	287	1,500
24T	Fred Marti	70	74	70	74	288	1,215
24T	David Graham	71	73	70	74	288	1,215
24T	Brian Allin	72	71	71	74	288	1,215
24T	Art Wall Jr.	73	70	73	72	288	1,215
24T	BertYancey	71	72	71	74	288	1,215
24T	Orville Moody	71	74	75	68	288	1,215
24T	Lanny Wadkins	71	73	73	71	288	1,215
31T	Johnny Miller	74	71	70	74	289	952
31T	Dick Lotz	72	71	74	72	289	952
31T	Tom Kite	71	75	72	71	289	952
31T	Tom Jenkins	73	71	76	69	289	952
35T	Bobby Nichols	69	75	70	76	290	741
35T	Dave Stockton	70	72	72	76	290	741
35T	John Schlee	75	70	73	72	290	741
35T	Larry Hinson	74	71	73	72	290	741
35T	Al Geiberger	74	73	73	70	290	741
35T	Homero Blancas	70	72	78	70	290	741
35T	Gardner Dickinson	70	71	75	74	290	741
42T	Rik Massengale	73	69	75	74	291	555
42T	Bob Murphy	71	71	75	74	291	555
42T	Jim Jamieson	75	71	73	72	291	555
42T	Bob Goalby	72	71	75	73	291	555
42T	Butch Baird	70	76	75	70	291	555
42T	Billy Casper	75	73	74	69	291	555
48T	Tommy Aaron	76	70	72	74	292	406
48T	Ron Cerrudo	77	71	72	72	292	406
48T	Chi Chi Rodriguez	73	75	75	69	292	406
48T	Jerry McGee	74	72	71	75	292	406
48T	Miller Barber	71	70	74	77	292	406
53T	Bob Lunn	71	74	75	73	293	356
53T	Frank Beard	72	70	79	72	293	356
55T	Dale Douglass	73	69	72	80	294	330
55T	Don January	73	74	73	74	294	330
55T	Roy Pace	71	73	76	74	294	330
55T	Lee Trevino	71	73	76	74	294	330
55T	Chris Blocker	72	76	73	73	294	330
60T	Jim Simons	79	69	72	75	295	303
60T	Gibby Gilbert	69	74	73	79	295	303
62T	*John Granger*	73	72	75	76	296	
62T	Dwight Nevil	78	70	70	78	296	281
62T	Dave Eichelberger	75	72	73	76	296	281
62T	Grier Jones	70	75	75	76	296	281
62T	Doug Sanders	76	71	75	74	296	281
67	Dave Hill	73	75	77	72	297	263
68	Babe Hiskey	77	66	79	76	298	255
69T	Tom Watson	73	73	74	79	299	243
69T	Rod Curl	72	74	75	78	299	243
71	Don Bies	72	72	79	77	300	233
72	Bob Barbarossa	74	74	75	78	301	225
73T	George Knudson	70	78	74	80	302	-
73T	Chuck Courtney	76	71	77	78	302	-
75	Marty Fleckman	70	76	84	81	311	-
76	Mike Hill	76	72	78	wd		-

DID NOT MAKE CUT

149 Larry Wood, DeWitt Weaver Jr, Hubert Green, Curtis Sifford, Bob E. Smith, Don Iverson, Ralph Johnston
150 Bobby Mitchell, George Johnson, Tom Ulozas, *Vinnie Giles*, Forrest Felzer
151 Ed Sneed, Jack Montgomery, John Schroeder
152 Don Cherry, Bob Charles, Steve Melnyk, Andy North, Cesar Sanudo
153 Allen Miller, Lionel Hebert
154 Tom Shaw
158 Dave Marr
78-nc J.C. Snead
80-wd Gay Brewer
82-wd B.R. McLendon
nc Larry Ziegler

1974
May 16-19

Rank	Player	1R	2R	3R	4R	Total	Money
1	Rod Curl	70	67	71	68	276	$50,600
2	Jack Nicklaus	71	69	69	68	277	28,500
3	Chuck Courtney	70	66	70	72	278	17,750
4	Julius Boros	69	70	72	68	279	11,750
5	Lee Trevino	72	69	71	68	280	10,250
6	Gary Player	74	68	70	70	282	9,000
7T	Gary McCord	72	74	66	71	283	7,094
7T	Lou Graham	74	72	71	66	283	7,094
7T	Charles Coody	68	72	74	69	283	7,094
7T	Steve Melnyk	72	69	72	70	283	7,094
11T	Tom Weiskopf	70	68	72	74	284	5,063
11T	Jack Ewing	76	69	71	68	284	5,063
11T	Bud Allin	74	68	74	68	284	5,063
11T	Chi Chi Rodriguez	72	71	72	69	284	5,063
15T	Bruce Devlin	71	71	73	70	285	3,875
15T	Jim Simons	74	72	71	68	285	3,875
15T	Orville Moody	69	72	72	72	285	3,875
15T	David Graham	73	69	70	73	285	3,875
19T	Gay Brewer	72	68	75	71	286	2,589
19T	Bobby Mitchell	75	71	70	70	286	2,589
19T	Tom Watson	73	69	73	71	286	2,589
19T	Dan Sikes	71	68	74	73	286	2,589
19T	Lionel Hebert	71	73	70	72	286	2,589
19T	Hubert Green	68	73	71	74	286	2,589
19T	Hale Irwin	65	72	73	76	286	2,589
26T	Lee Elder	71	69	75	72	287	1,850
26T	Dale Douglass	73	70	74	70	287	1,850
26T	Bob Menne	72	68	78	69	287	1,850
26T	Dave Hill	72	73	70	72	287	1,850
26T	Larry Hinson	68	72	72	75	287	1,850
31T	Monty Kaser	73	73	66	76	288	1,418
31T	Bert Greene	71	74	71	72	288	1,418
31T	Mason Rudolph	74	66	76	72	288	1,418
31T	Bobby Nichols	68	73	75	72	288	1,418
31T	Larry Zeigler	70	74	73	71	288	1,418
31T	Tom Kite	73	71	73	71	288	1,418
31T	Ray Floyd	76	69	73	70	288	1,418
38T	Kermit Zarley	71	74	73	71	289	1,100
38T	Ken Still	72	71	74	72	289	1,100
38T	Pat Fitzsimons	71	73	75	70	289	1,100
38T	Jim Dent	74	70	71	74	289	1,100
42T	Larry Nelson	70	73	73	74	290	850
42T	Phil Rodgers	69	77	71	73	290	850
42T	Butch Baird	69	76	72	73	290	850
42T	Frank Beard	69	75	74	72	290	850
42T	Joe Inman	73	73	74	70	290	850
42T	John Mahaffey	76	69	72	73	290	850
48T	Dave Stockton	70	71	75	75	291	641
48T	Rik Massengale	71	72	72	76	291	641
48T	Don Bies	72	72	74	73	291	641
48T	J. C. Snead	74	68	76	73	291	641
52T	Homero Blancas	74	69	74	75	292	575
52T	Jerry Heard	73	73	73	73	292	575
52T	Billy Casper	68	76	74	74	292	575
52T	Andy North	72	70	77	73	292	575
52T	Randy Erskine	74	72	73	73	292	575
57T	Artie McNickle	75	70	73	75	293	519
57T	Ross Randall	71	74	75	73	293	519
57T	Gibby Gilbert	74	72	77	70	293	519
57T	Mike Morley	72	73	70	78	293	519
61T	Bob Eastwood	72	73	73	76	294	475
61T	David Barber	75	71	73	75	294	475
61T	Richard Crawford	72	72	77	73	294	475
64	Lyn Lott	71	74	76	74	295	450
65	Bob Payne	71	73	74	78	296	437
66T	Bob Stanton	69	77	73	78	297	413
66T	Art Wall Jr.	71	74	77	75	297	413
66T	Tom Shaw	71	74	75	77	297	413
69	Forrest Fezler	74	71	79	74	298	387
70T	Rick Rhoads	73	71	77	78	299	188
70T	John Schroeder	72	73	81	73	299	188
72	Roger Parker	75	69	81	77	302	-
73	Bruce Crampton	71	73	75	wd		
74	Bert Yancey	68	75	dq			

DID NOT MAKE CUT

147 A. Palmer, Marr, Schlee, Eichelberger, Wiechers, M. Hayes, Allard, Knudson, Geiberger, Jones
148 Charles, Masserio, Mast, M. Hill, Sneed, Rhyan, McGee, Pearce
149 Littler, Burke, Archer, Lister, Kallam, M. Barber, L. Thompson, Cerrudo
150 Novak, T. Evans, Brown, Bohen, Unger, McBee, Davis, Aaron, Jamieson, Charles Sifford, Fleisher, Crenshaw
151 Comstock, Nevil, Rosburg, Ford, Wadkins, Allen, D. Lotz, Goalby, Curtis Sifford
152 Moran, S. Adams, Ziobro
153 B. Smith, Funseth, Dickson, Venturi
154 R. Ellis, Armstrong, Zender, D. Weaver, Morgan
155 Goetz, Stubblefield, Cain
156 *Simmons, Harris*
157 Hiskey
158 Pace
160 Acton
165 Dugger
167 J. Collins
WD B. Wynn, Lunn, Chancellor, M. Higgins, J. Miller, McCullough, Regalado

**Names in italics designate amateurs.*

1970s

1975 August 21-24

Rank	Player	1R	2R	3R	4R	Total	Money
1	Al Geiberger	66	68	67	69	270	$50,000
2	Dave Stockton	72	64	68	69	273	28,500
3	Hubert Green	71	65	70	69	275	17,750
4T	Mason Rudolph	69	70	72	70	281	10,333
4T	Bob Dickson	67	69	72	73	281	10,333
4T	Bob Murphy	73	69	71	68	281	10,333
7	Hale Irwin	67	72	72	72	283	8,000
8T	Joe Porter	72	72	68	72	284	6,792
8T	Bobby Wadkins	76	69	68	71	284	6,792
8T	Tom Watson	73	69	75	67	284	6,792
11T	John Mahaffey	69	75	69	72	285	5,063
11T	Bud Allin	68	73	71	73	285	5,063
11T	Gene Littler	73	71	70	71	285	5,063
11T	Bill Rogers	69	70	76	70	285	5,063
15T	John Schlee	69	68	76	73	286	4,000
15T	John Lister	72	71	71	72	286	4,000
15T	Billy Casper	73	68	73	72	286	4,000
18T	Jack Nicklaus	67	75	70	75	287	3,250
18T	Leonard Thompson	74	73	69	71	287	3,250
18T	Gibby Gilbert	72	71	74	70	287	3,250
21T	Roger Maltbie	71	71	71	75	288	2,206
21T	Gary Player	71	72	72	73	288	2,206
21T	Jerry Heard	77	69	69	73	288	2,206
21T	Mike Hill	76	69	70	73	288	2,206
21T	Randy Erskine	71	69	76	72	288	2,206
21T	Ray Floyd	73	72	72	71	288	2,206
21T	Peter Oosterhuis	72	73	73	70	288	2,206
21T	Don Iverson	74	71	73	70	288	2,206
29T	Charles Coody	73	70	68	78	289	1,625
29T	Tom Weiskopf	75	71	70	73	289	1,625
29T	Mike Morley	71	75	71	72	289	1,625
29T	Miller Barber	71	72	75	71	289	1,625
29T	Lou Graham	75	71	73	70	289	1,625
34T	Bob Payne	70	71	74	75	290	1,263
34T	Bruce Crampton	75	72	69	74	290	1,263
34T	Dan Sikes	73	72	72	73	290	1,263
34T	Andy North	69	76	72	73	290	1,263
34T	Jim Simons	71	73	74	72	290	1,263
34T	J. C. Snead	71	73	76	70	290	1,263
40T	Jerry McGee	72	73	69	77	291	975
40T	Larry Ziegler	69	71	76	75	291	975
40T	Julius Boros	73	73	74	71	291	975
40T	Tom Kite	72	70	77	72	291	975
40T	Ron Cerrudo	74	73	74	70	291	975
45T	Mike McCullough	72	74	70	76	292	730
45T	Mike Wynn	68	74	77	73	292	730
45T	Tom Shaw	71	72	76	73	292	730
45T	Sammy Rachels	71	76	72	73	292	730
45T	Ralph Johnston	72	73	76	71	292	730
50T	Bobby Nichols	74	70	74	75	293	600
50T	Lee Trevino	75	70	75	73	293	600
50T	Don January	74	72	73	74	293	600
50T	Dale Douglass	75	71	74	73	293	600
50T	Allen Miller	71	73	81	68	293	600
55T	B. R. McLendon	74	72	73	75	294	538
55T	Spike Kelley	70	76	72	76	294	538
55T	Ben Crenshaw	73	72	74	75	294	538
55T	Nate Starks	75	72	73	74	294	538
55T	Jim Wiechers	68	79	78	69	294	538
60T	Lyn Lott	74	69	74	78	295	481
60T	George Cadle	73	69	76	77	295	481
60T	Pat Fitzsimons	77	70	73	75	295	481
60T	Bobby Cole	74	72	75	74	295	481
64T	Danny Edwards	73	72	73	78	296	437
64T	Lionel Hebert	72	74	77	73	296	437
64T	Bob Eastwood	75	70	79	72	296	437
67T	David Graham	70	75	75	77	297	407
67T	Ed Dougherty	72	75	73	77	297	407
69	Bruce Devlin	73	73	73	79	298	387
70	Babe Hiskey	73	73	80	73	299	375
71T	Tim Collins	75	71	80	75	301	—
71T	Larry Nelson	73	74	77	77	301	—
73	Tommy Aaron	72	74	77	80	303	—

DID NOT MAKE CUT

148 Fezler, Wall, Zender, M. Hayes, Schroeder, Menne, Masserio, Lietzke
149 Eichelberger, Curtis Sifford, Regalado, Dent, Walzel, Curl, Hinson, A. Palmer, Inman
150 B. Smith, Knudson, Nevil, Archer, Blancas, Ewing, Bies, Zarley, Morgan
151 Reasor, Marti, Glenz, Armstrong, Rhyan, Goalby, Baird, Jacklin, Diehl, Groh, Still
152 D. Weaver, Unger, D. Lotz, Beard
153 Elder, B. Thompson, Zoeller, Crawford
154 Pace, Mitchell, Jenkins
155 Brewer, Evans, Stanton, Tapie
156 Rodriguez, Fleisher, McCord
158 R. Massengale
160 Greenwood
162 Rodgers
WD S. Adams, B. Wynn, Pearce, G. Johnson, Courtney, Colbert, D. Hill, L. Wadkins, Dill, Conner, Melnyk
DQ Ziobro, Green

1976 May 13-16

Rank	Player	1R	2R	3R	4R	Total	Money
1	Lee Trevino	68	64	68	73	273	$40,000
2	Mike Morley	70	68	67	69	274	22,800
3T	Don January	68	68	69	72	277	11,800
3T	Tom Weiskopf	68	71	67	71	277	11,800
5T	Tom Kite	69	68	72	69	278	7,267
5T	Bob Gilder	69	73	66	70	278	7,267
5T	John Mahaffey	69	72	68	69	278	7,267
8T	Grier Jones	72	69	71	67	279	5,225
8T	Bob E. Smith	70	72	68	69	279	5,225
8T	Hubert Green	67	72	70	70	279	5,225
8T	Miller Barber	68	65	70	76	279	5,225
12T	John Schlee	74	67	69	71	281	4,000
12T	Barry Jaeckel	68	73	69	71	281	4,000
14T	David Graham	71	72	69	70	282	3,300
14T	Jerry Pate	72	70	68	72	282	3,300
14T	Ed Sneed	72	71	66	73	282	3,300
14T	Charles Coody	72	70	67	73	282	3,300
18T	Jerry McGee	70	68	76	69	283	2,600
18T	Gary Player	70	67	74	72	283	2,600
18T	Peter Oosterhuis	68	73	68	74	283	2,600
21T	Ray Floyd	71	70	73	70	284	2,027
21T	Gay Brewer	71	71	68	74	284	2,027
21T	Marty Fleckman	71	67	69	77	284	2,027
24T	Kermit Zarley	73	69	73	70	285	1,608
24T	Lou Graham	74	68	73	70	285	1,608
24T	Art Wall, Jr.	73	68	73	71	285	1,608
24T	Don Iverson	70	70	74	71	285	1,608
24T	Rik Massengale	72	72	69	72	285	1,608
29T	Bob Dickson	69	71	76	70	286	1,272
29T	Bill Rogers	74	69	74	69	286	1,272
29T	B. R. McLendon	72	71	72	71	286	1,272
29T	Rod Curl	70	70	75	71	286	1,272
29T	Forrest Fezler	71	74	69	72	286	1,272
29T	Lyn Lott	72	68	71	75	286	1,272
35T	Al Geiberger	74	72	71	70	287	944
35T	Terry Diehl	74	72	69	72	287	944
35T	Bruce Lietzke	72	74	69	72	287	944
35T	Lanny Wadkins	72	72	71	72	287	944
35T	Julius Boros	75	66	73	73	287	944
35T	Tom Watson	72	71	71	73	287	944
35T	Don Bies	69	71	70	77	287	944
42T	Ben Crenshaw	74	70	74	70	288	680
42T	Gibby Gilbert	73	72	71	72	288	680
42T	Larry Nelson	72	69	73	74	288	680
42T	Bobby Wadkins	69	73	72	74	288	680
42T	Lee Elder	74	67	71	76	288	680
42T	Dave Stockton	67	69	75	77	288	680
48T	Chi Chi Rodriguez	72	74	73	70	289	506
48T	Wally Armstrong	69	73	74	73	289	506
48T	Roger Maltbie	71	73	72	73	289	506
48T	Ken Still	74	72	69	74	289	506
48T	Hale Irwin	71	70	70	78	289	506
53T	Steve Melnyk	77	69	70	74	290	455
53T	Butch Baird	72	74	70	74	290	455
53T	Tommy Aaron	70	71	74	75	290	455
53T	Bobby Cole	74	71	70	75	290	455
57T	Larry Hinson	71	73	76	71	291	400
57T	Jim Masserio	71	73	74	73	291	400
57T	Larry Ziegler	71	71	76	73	291	400
57T	Frank Beard	76	70	73	72	291	400
57T	Howard Twitty	72	71	73	75	291	400
57T	Victor Regalado	72	73	71	75	291	400
57T	Fred Marti	71	73	71	76	291	400
64T	Leonard Thompson	72	74	77	69	292	340
64T	Eddie Pearce	74	71	74	73	292	340
64T	Gary McCord	69	77	74	72	292	340
64T	Alan Tapie	74	71	73	74	292	340
64T	Jim Dent	72	72	70	78	292	340
69T	Gil Morgan	71	73	75	74	293	305
69T	Tom Jenkins	70	74	72	77	293	305
71T	Mark Hayes	76	70	76	72	294	—
71T	Gary Koch	75	70	74	75	294	—
73	Bobby Mitchell	72	74	77	72	295	—

DID NOT MAKE THE CUT

147 Jim Simons, George Burns, Gene Littler, Danny Edwards
147 Ed Dougherty, Dean Refram
148 Homero Blancas, Andy North, Bob Murphy, Bruce Devlin
148 Doug Sanders, Keith Fergus
149 Allen Miller, Billy Casper
150 Dale Douglass, Gary Groh, Joe Inman, Lionel Hebert, Dave Newquist
151 Tom Shaw, John Grace
152 Bud Allin, George Cadle
153 Dennie Meyer, John Schroeder, Andy Bean
154 Labron Harris
157 Bruce Crampton
78-wd Mike Hill

1977 May 12-15

Rank	Player	1R	2R	3R	4R	Total	Money
1	Ben Crenshaw	65	70	68	69	272	$40,000
2	John Schroeder	66	65	71	71	273	22,800
3	Tom Watson	67	72	68	67	274	14,200
4T	Al Geiberger	65	71	73	68	277	8,800
4T	Lyn Lott	72	72	67	66	277	8,800
6T	Butch Baird	68	73	68	70	279	6,500
6T	Ed Sneed	67	70	71	71	279	6,500
6T	Miller Barber	69	73	69	68	279	6,500
9T	Hubert Green	69	73	70	68	280	5,200
9T	Wally Armstrong	70	73	69	68	280	5,200
11T	Rik Massengale	72	66	72	71	281	3,800
11T	Tom Kite	67	71	72	71	281	3,800
11T	B. R. McLendon	68	74	69	70	281	3,800
11T	Bruce Lietzke	71	71	72	67	281	3,800
11T	Lee Trevino	70	67	73	71	281	3,800
11T	Chi Chi Rodriguez	66	70	73	72	281	3,800
17T	Jim Masserio	68	71	71	73	283	2,800
17T	George Archer	71	71	71	70	283	2,800
17T	Gil Morgan	72	71	71	69	283	2,800
20T	George Cadle	69	70	73	72	284	1,983
20T	Jerry McGee	70	75	69	70	284	1,983
20T	Bruce Devlin	69	74	71	70	284	1,983
20T	Woody Blackburn	76	70	69	69	284	1,983
20T	Joe Inman	71	70	73	70	284	1,983
20T	Bill Rogers	71	70	75	68	284	1,983
26T	Stan Lee	73	70	67	75	285	1,390
26T	Roger Maltbie	66	70	75	74	285	1,390
26T	Don January	72	68	73	72	285	1,390
26T	Tom Weiskopf	72	70	72	71	285	1,390
26T	Gary McCord	67	76	72	70	285	1,390
26T	Julius Boros	68	72	75	70	285	1,390
26T	Doug Tewell	73	69	73	70	285	1,390
26T	Bob E. Smith	70	72	73	70	285	1,390
34T	Ed Dougherty	69	70	73	74	286	1,010
34T	Gary Player	71	72	72	71	286	1,010
34T	Grier Jones	70	71	74	71	286	1,010
34T	Rod Curl	68	77	71	70	286	1,010
34T	Bill Kratzert	70	74	72	70	286	1,010
34T	Lee Elder	68	75	74	69	286	1,010
40T	Dave Eichelberger	69	70	73	75	287	800
40T	Bob Dickson	72	74	70	71	287	800
40T	Bob Gilder	75	70	71	71	287	800
40T	Dave Stockton	72	70	74	71	287	800
44T	Ray Floyd	72	70	69	77	288	640
44T	Johnny Miller	73	69	71	75	288	640
44T	Lou Graham	70	70	72	76	288	640
44T	Hale Irwin	71	73	70	74	288	640
48T	Danny Edwards	73	73	69	74	289	520
48T	Graham Marsh	73	71	71	74	289	520
48T	Andy North	70	71	74	74	289	520
48T	*Lindy Miller*	75	71	74	69	289	
52T	Bobby Wadkins	70	69	77	74	290	480
52T	Gibby Gilbert	69	74	75	72	290	480
52T	Mike McCullough	72	72	73	73	290	480
55T	Fred Marti	72	72	70	77	291	435
55T	Lanny Wadkins	72	71	72	76	291	435
55T	Ron Cerrudo	71	72	72	76	291	435
55T	Fuzzy Zoeller	73	72	72	74	291	435
55T	Kermit Zarley	73	73	74	71	291	435
55T	John Schlee	72	74	76	69	291	435
61T	Lon Hinkle	71	71	73	77	292	390
61T	Gay Brewer	72	71	75	74	292	390
61T	Craig Stadler	74	72	74	72	292	390
64T	Ed Sabo	71	75	75	72	293	365
64T	Bobby Walzel	71	74	76	72	293	365
66	Mark Lye	72	74	75	74	295	350
67	Jay Haas	72	73	77	74	296	340
68	Bill Mallon	71	74	77	75	297	330
69	Keith Fergus	70	71	78	81	300	320
70T	Bob Wynn	70	74	78	79	301	305
70T	Don Bies	74	71	77	79	301	305
72	Jim Simons	73	71	dq			

DID NOT MAKE CUT

147 Peter Oosterhuis, Bobby Cole, Leonard Thompson, Tom Jenkins, John Jacobs, HowardTwitty, Tommy Aaron
148 Mark Hayes, Victor Regalado, Alan Tapie, Steve Melnyk, Dwight Nevil, Gene Littler, Jim Dent
149 Charles Coody, Doug Sanders, Tom Purtzer
150 Barry Jaeckel, Joe Porter, Bob Murphy, Forrest Fezler
151 Bill Sander
152 Homero Blancas, Larry Nelson
153 Dale Hayes, Mike Reid
154 Eddie Pearce
76-wd Bud Allin, Terry Diehl
wd Ken Still

1978
May 11–14

RANK	PLAYER	1R	2R	3R	4R	TOTAL	MONEY
1	Lee Trevino	66	68	68	66	268	$40,000
2T	Jerry Pate	69	67	71	65	272	18,500
2T	Jerry Heard	67	66	71	68	272	18,500
4T	Tom Watson	69	68	68	68	273	8,800
4T	Steve Melnyk	65	68	70	70	273	8,800
6	Tom Weiskopf	72	68	71	65	276	7,200
7	Gary Koch	70	69	69	69	277	6,400
8T	Tom Purtzer	70	68	68	73	279	5,020
8T	Jim Simons	70	67	71	71	279	5,020
8T	Tom Kite	68	69	70	72	279	5,020
8T	Andy Bean	67	70	73	69	279	5,020
8T	John Mahaffey	71	69	72	67	279	5,020
13T	Jack Renner	69	71	69	71	280	3,600
13T	Don January	72	68	70	70	280	3,600
13T	Alan Tapie	68	73	70	69	280	3,600
16T	Fuzzy Zoeller	66	69	72	74	281	2,800
16T	Danny Edwards	67	68	72	74	281	2,800
16T	Mike Morley	67	69	73	72	281	2,800
16T	Mike Sullivan	66	69	75	71	281	2,800
16T	Curtis Strange	67	71	72	71	281	2,800
21T	Ray Floyd	70	71	71	70	282	2,100
21T	Hubert Green	73	69	69	71	282	2,100
23T	Bobby Cole	69	72	73	69	283	1,688
23T	Craig Stadler	68	73	73	69	283	1,688
23T	Ed Fiori	67	77	71	68	283	1,688
23T	Barry Jaeckel	72	70	73	68	283	1,688
23T	Doug Tewell	68	73	74	68	283	1,688
28T	Charles Coody	67	72	73	72	284	1,301
28T	Bruce Devlin	70	70	72	72	284	1,301
28T	Howard Twitty	74	68	71	71	284	1,301
28T	Al Geiberger	70	73	71	70	284	1,301
28T	Victor Regalado	70	73	72	69	284	1,301
28T	John Schroeder	71	68	76	69	284	1,301
28T	Mac McLendon	72	73	72	67	284	1,301
35	Mike Reid	69	72	75	69	285	1,080
36T	J. C. Snead	70	73	69	74	286	942
36T	Wally Armstrong	70	75	69	72	286	942
36T	Fred Marti	70	70	75	71	286	942
36T	Jeff Mitchell	73	69	74	70	286	942
36T	Lou Graham	72	71	74	69	286	942
41T	Grier Jones	71	68	70	78	287	680
41T	Kermit Zarley	71	67	76	73	287	680
41T	Mark Hayes	68	76	75	68	287	680
41T	Morris Hatalsky	72	72	73	70	287	680
41T	Lon Hinkle	70	72	73	72	287	680
41T	Jay Haas	72	67	75	73	287	680
41T	Bob Gilder	70	73	70	74	287	680
41T	Bill Rogers	73	69	71	74	287	680
49T	Keith Fergus	71	71	77	69	288	476
49T	*Lindy Miller*	72	72	73	71	288	
49T	Don Pooley	72	70	73	73	288	476
49T	Roger Maltbie	69	73	74	72	288	476
49T	Gary Player	73	69	74	72	288	476
49T	Rik Massengale	69	72	74	73	288	476
49T	Leonard Thompson	75	70	70	73	288	476
49T	Mark Pfeil	71	69	75	73	288	476
49T	Terry Diehl	71	73	77	71	288	476
58T	John Lister	72	70	75	72	289	420
58T	John Fought III	73	70	74	72	289	420
58T	Gil Morgan	66	71	77	75	289	420
61T	Don Bies	70	69	74	77	290	390
61T	Gary McCord	71	72	73	74	290	390
61T	George Burns	70	73	75	72	290	390
64	Peter Oosterhuis	71	71	76	73	291	370
65T	Homero Blancas	72	69	73	78	292	355
65T	Gene Littler	73	71	74	74	292	355
67T	Forrest Fezler	71	74	75	73	293	335
67T	Lee Elder	73	69	76	75	293	335
69T	Bob E. Smith	73	68	76	77	294	310
69T	Larry Ziegler	68	69	75	78	294	310
69T	Butch Baird	70	74	78	72	294	310
72	Bobby Walzel	71	74	74	76	295	—

DID NOT MAKE CUT

146 Julius Boros, Bill Kratzert, Chi Chi Rodriguez, Bob Wynn, Larry Nelson, Bobby Wadkins
147 Lyn Lott, Bruce Lietzke, Jim Colbert, Dave Stockton, Rod Curl, Orville Moody, Phil Hancock
148 Rex Caldwell, Ben Crenshaw, Bob Shearer, Joe Inman, Bob Eastwood, Ken Still, Ed Sneed
150 Bill Calfee, Tim Simpson
151 Dave Eichelberger
153 Doug Sanders
157 *Gary Hallberg*
158 Joe Porter

1979
May 17–20

RANK	PLAYER	1R	2R	3R	4R	TOTAL	MONEY
1	Al Geiberger	68	69	64	73	274	$54,000
2T	Gene Littler	70	70	67	68	275	26,400
2T	Don January	72	70	65	68	275	26,400
4T	Tom Watson	71	73	65	67	276	13,200
4T	Jim Colbert	70	73	64	69	276	13,200
6T	Leonard Thompson	65	68	73	72	278	10,425
6T	Fuzzy Zoeller	70	68	70	70	278	10,425
8T	Wayne Levi	68	71	71	69	279	8,400
8T	Ed Sneed	69	74	69	67	279	8,400
8T	Lindy Miller	68	74	70	67	279	8,400
8T	Jack Renner	70	74	66	69	279	8,400
12T	Gil Morgan	69	67	71	73	280	6,600
12T	D. A. Weibring	70	69	69	72	280	6,600
14T	Howard Twitty	72	68	69	72	281	4,950
14T	Barry Jaeckel	70	67	68	76	281	4,950
14T	Bob Shearer	73	71	69	68	281	4,950
14T	Bruce Lietzke	66	73	74	68	281	4,950
14T	Ben Crenshaw	70	70	70	71	281	4,950
14T	Keith Fergus	71	69	70	71	281	4,950
20T	Grier Jones	67	69	72	74	282	3,250
20T	Bruce Devlin	70	69	71	72	282	3,250
20T	Hale Irwin	70	72	69	71	282	3,250
20T	Alan Tapie	74	70	69	69	282	3,250
20T	Buddy Gardner	71	72	71	68	282	3,250
20T	Lee Elder	73	72	70	67	282	3,250
20T	*Bobby Clampett*	71	72	69	70	282	
27T	Mike Sullivan	70	66	74	73	283	2,042
27T	Gibby Gilbert	68	73	71	71	283	2,042
27T	Hubert Green	72	70	70	71	283	2,042
27T	Mark Hayes	73	68	72	70	283	2,042
27T	Bobby Wadkins	66	73	72	72	283	2,042
27T	Jim Nelford	69	71	71	72	283	2,042
27T	Jerry Pate	68	72	72	72	283	2,042
27T	Orville Moody	71	72	70	70	283	2,042
27T	Lee Trevino	66	73	74	70	283	2,042
36T	Mark Lye	75	70	64	75	284	1,447
36T	Tom Purtzer	69	76	68	71	284	1,447
36T	Bill Rogers	73	72	71	68	284	1,447
36T	Jay Haas	68	73	70	73	284	1,447
36T	Craig Stadler	72	72	69	71	284	1,447
36T	Kermit Zarley	69	74	77	64	284	1,447
42T	David Graham	69	73	73	70	285	1,050
42T	J. C. Snead	70	72	72	71	285	1,050
42T	Jerry McGee	69	69	72	75	285	1,050
42T	Bobby Walzel	74	71	71	69	285	1,050
42T	Tom Weiskopf	72	69	72	72	285	1,050
42T	Charles Coody	71	73	68	73	285	1,050
42T	David Edwards	74	70	74	67	285	1,050
49T	Bob E. Smith	70	72	74	70	286	763
49T	Tom Kite	70	72	70	74	286	763
49T	Lanny Wadkins	71	72	70	73	286	763
49T	Julius Boros	71	71	72	72	286	763
49T	Mac McLendon	69	73	74	70	286	763
54T	Rod Curl	71	72	66	78	287	694
54T	Artie McNickle	68	70	76	73	287	694
54T	Jim Thorpe	72	72	68	75	287	694
54T	Tommy Aaron	71	73	73	70	287	694
58T	Dave Stockton	74	67	70	77	288	675
58T	Wally Armstrong	69	73	72	74	288	675
60T	Jack Newton	68	73	75	73	289	660
60T	Peter Jacobsen	71	72	74	72	289	660
60T	Gary Koch	73	70	74	72	289	660
63T	Fred Marti	69	71	78	72	290	642
63T	Chi Chi Rodriguez	73	70	74	73	290	642
63T	Pat McGowan	73	70	73	74	290	642
66	Mark McCumber	71	70	74	77	292	630
67	Mike McCullough	71	74	76	72	293	624
68T	Jeff Hewes	71	74	72	77	294	612
68T	Tim Simpson	70	71	77	76	294	612
68T	Jim Simons	73	72	78	71	294	612
71	John Schroeder	75	70	79	75	299	600

DID NOT MAKE CUT

146 Bill Kratzert, Bob Mann, Doug Tewell, Phil Hancock, Bob Zender, Mike Reid, Bob Gilder, Bob Murphy
147 Scott Simpson, Ken Still, Frank Conner
148 Mike Morley, Dave Eichelberger, Larry Nelson, Lou Graham, Jim Dent, Victor Regalado
149 Homero Blancas, Morris Hatalsky, Curtis Strange
150 Rex Caldwell, Miller Barber, *Payne Stewart*
151 Ron Streck, Jerry Heard, John Mahaffey
152 Marty Fleckman
154 Bob Byman
155 Brad Bryant
156 Lon Hinkle
74-wd Steve Melnyk

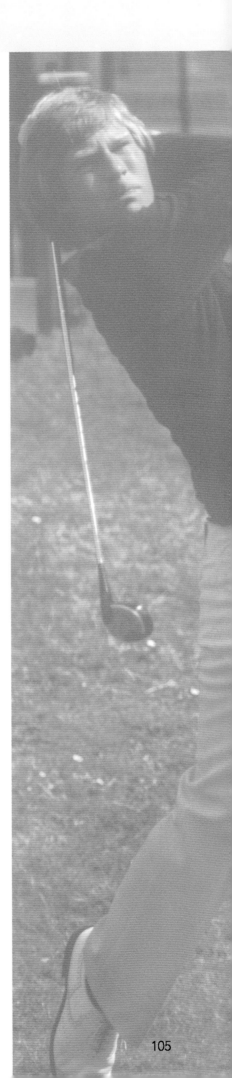

THE 1980s

THE DECADE OF RECORDS AND RAIN

The decade of the 1980s couldn't even get started without a rain delay, then climaxed with one of the tournament's most exciting finishes ever. Amazingly, Colonial had gone 15 years without losing a day to rain, but the first NIT of the '80s actually began on a Friday, and the tournament experienced some sort of rain delay almost every year of the decade.

With tees up and greens soft, Bruce Lietzke blitzed the course with a record-tying 63 that Friday in 1980, including an ace on #16. He then tied the tourney's 36-hole record, with Ben Crenshaw and Tom Watson breathing down his neck. Watson had won the previous week in Dallas, and looked to capture a new "Texas Bonanza" bonus of $200,000 for winning both tournaments.

The 36-hole Sunday finish featured fishing buddies Lietzke and Crenshaw duking it out, and Lietzke had a precarious one-shot lead at the mid-day break. Crenshaw birdied #12 for the lead, then Lietzke almost aced #16 again. His tap-in birdie tied for the lead. Both

ABOVE:
Bruce Lietzke won his first Colonial championship in 1980; pictured with Colonial President Charlie Floyd.
FACING PAGE:
Jack Nicklaus captured his Colonial title in 1982.

ABOVE:
Fuzzy Zoeller won at Colonial in 1981.

parred the 17th, but Lietzke drained a thrilling 25-footer for the win at 18. It marked the first time in history that a Colonial champ birdied the 72nd hole for the win. Watson finished tied for fourth, unable to make any key putts. "I've finished third or fourth here for the last four years," Watson commented about his "rut" of high, but not winning, finishes at Colonial. "This is a great golf course; I'll just look forward to it next year and every year." He went on to win six Tour events, the British Open and PGA Player of the Year honors.

The 1981 event featured a rain-delayed second round and another 36-hole Sunday finish. Colonial celebrated the 40th anniversary of its 1941 U.S. Open by hosting a 9-hole exhibition

featuring such memorable players as Byron Nelson, Fred Haas, Toney Penna, Herman Keiser, Dick Metz, Henry Ransom, and Johnny Revolta - all veterans of the '41 championship.

Afternoon rain and lightning suspended Friday's play, with most players still on the course. Following Saturday's completion of the second round, 1979 Masters champion Fuzzy Zoeller held a slim one-shot lead over 1979 U.S. Open winner Hale Irwin. Sunday was hot and humid, which helped Zoeller's temperamental back, but the popular star had never played a 36-hole day in his competitive career. At the mid-day break, he held a three-shot lead over Curtis Strange, and then expanded it to six shots on the front nine of the afternoon

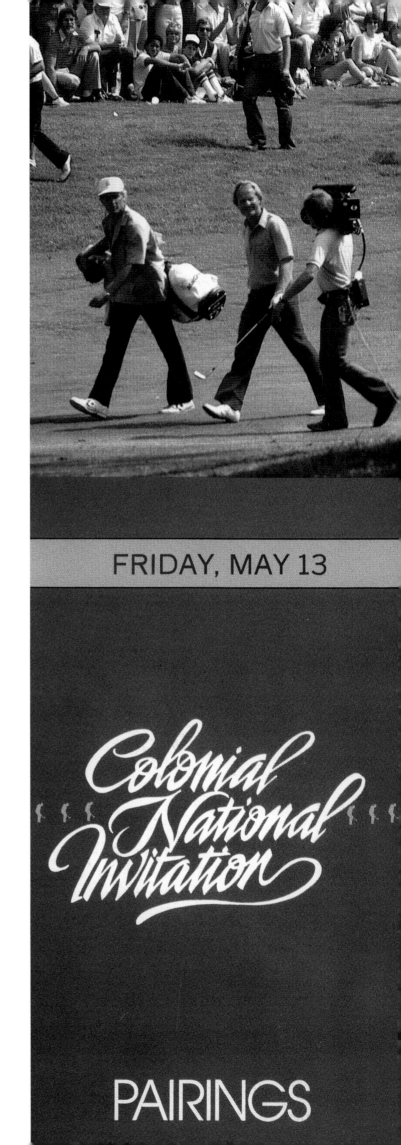

round. That lead plummeted to just one shot with seven holes left, but birdies at #12, 14, and 15 iced the win.

"It was a day of patience, mentally and physically," Zoeller said of his up-and-down day. "I may be sore in the morning, but I'm just going home to sleep and have a few glasses of champagne."

Excitement reigned in 1982 when Arnold Palmer and Jack Nicklaus entered after six-year absences. Both superstars broke par Thursday to highlight a crowded leaderboard and spur the tournament to its first $1 million gate. By Saturday, Nicklaus and David Edwards were nipping at the heels of 1978 U.S. Open champ Andy North, who led by two. North and Edwards were tied for the lead after eight holes Sunday, but blew up together on #9. Nicklaus claimed the lead with a birdie on #10, but was caught by North with birdies on 11 and 12. Then, right after missing a short par putt on #15, North saw his title hopes vanish with the Golden Bear's dramatic, curling birdie putt at #16. At age 47, with son Steve caddying for him, Nicklaus finally conquered Hogan's Alley and buried the ghosts of 1974, when he lost by one.

Marvin Leonard's widow, Mary, observing the legendary golfer's victory, turned to daughter Marty and exclaimed, "Wouldn't your daddy be proud!"

Writing to chairman Rodney Johnston the following week, Nicklaus said, "It may have taken me ten times to be successful at Colonial, but believe me it was truly a pleasure! My first win at age 42 will certainly be savored, and your ring will find a prominent place in my trophy case."

FRIDAY, MAY 13

Colonial National Invitation

PAIRINGS

ABOVE:
The CBS television crew provides western Fort Worth flavor for the broadcast. L-R: Verne Lundquist, Steve Melnyk, Pat Summerall, Tom Weiskopf, Ben Wright.

The 1983 tournament was a logjam from start to finish, highlighted by crazy weather in the third round with a 21-degree temperature drop that carried wind and rain along with it. Defending champion Nicklaus led the first round with a 66, but ballooned to a 75 Friday. Fuzzy Zoeller and Jim Colbert anchored a five-way tie for first after the third round, and swirling Sunday winds guaranteed a battle for survival.

Both players held their own, but stumbled in with bogeys on #18 to tie and force Colonial's first sudden-death playoff. A nerve-racking, six-hole battle ensued, finally won by Colbert when Zoeller bogeyed #18 again. Colbert then almost apologized to Zoeller, "I didn't care about the money; I just wanted the title." To which the former champ replied, "Why didn't you just say so!?" It is still the only Colonial playoff not won with a birdie.

"This is the biggest championship I've won, because of the tradition and the golf course," claimed six-time Tour winner Colbert, who then won the Texas Open that fall for career victory number seven. "It's as hard to win this tournament as a major."

Peter Jacobsen, who had been in that five-way tie with 18 holes to go in 1983, roared back in 1984 with an opening 64. In the rain-interrupted second round, Gil Morgan and a red-hot Payne Stewart took the lead. A record purse of $500,000 awaited the field. After settling into a two-man race with Stewart after three rounds, Jacobsen informed the public that he was dedicating the tournament to his ill father, who had just been diagnosed with cancer.

Former champ Ben Crenshaw started the excitement Sunday by becoming the first player in history to eagle the defiant hole #5 during the tournament. Stewart, who led by two after setting a 54-hole record of 12-under 198, lost the lead on #6 to Jacobsen. They played tag all day, and Stewart led by one stroke at the 18th tee. His drive, however, strayed right and under a bridge, allowing Jacobsen's par to tie. Jacobsen cleaned up quickly, birdieing the first playoff hole for the win.

"I felt nervous, but is was a good nervous," Jacobsen said. "When that last putt went in I thought about my dad. There are no accidents in this world, and no luck either."

In 1985, Mother Nature finally smiled on Colonial, and the Tour's 1984 Rookie of the Year, Corey Pavin, took advantage. Course records fell like gimmie putts all week as windless conditions prevailed. Pavin started with a 66 to tie Mark O'Meara and others, as nearly half the field played below par. His second-round 64 opened up a four-shot lead.

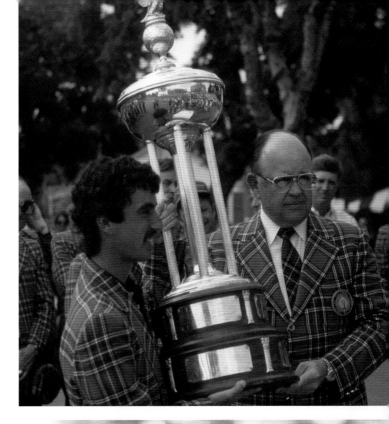

TOP:
Corey Pavin captured his first Colonial win in record fashion in 1985; pictured with Colonial President M.C. Hamilton Jr.
MIDDLE:
Jim Colbert won the Colonial title in 1983; pictured with wife Marcia.
BOTTOM:
1984 champion Peter Jacobsen shakes hands with runner-up Payne Stewart after their playoff.

Pavin never looked back, lowering the 72-hole course record by three shots, and carding only two bogeys the entire tournament. His 14-under total, along with his 36-hole record of 10-under, would stand for eight years. Joey Sindelar's eight-under 62 (with a bogey on #5) and Tom Watson's front nine 29 also hit the record books, but never threatened Pavin's march. On Sunday, veteran Ray Floyd charged out of the gate by birdieing the first five holes, but disappeared with a double-bogey on #8 and a quad on #9. At 25 years, six months and three days, Pavin became Colonial's youngest champion, besting Dave Stockton (1967) by four days.

"To shoot 14 under par here is a dream tournament," Pavin noted. "I came out here and played the best golf I've ever played. This course is so demanding; maybe the most demanding in the United States."

Windy conditions prevailed for the first two rounds in 1986, bunching up the field for a horse race. Then rain on Saturday kept the starting gates closed and forced Colonial officials to go for a shortened, 54-hole event, as a poor forecast for Sunday threatened the chance of getting in even 18 more holes. A scheduled early TV finish Sunday also played heavily into the decision. Thirteen players crowded within four shots at the top, including Danny Edwards, Dan Pohl, Bill Rogers, Bob Tway, Corey Pavin, Payne Stewart, and German Bernhard Langer.

TOP:
Dan Pohl won at Colonial in 1986 in a sudden-death playoff.
MIDDLE:
Tom Kite notched four top 10 finishes at Colonial in the 1980s.
BOTTOM:
1987 champion Keith Clearwater shot an incredible 64-64 in the 36-hole Sunday finish.

A cool and windy day greeted the contestants for the final round, but thankfully the rain stayed away. Stewart fired a stout 66 and waited in the clubhouse with the lead. Tom Watson (64) and Langer (67) mounted fierce charges but tied for third with Rogers, two shots behind. The long-hitting Pohl birdied #16 to tie Stewart and force a sudden-death playoff. He then promptly birdied it again to win on the first extra hole, his first career victory. Watson's finish marked the sixth time in his last eight Colonial appearances that he finished in the top five. Stewart's second loss in three years was as close as he came to winning at Colonial, though he notched three more top 10 finishes over the next 10 years.

The third 36-hole finish of the decade, and its most famous, highlighted the 1987 Colonial tournament. Friday's play was washed out and, after the record-low cut of even-par 140 on Saturday, 63 players were within seven shots of the lead. On a hot and humid Sunday, Ben Crenshaw seized the lead after 54 holes as players teed off holes #1 and #10, and could not re-pair between rounds. Thus, unknown Keith Clearwater, who had shot an incredible 64 that morning to overtake 23 players and tie Doug Tewell and defending champ Dan Pohl for second place, remained in obscurity teeing off on #10, far away from the leaders. Davis Love III, firing an equally hot 65 to tie for fifth position, also began the last round on the back nine.

ABOVE:
Ian Baker- Finch won the 1989 Colonial title; pictured with Colonial President Sam Day.

That obscurity didn't last long, however, as both players kept up their torrid pace all afternoon. Clearwater's winning 64-64 finish overshadowed the stellar 65-66 performance by Love, who placed second. Clearwater, a 1981 all-America at Brigham Young, was the third player to win at Colonial on his first try, and is the only champ to finish on the ninth hole. His 266 total tied Pavin's record from two years earlier.

If you had tried to pick the 1988 Colonial winner you would have lost a bundle. He had played the tournament so poorly in the past that he took two years off in order to arrive with a fresh attitude. He had never broken par in 11 years and 35 rounds at Colonial, missing the cut in 1984 and '85. Menacing winds made the tournament an exciting dogfight from start to finish.

Dallas' Lanny Wadkins opened with a leading 67, and still clung to the top spot after 36 holes. A record $750,000 purse was on the line. "I don't have any reason for not playing well here in the past," Wadkins stated. "I like the golf course, and I think it's the kind of course that if I play well I should do okay."

A brilliant closing 65 by Wadkins in a difficult wind Sunday overtook Ben Crenshaw and Joey Sindelar, who finished one shot back with Mark Calcavecchia. Wadkins' dramatic birdie on #18 averted a four-man playoff. Ever-popular Crenshaw ignited the crowd with four consecutive closing birdies, including an incredible 40-footer on 18. The ensuing roar rattled the bricks of Colonial's stately clubhouse.

The Tuesday Shootout was a popular event with players and fans in the 1980s.
L - R: Ben Crenshaw, Bruce Lietzke, Hal Sutton, Tom Watson, Lee Trevino, Payne Stewart, Curtis Strange, Peter Jacobsen, Jim Colbert, Tom Kite.

The decade closed with some new faces and another surprise winner in 1989. Masters champion Nick Faldo made his Colonial debut. Rising PGA Tour purses brought Southwestern Bell Corporation to title sponsorship of the event, the first time Colonial members shared the spotlight as host. A familiar face this year was the wind, and blowing in it was a record $1 million purse.

A top Australian player named Ian Baker-Finch, playing in the tournament on a special exemption from Colonial, opened with a 65 to lead by one. He had been recommended by fellow Aussie and 1986 British Open champion Greg Norman. After Friday, two players from another British colony, Nick Price and David Frost, were just one back of the Aussie. But another

65 on Saturday separated Baker-Finch from the field and he coasted in on Sunday with a four-shot victory. He joined countrymen Bruce Devlin and Bruce Crampton as Colonial champs from "Down Under." It was his first victory in America, but his 10th worldwide. The first foreign winner at Colonial in 23 years, Baker-Finch remains the last champion to lead the event wire-to-wire.

1980s

results

1980
May 16-18

RANK	PLAYER	1R	2R	3R	4R	TOTAL	MONEY
1	Bruce Lietzke	63	68	71	69	271	$54,000
2	Ben Crenshaw	67	66	70	69	272	32,400
3	Jeff Mitchell	65	73	70	65	273	20,400
4T	Tom Watson	66	68	71	69	274	13,200
4T	Doug Tewell	71	65	69	69	274	13,200
6	Andy Bean	70	67	71	67	275	10,800
7T	Lon Hinkle	71	64	72	69	276	9,675
7T	Bob Murphy	70	69	67	70	276	9,675
9T	Tom Kite	67	71	67	72	277	7,800
9T	Ed Sneed	68	71	70	67	277	7,800
9T	Lee Trevino	66	72	69	70	277	7,800
9T	Ed Fiori	70	69	68	70	277	7,800
13T	Fuzzy Zoeller	67	72	70	69	278	5,800
13T	Mike Reid	70	71	67	70	278	5,800
13T	Peter Jacobsen	70	71	68	69	278	5,800
16T	David Graham	68	71	68	72	279	4,209
16T	Frank Conner	67	74	72	66	279	4,209
16T	Terry Mauney	69	73	70	67	279	4,209
16T	Bill Rogers	71	70	67	71	279	4,209
16T	Dan Pohl	72	70	69	68	279	4,209
16T	John Fought	72	71	68	68	279	4,209
16T	Jerry Pate	70	69	71	69	279	4,209
23T	Mark Pfeil	72	71	67	70	280	2,880
23T	David Edwards	69	73	69	69	280	2,880
23T	Curtis Strange	70	68	71	71	280	2,880
26T	Bruce Devlin	71	71	69	70	281	2,220
26T	Bill Kratzert	70	72	70	69	281	2,220
26T	Chi Chi Rodriguez	68	68	73	72	281	2,220
26T	George Cadle	70	70	70	71	281	2,220
26T	Jay Haas	70	71	69	71	281	2,220
31T	Tom Weiskopf	69	67	70	76	282	1,779
31T	Gil Morgan	72	65	67	78	282	1,779
31T	Jim Colbert	69	66	71	76	282	1,779
31T	Bud Allin	73	70	67	72	282	1,779
31T	Gary Koch	71	70	70	71	282	1,779
36T	Bob Byman	70	72	74	67	283	1,352
36T	Don Pooley	70	70	69	74	283	1,352
36T	Howard Twitty	73	67	72	71	283	1,352
36T	Victor Regalado	70	70	70	73	283	1,352
36T	John Mahaffey	72	70	67	74	283	1,352
36T	Artie McNickle	70	72	69	72	283	1,352
36T	Andy North	68	72	73	70	283	1,352
43T	Bobby Wadkins	68	74	69	73	284	990
43T	Ray Floyd	70	70	73	71	284	990
43T	John Cook	69	72	71	72	284	990
43T	Craig Stadler	75	67	72	70	284	990
43T	Lou Graham	71	69	72	72	284	990
48T	Charles Coody	70	73	69	73	285	763
48T	J. C. Snead	69	71	71	74	285	763
48T	Wayne Levi	74	69	73	69	285	763
48T	Gibby Gilbert	71	69	70	75	285	763
48T	Scott Simpson	72	69	71	73	285	763
53T	Dan Halldorson	71	69	74	72	286	691
53T	Jim Thorpe	70	73	72	71	286	691
53T	Mike Morley	71	69	77	69	286	691
53T	Homero Blancas	70	72	73	71	286	691
53T	Bob E. Smith	69	72	73	72	286	691
58T	Al Geiberger	72	71	72	72	287	660
58T	Mike Sullivan	70	73	72	72	287	660
58T	Terry Diehl	72	71	69	75	287	660
58T	Alan Tapie	70	68	72	72	287	660
58T	Tom Purtzer	71	70	74	72	287	660
63	Dave Stockton	67	72	71	79	289	642
64	Steve Melnyk	71	71	74	74	290	636
65	Mark McCumber	75	68	71	81	295	630

DID NOT MAKE CUT

144   Keith Fergus, D.A. Weibring, Grier Jones, Jerry McGee, Miller Barber, Tommy Aaron, Gene Littler, Dave Eichelberger
145   Joe Inman, Jack Renner, Bobby Walzel, Rex Caldwell
146   Jack Newton, Bill Calfee, Kermit Zarley, Mark Hayes, Larry Nelson, Don January
147   Lee Elder, *Mark O'Meara*, Peter Oosterhuis, Morris Hatalsky, Ron Streck, Bob Gilder, Mark Lye
148   Jim Simons, Jim Boros, Jim Nelford, Buddy Gardner
149   Brad Bryant, Mike Brannan
150   Lindy Miller
152   *Ray Barr*, Orville Moody
153   John Schroeder
78-wd   Wally Armstrong
78-wd   Rod Curl

1981
May 14-17

RANK	PLAYER	1R	2R	3R	4R	TOTAL	MONEY
1	Fuzzy Zoeller	67	69	68	70	274	$54,000
2	Hale Irwin	69	68	71	70	278	32,400
3T	Tom Kite	67	71	71	70	279	15,600
3T	Scott Simpson	69	70	70	70	279	15,600
3T	Curtis Strange	69	71	67	72	279	15,600
6	Frank Conner	70	72	68	70	280	10,800
7T	Don January	70	69	70	72	281	9,675
7T	Ray Floyd	66	74	71	70	281	9,675
9T	Rod Curl	67	73	74	68	282	8,400
9T	Jerry Heard	74	65	72	71	282	8,400
11T	Jack Renner	73	70	70	70	283	6,150
11T	Vance Heafner	72	71	68	72	283	6,150
11T	Bob Murphy	70	73	67	73	283	6,150
11T	Jim Colbert	70	73	71	69	283	6,150
11T	Bill Rogers	72	68	75	68	283	6,150
11T	Ron Streck	71	69	71	72	283	6,150
17T	Mike Reid	73	69	72	70	284	4,650
17T	Craig Stadler	69	71	71	73	284	4,650
19T	Tom Weiskopf	70	72	69	74	285	4,050
19T	Mark Lye	69	72	70	74	285	4,050
21T	Fred Couples	71	70	72	73	286	3,000
21T	Tom Jenkins	73	70	74	69	286	3,000
21T	Keith Fergus	68	70	71	77	286	3,000
21T	George Archer	74	70	73	69	286	3,000
21T	Chi Chi Rodriguez	71	73	69	73	286	3,000
21T	Bobby Clampett	72	72	69	73	286	3,000
27T	Mark McCumber	72	70	71	74	287	2,040
27T	Jeff Mitchell	71	71	72	73	287	2,040
27T	Barry Jaeckel	68	74	73	72	287	2,040
27T	Mark O'Meara	71	72	72	72	287	2,040
27T	Mark Pfeil	76	68	72	71	287	2,040
27T	Danny Edwards	73	71	71	72	287	2,040
27T	Jay Haas	72	72	71	72	287	2,040
34T	Bob Eastwood	73	69	70	76	288	1,515
34T	George Cadle	73	70	72	73	288	1,515
34T	Rik Massengale	76	64	76	72	288	1,515
34T	Jerry Pate	73	67	76	72	288	1,515
34T	Lon Hinkle	73	71	70	74	288	1,515
34T	David Graham	77	67	69	75	288	1,515
40T	Howard Twitty	69	74	72	74	289	1,140
40T	Lee Trevino	73	71	71	74	289	1,140
40T	Dan Pohl	71	72	71	75	289	1,140
40T	George Burns	68	75	72	74	289	1,140
40T	Gary Koch	73	70	72	74	289	1,140
40T	Dan Halldorson	71	72	71	75	289	1,140
46T	John Mahaffey	69	72	74	75	290	850
46T	Bud Allin	71	69	76	74	290	850
46T	John Schroeder	72	72	72	74	290	850
46T	Brad Bryant	71	73	73	73	290	850
50	Tommy Valentine	69	72	75	75	291	756
51T	Mike Sullivan	66	75	75	76	292	715
51T	Scott Hoch	74	69	72	77	292	715
51T	David Edwards	72	72	72	76	292	715
51T	Ed Sneed	69	75	76	72	292	715
55T	Terry Mauney	68	75	72	78	293	687
55T	Lanny Wadkins	73	71	75	74	293	687
57T	Dave Eichelberger	69	75	71	79	294	675
57T	Barney Thompson	74	70	75	75	294	675
59	Gary Hallberg	69	75	76	76	296	666
60T	John Fought	71	72	75	79	297	657
60T	Miller Barger	69	75	79	74	297	657
62	Mike Morley	70	74	77	77	298	648

DID NOT MAKE CUT

145   Bruce Devlin, Tom Watson, Al Geiberger, Tom Purtzer, Larry Nelson, Jim Simons
146   Rex Caldwell, Hubert Green, Artie McNickle, Charles Coody, John Cook, Ben Crenshaw
147   Morris Hatalsky, Roger Maltbie, Leonard Thompson, Dave Stockton, Bobby Wadkins, Terry Diehl
148   Bruce Lietzke, Johnny Miller, Ed Fiori, Lindy Miller, Calvin Peete, Gene Littler, *Ray Barr*, Mark Hayes, Lou Graham
149   Bobby Walzel
150   Larry Ziegler
151   Peter Jacobsen, Don Pooley
153   *Hal Sutton*
157   Mike Donald
71-wd   Jack Newton
74-wd   Gibby Gilbert
75-wd   Bob Gilder
76-wd   Doug Tewell, Phil Hancock
78-wd   Victor Regalado
79-wd   D.A. Weibring

1982
May 13-16

Rank	Player	1R	2R	3R	4R	Total	Money
1	Jack Nicklaus	66	70	70	67	273	$63,000
2	Andy North	68	69	67	72	276	37,800
3	Jerry Pate	68	69	68	71	277	23,800
4	Tom Kite	68	68	74	68	278	16,800
5T	Lennie Clements	66	69	75	70	280	12,294
5T	Bob Eastwood	74	71	70	65	280	12,294
5T	Joe Inman	68	73	70	69	280	12,294
5T	Tom Purtzer	69	74	67	70	280	12,294
9T	Danny Edwards	72	68	66	75	281	9,800
9T	Lee Trevino	72	74	67	68	281	9,800
11T	Frank Conner	71	70	69	72	282	7,700
11T	Hubert Green	73	66	76	67	282	7,700
11T	Steve Melnyk	74	69	69	70	282	7,700
11T	Curtis Strange	72	71	69	70	282	7,700
15T	Chip Beck	73	74	69	67	283	5,600
15T	George Burns	73	72	71	67	283	5,600
15T	Bruce Lietzke	71	74	69	69	283	5,600
15T	Roger Maltbie	73	69	68	73	283	5,600
15T	Bobby Wadkins	70	72	70	71	283	5,600
20T	John Cook	71	73	70	70	284	3,531
20T	Bruce Fleisher	72	70	72	70	284	3,531
20T	John Mahaffey	70	70	74	70	284	3,531
20T	Peter Oosterhuis	69	70	76	69	284	3,531
20T	Ben Crenshaw	72	72	70	70	284	3,531
20T	Don January	70	74	69	71	284	3,531
20T	Bob Murphy	69	71	71	73	284	3,531
20T	Mike Reid	73	72	69	70	284	3,531
28T	George Archer	68	72	73	72	285	2,328
28T	Jim Booros	68	77	74	66	285	2,328
28T	Mike Donald	71	70	72	72	285	2,328
28T	Scott Hoch	69	72	73	71	285	2,328
28T	Greg Powers	70	75	71	69	285	2,328
28T	John Schroeder	74	70	70	71	285	2,328
34T	Bobby Clampett	70	73	71	72	286	1,890
34T	Barry Jaeckel	68	77	72	69	286	1,890
34T	Tommy Valentine	73	72	70	71	286	1,890
37T	Jay Haas	71	74	74	68	287	1,575
37T	Vance Heafner	65	76	70	76	287	1,575
37T	Tom Jenkins	72	75	68	72	287	1,575
37T	Gene Littler	70	73	73	71	287	1,575
37T	Fuzzy Zoeller	69	72	72	74	287	1,575
42T	Fred Couples	77	70	71	70	288	1,018
42T	Al Geiberger	73	72	73	70	288	1,018
42T	Doug Tewell	69	76	72	71	288	1,018
42T	Bill Britton	70	73	72	73	288	1,018
42T	Brad Bryant	68	73	75	72	288	1,018
42T	Charles Coody	70	71	71	76	288	1,018
42T	Bob Gilder	70	72	71	75	288	1,018
42T	Gil Morgan	74	71	71	72	288	1,018
42T	Larry Nelson	68	76	72	72	288	1,018
42T	Dan Pohl	72	73	72	71	288	1,018
42T	Ed Sneed	71	76	70	71	288	1,018
42T	Ron Streck	69	70	75	74	288	1,018
42T	Mike Sullivan	72	73	71	72	288	1,018
55T	Hale Irwin	73	73	72	71	289	798
55T	Bill Kratzert	76	71	73	69	289	798
55T	Leonard Thompson	69	74	73	73	289	798
58T	Terry Diehl	75	72	72	71	290	774
58T	Jerry Heard	71	73	72	74	290	774
58T	Craig Stadler	77	70	71	72	290	774
58T	Hal Sutton	74	73	72	71	290	774
62T	Dave Eichelberger	68	70	74	79	291	746
62T	Jack Renner	71	71	73	76	291	746
62T	Bill Rogers	74	72	73	72	291	746
62T	Tim Simpson	73	74	73	71	291	746
66T	David Edwards	72	73	71	76	292	714
66T	Keith Fergus	75	70	73	74	292	714
66T	Peter Jacobsen	69	76	73	74	292	714
66T	Chi Chi Rodriguez	73	74	76	69	292	714
66T	Howard Twitty	69	76	75	72	292	714
71T	Bruce Devlin	71	73	75	74	293	686
71T	Jeff Mitchell	72	73	72	76	293	686
71T	Lanny Wadkins	73	70	75	75	293	686
74T	Dave Barr	75	72	76	71	294	669
76T	Ed Fiori	73	73	78	71	295	655
76T	Arnold Palmer	68	73	78	76	295	655
78	Miller Barber	71	73	76	76	296	644
79	D. A. Weibring	70	77	75	75	297	637
80	David Graham	73	71	76	79	299	630
81	Jim Thorpe	73	71	81	78	303	623

DID NOT MAKE CUT

148 Denis Watson, Gary Hallberg
149 Lee Elder, Bob Shearer
150 Scott Simpson, Jim Colbert, *Willie Wood*, Rex Caldwell
Ray Floyd, Dan Halldorson
151 Lon Hinkle, Don Pooley, Rod Curl
152 Lyn Lott, Mike McCullough
153 Mike Holland
154 Mark Hayes, Mark O'Meara, Dave Stockton
155 *Danny Briggs*
156 Mark Lye

1983
May 12-15

Rank	Player	1R	2R	3R	4R	Total	Money
1	Jim Colbert	69	67	70	72	278*	$72,000
2	Fuzzy Zoeller	68	70	68	72	278*	43,200
3T	Lon Hinkle	70	72	67	70	279	23,200
3T	Bruce Lietzke	69	67	72	71	279	23,200
5T	Peter Jacobsen	70	69	67	74	280	12,657
5T	Bob Murphy	70	66	75	69	280	12,657
5T	Bobby Wadkins	68	64	74	74	280	12,657
5T	Gary Hallberg	66	67	75	72	280	12,657
5T	Gary Koch	69	69	72	70	280	12,657
5T	Mark McNulty	70	67	72	71	280	12,657
5T	Mike Reid	67	69	70	74	280	12,657
12T	Hale Irwin	67	72	71	71	281	7,600
12T	Bobby Clampett	72	73	65	71	281	7,600
12T	John Mahaffey	71	68	69	73	281	7,600
12T	Thomas Gray	70	67	71	73	281	7,600
12T	Bob Eastwood	69	68	74	70	281	7,600
12T	Tom Kite	68	73	70	70	281	7,600
18T	Frank Conner	70	69	71	72	282	4,700
18T	Mike Sullivan	68	70	72	72	282	4,700
18T	Joe Inman	66	72	69	75	282	4,700
18T	Keith Fergus	69	70	72	71	282	4,700
18T	Bruce Devlin	73	69	70	70	282	4,700
18T	Gil Morgan	68	69	74	71	282	4,700
18T	Chip Beck	72	72	70	68	282	4,700
18T	Jim Nelford	68	67	75	72	282	4,700
26T	Rex Caldwell	67	68	75	73	283	3,140
26T	Ed Fiori	69	66	75	73	283	3,140
28T	Jack Nicklaus	66	75	74	69	284	2,720
28T	George Archer	69	73	72	70	284	2,720
28T	Al Geiberger	71	70	69	74	284	2,720
28T	Howard Twitty	69	74	68	73	284	2,720
28T	Fred Couples	73	68	75	68	284	2,720
33T	Andy North	69	72	68	76	285	2,260
33T	Danny Edwards	71	71	69	74	285	2,260
33T	Brad Bryant	70	74	70	71	285	2,260
36T	David Edwards	70	68	71	77	286	2,010
36T	Mike McCullough	67	72	73	74	286	2,010
38T	Peter Oosterhuis	70	72	73	72	287	1,760
38T	Ed Sneed	70	70	72	75	287	1,760
38T	Donnie Hammond	72	71	74	70	287	1,760
38T	Miller Barber	73	69	73	72	287	1,760
42T	Mike Donald	71	73	72	72	288	1,322
42T	Mike Nicolette	68	74	72	74	288	1,322
42T	Larry Mize	72	70	72	74	288	1,322
42T	Dan Pohl	68	73	71	76	288	1,322
42T	*Brandel Chamblee*	75	70	70	73	288	1,322
42T	Andy Bean	70	74	71	73	288	1,322
42T	Bill Rogers	72	73	69	74	288	1,322
42T	John Cook	70	68	74	76	288	1,322
50T	Bruce Fleisher	73	69	75	72	289	987
50T	Jay Haas	72	73	73	71	289	987
50T	David Graham	75	69	72	73	289	987
50T	Woody Blackburn	73	71	72	73	289	987
50T	Mark McCumber	67	72	75	75	289	987
55T	Barry Jaeckel	76	68	73	73	290	920
55T	Mark Lye	72	70	73	75	290	920
55T	Charles Coody	74	70	71	75	290	920
58T	Pat McGowan	72	70	74	75	291	884
58T	Leonard Thompson	75	70	71	75	291	884
58T	John Fought	70	71	74	76	291	884
58T	Mark Pfeil	71	73	71	76	291	884
58T	Ben Crenshaw	69	69	80	73	291	884
58T	Denis Watson	72	71	72	76	291	884
64	Victor Regalado	71	72	75	74	292	856
65T	Dan Halldorson	72	70	72	79	293	840
65T	Dave Stockton	73	70	73	77	293	840
65T	Mark Hayes	73	72	75	73	293	840
68T	Larry Rinker	77	68	74	75	294	820
68T	Jerry Heard	71	71	72	80	294	820
70T	Tom Weiskopf	73	66	75	81	295	800
70T	Jim Thorpe	69	75	75	76	295	800
70T	Bob Gilder	71	73	73	78	295	800
73	Doug Tewell	71	73	71	81	296	784

*In sudden death playoff, Colbert beat Zoeller with par on sixth hole.

DID NOT MAKE CUT

146 Lee Trevino, Gene Littler, Jim Simons, George Burns
Hal Sutton, Brad Shearer
147 Roger Maltbie, Tim Norris, Don January, John Adams,
Tim Simpson, Jack Renner,
148 Tommy Valentine
149 Mark O'Meara, Morris Hatalsky, Chi Chi Rodriguez
Mark Brooks, Jodie Mudd, Vance Heafner
150 Mike Holland
151 Rod Curl
152 Dave Eichelberger, Lennie Clements
153 Mac O'Grady, Steve Melnyk, Tom Jenkins
161 Bill Britton
75-dq Tom Purtzer
76-wd Curtis Strange

1984
May 17-20

Rank	Player	1R	2R	3R	4R	Total	Money
1	Peter Jacobsen	64	71	65	70	270*	$90,000
2	Payne Stewart	68	66	64	72	270*	54,000
3	Gil Morgan	66	67	70	72	275	34,000
4T	Tom Watson	66	72	69	70	277	18,850
4T	Tom Kite	70	69	67	71	277	18,850
4T	Tony Sills	67	71	69	70	277	18,850
4T	Mark Pfeil	72	67	69	69	277	18,850
4T	Ben Crenshaw	69	71	68	69	277	18,850
9T	Ray Floyd	72	68	69	69	278	14,000
9T	Mike Sullivan	68	71	70	69	278	14,000
11T	Rex Caldwell	69	68	73	69	279	11,000
11T	D. A. Weibring	66	71	70	72	279	11,000
11T	Mark Lye	66	70	73	70	279	11,000
11T	Mike Reid	66	71	74	68	279	11,000
15T	Scott Hoch	69	67	74	70	280	8,500
15T	Sammy Rachels	68	67	74	71	280	8,500
15T	Dan Pohl	69	68	74	69	280	8,500
18T	Seve Ballesteros	68	70	73	70	281	5,485
18T	Peter Oosterhuis	69	70	71	71	281	5,485
18T	Corey Pavin	70	69	73	69	281	5,485
18T	Fuzzy Zoeller	69	73	70	69	281	5,485
18T	George Burns	74	70	71	66	281	5,485
18T	George Archer	70	70	70	71	281	5,485
18T	Ron Streck	71	69	68	73	281	5,485
18T	Russ Cochran	70	71	73	67	281	5,485
18T	Curtis Strange	67	71	71	72	281	5,485
18T	Bruce Lietzke	68	72	70	71	281	5,485
28T	Bill Rogers	71	71	67	73	282	3,400
28T	Mark McCumber	69	72	69	72	282	3,400
28T	Brad Bryant	73	72	67	70	282	3,400
28T	Bobby Wadkins	68	71	70	73	282	3,400
28T	Mike Donald	72	67	70	73	282	3,400
33T	Larry Nelson	70	72	71	70	283	2,585
33T	Craig Stadler	70	67	72	74	283	2,585
33T	Chi Chi Rodriguez	70	68	72	73	283	2,585
33T	John Cook	70	68	73	72	283	2,585
33T	David Edwards	68	71	72	72	283	2,585
33T	Jim Thorpe	69	71	72	71	283	2,585
33T	Jim Colbert	70	69	73	71	283	2,585
40T	Danny Edwards	67	74	71	72	284	1,950
40T	Bill Kratzert	68	77	69	70	284	1,950
40T	Dave Stockton	71	70	69	74	284	1,950
40T	Gary Koch	72	68	71	73	284	1,950
40T	Mike Nicolette	72	73	69	70	284	1,950
45T	Tim Simpson	75	70	73	67	285	1,600
45T	Mark Hayes	71	69	75	70	285	1,600
47T	John Adams	70	72	69	75	286	1,244
47T	Larry Mize	74	70	69	73	286	1,244
47T	Pat McGowan	70	69	76	71	286	1,244
47T	Johnny Miller	69	68	76	73	286	1,244
47T	Chip Beck	68	73	71	74	286	1,244
47T	Ronnie Black	71	68	73	74	286	1,244
47T	Mark O'Meara	71	72	75	68	286	1,244
47T	Greg Norman	75	70	73	68	286	1,244
47T	David Graham	73	68	74	71	286	1,244
47T	Charles Coody	73	71	71	71	286	1,244
57T	Ed Fiori	69	69	75	74	287	1,125
57T	Tom Purtzer	73	71	71	72	287	1,125
59T	Keith Fergus	72	71	74	71	288	1,105
59T	Tim Norris	71	67	72	78	288	1,105
59T	*Steve Elkington*	68	73	73	74	288	1,105
62T	Doug Tewell	70	73	69	77	289	1,075
62T	Jack Renner	74	70	73	72	289	1,075
62T	Lee Trevino	75	70	74	70	289	1,075
62T	Donnie Hammond	73	70	72	74	289	1,075
66T	Jim Nelford	73	70	73	74	290	1,045
66T	Buddy Gardner	69	75	71	75	290	1,045
68T	Tom Weiskopf	71	71	74	75	291	1,015
68T	Al Geiberger	72	72	70	77	291	1,015
68T	Nick Price	69	74	75	73	291	1,015
68T	Larry Rinker	69	73	74	75	291	1,015
72	Pat Lindsey	70	75	73	75	293	990
73T	Vance Heafner	70	74	73	77	294	975
73T	Gary Hallberg	69	71	74	80	294	975
75	Joey Sindelar	68	75	74	80	297	960
76	Ed Sneed	75	69	76	80	300	950

*In sudden death playoff, Jacobsen beat Stewart with birdie on first hole.

DID NOT MAKE CUT

146 Jay Haas, Roger Maltbie, Bobby Clampett, John Mahaffey
Mac O'Grady, Frank Conner, Willie Wood, Bob Eastwood
Hal Sutton
147 *Danny Mijovic*, Lanny Wadkins, J. C. Snead, Steve Melnyk
148 Don Pooley, Gary McCord
149 Andy North, Bob Gilder
150 Leonard Thompson
151 Dave Eichelberger
153 Barry Jaeckel, Mark Brooks, Bob Murphy, Bruce Devlin
142-dq Scott Simpson
74-wd Phil Hancock
80-wd Lon Hinkle

Names in italics designate amateurs.

1980s

1985
May 16-19

Rank	Player	1R	2R	3R	4R	Total	Money
1	Corey Pavin	66	64	68	68	266	$90,000
2	Bob Murphy	68	70	65	67	270	54,000
3	Scott Hoch	69	68	66	69	272	34,000
4T	Nick Price	69	70	70	64	273	22,000
4T	Mark O'Meara	66	68	71	68	273	22,000
6	Larry Mize	71	70	65	68	274	18,000
7T	Buddy Gardner	68	70	68	69	275	15,063
7T	Joey Sindelar	71	72	62	70	275	15,063
7T	Willie Wood	66	69	72	68	275	15,063
7T	John Mahaffey	70	66	71	68	275	15,063
11T	D.A.Weibring	73	67	68	68	276	11,000
11T	Mike Donald	68	68	68	72	276	11,000
11T	Tim Norris	69	66	70	71	276	11,000
11T	Mike Smith	67	69	74	66	276	11,000
15T	Mark Pfeil	71	67	72	68	278	8,250
15T	Hal Sutton	70	68	67	73	278	8,250
15T	Larry Nelson	70	68	71	69	278	8,250
15T	Lee Trevino	70	69	68	71	278	8,250
19T	Keith Fergus	72	70	68	69	279	5,643
19T	Ray Floyd	72	66	70	71	279	5,643
19T	Bill Kratzert	68	70	70	71	279	5,643
19T	Mike Reid	72	67	69	71	279	5,643
19T	Lon Hinkle	68	69	71	71	279	5,645
19T	Peter Jacobsen	67	73	69	70	279	5,643
19T	Payne Stewart	71	71	66	71	279	5,643
26T	Gibby Gilbert	71	72	69	68	280	3,403
26T	Chip Beck	67	70	68	75	280	3,403
26T	Rex Caldwell	70	68	71	71	280	3,403
26T	Roger Maltbie	69	69	70	72	280	3,403
26T	Bill Glasson	68	71	64	77	280	3,403
26T	Jim Thorpe	66	72	69	73	280	3,403
26T	Mac O'Grady	68	70	74	68	280	3,403
26T	Tim Simpson	69	73	71	67	280	3,403
26T	Paul Azinger	70	67	70	73	280	3,403
35T	Donnie Hammond	70	68	71	72	281	2,465
35T	Ron Streck	68	69	69	75	281	2,465
35T	Tom Watson	74	66	73	68	281	2,465
35T	Howard Twitty	72	69	72	68	281	2,465
35T	Don Pooley	73	68	71	69	281	2,465
40T	Dan Halldorson	68	67	75	72	282	1,900
40T	Russ Cochran	71	70	73	68	282	1,900
40T	Danny Edwards	74	69	65	74	282	1,900
40T	David Edwards	70	71	67	74	282	1,900
40T	Doug Tewell	71	71	68	72	282	1,900
40T	Bobby Wadkins	69	69	71	73	282	1,900
46T	Tommy Nakajima	70	67	74	72	283	1,500
46T	Bruce Lietzke	70	73	66	74	283	1,500
48T	Charles Coody	69	73	72	70	284	1,290
48T	Andy Bean	72	68	73	71	284	1,290
48T	John Adams	70	69	75	70	284	1,290
48T	Jim Nelford	74	69	72	69	284	1,290
52T	George Archer	72	68	70	75	285	1,143
52T	Dave Stockton	70	69	70	76	285	1,143
52T	Ralph Landrum	71	70	72	72	285	1,143
52T	Ian Baker-Finch	71	71	69	74	285	1,143
52T	Tom Kite	72	71	69	73	285	1,143
52T	Dave Barr	72	71	72	70	285	1,143
52T	David Graham	67	70	74	74	285	1,143
52T	Gary Hallberg	69	68	75	73	285	1,143
52T	Gil Morgan	71	72	69	73	285	1,143
61T	Larry Rinker	70	72	71	73	286	1,080
61T	Chi Chi Rodriguez	68	74	71	73	286	1,080
61T	Tom Purtzer	69	71	74	72	286	1,080
61T	*Steve Elkington*	73	68	74	71	286	1,080
65T	Curtis Strange	72	69	70	76	287	1,045
65T	George Burns	71	69	75	72	287	1,045
65T	Vance Heafner	73	70	71	73	287	1,045
65T	Tony Sills	70	70	75	72	287	1,045
69T	John Cook	69	71	74	74	288	1,010
69T	Bob Lohr	73	69	71	75	288	1,010
69T	Fred Couples	73	68	77	70	288	1,010
72	Pat McGowan	67	76	71	75	289	990

DID NOT MAKE CUT

144 Brad Faxon, Hale Irwin, Loren Roberts, Bill Rogers
Gary Koch
145 J.C. Snead, Bob Eastwood, Jack Renner, Dan Pohl
Ed Fiori, Mark Lye, Jim Colbert, Barry Jaeckel
Peter Oosterhuis, *Scott Verplank*
146 Al Geiberger, Ronnie Black, Mark McCumber
147 Jerry Pate, Andy North, Lanny Wadkins
148 Fuzzy Zoeller
149 Clarence Rose, Woody Blackburn, Dan Forsman
Gary McCord
150 David Frost
151 Jim Simons
153 Phil Blackmar
154 Ben Crenshaw

1986
May 15-18

Rank	Player	1R	2R	3R	Total	Money
1	Dan Pohl	68	69	68	205*	$108,000
2	Payne Stewart	72	67	66	205*	64,800
3T	Tom Watson	75	68	64	207	31,200
3T	Bernhard Langer	70	70	67	207	31,200
3T	Bill Rogers	67	71	69	207	31,200
6T	David Frost	70	71	67	208	20,100
6T	Mike Sullivan	70	69	69	208	20,100
6T	Gene Sauers	66	72	70	208	20,100
9T	Paul Azinger	75	67	67	209	15,600
9T	Ronnie Black	71	68	70	209	15,600
9T	Bob Tway	69	68	72	209	15,600
9T	David Edwards	69	67	73	209	15,600
13T	Jim Colbert	72	70	68	210	10,920
13T	Barry Jaeckel	72	70	68	210	10,920
13T	Lee Trevino	73	68	69	210	10,920
13T	Bobby Wadkins	70	71	69	210	10,920
13T	Bob Gilder	73	65	72	210	10,920
18T	Steve Pate	72	71	68	211	7,302
18T	Bruce Lietzke	70	70	71	211	7,302
18T	Buddy Gardner	69	71	71	211	7,302
18T	Tony Sills	72	71	68	211	7,302
18T	Ken Green	74	66	71	211	7,302
18T	Nick Price	68	76	67	211	7,302
18T	Howard Twitty	68	68	75	211	7,302
25T	Ben Crenshaw	70	72	70	212	4,387
25T	Scott Simpson	68	74	70	212	4,387
25T	Lennie Clements	68	72	72	212	4,387
25T	Doug Tewell	69	70	73	212	4,387
25T	Jay Haas	70	70	72	212	4,387
25T	D.A. Weibring	68	70	74	212	4,387
25T	Bob Lohr	69	69	74	212	4,387
25T	Corey Pavin	70	68	74	212	4,387
33T	Curtis Strange	75	68	70	213	3,315
33T	Joey Sindelar	71	71	71	213	3,315
33T	Wayne Grady	73	69	71	213	3,315
33T	Calvin Peete	71	69	73	213	3,315
37T	Fuzzy Zoeller	74	68	72	214	2,640
37T	Jim Thorpe	68	73	73	214	2,640
37T	Keith Fergus	72	70	72	214	2,640
37T	Roger Maltbie	70	70	74	214	2,640
37T	Lon Hinkle	75	68	71	214	2,640
37T	Fred Couples	76	68	70	214	2,640
43T	Hal Sutton	70	71	74	215	1,788
43T	Bill Glasson	73	70	72	215	1,788
43T	Gil Morgan	76	68	71	215	1,788
43T	Denis Watson	73	71	71	215	1,788
43T	Tom Kite	72	72	71	215	1,788
43T	Gary Koch	72	72	71	215	1,788
43T	Mark Lye	71	73	71	215	1,788
43T	Larry Mize	72	73	70	215	1,788
43T	Bob Murphy	72	67	76	215	1,788
52T	Dan Halldorson	72	70	74	216	1,392
52T	Kenny Knox	70	71	75	216	1,392
52T	Mark Brooks	73	68	75	216	1,392
52T	Al Geiberger	74	69	73	216	1,392
52T	Mike Hulbert	73	67	76	216	1,392
52T	Charles Bolling	72	67	77	216	1,392
58T	Ron Streck	71	72	74	217	1,290
58T	David Graham	73	70	74	217	1,290
58T	Mark Wiebe	72	71	74	217	1,290
58T	Andy North	70	73	74	217	1,290
58T	Bill Kratzert	70	73	74	217	1,290
58T	Phil Blackmar	74	69	74	217	1,290
58T	Tim Norris	73	71	73	217	1,290
58T	Pat McGowan	74	71	72	217	1,290
58T	Mike Reid	72	73	72	217	1,290
58T	Peter Jacobsen	78	68	71	217	1,290
68T	Greg Ladehoff	75	67	76	218	1,206
68T	Danny Edwards	68	72	78	218	1,206
68T	Mac O'Grady	69	76	73	218	1,206
68T	George Archer	74	72	72	218	1,206
72T	Hale Irwin	74	72	73	219	1,164
72T	Mark Pfeil	71	75	73	219	1,164
72T	Ken Brown	74	72	73	219	1,164
75	Mike Donald	74	72	77	223	1,140

*In sudden death, Pohl beat Stewart with birdie on first extra hole.

DID NOT MAKE CUT

147 David Ogrin, Willie Wood, Rod Curl, Clarence Rose
148 *Jack Kay Jr.*, Ed Fiori, Tom Byrum, John Mahaffey,
Tom Weiskopf
149 Dave Barr, John Cook, Mike Smith, Leonard Thompson,
Davis Love III, Gary Hallberg, Bob Eastwood
150 Larry Rinker, Woody Blackburn
151 Jack Renner, Chip Beck
153 Brett Upper
155 Dan Forsman, Tom Sieckmann
156 *Jim Sorenson*
78-wd Charles Coody
80-wd Tom Purtzer
wd Tim Simpson

1987
May 14-17

Rank	Player	1R	2R	3R	4R	Total	Money
1	Keith Clearwater	67	71	64	64	266	$108,000
2	Davis Love III	69	69	65	66	269	64,800
3	Dan Pohl	69	67	66	68	270	40,800
4T	Scott Simpson	67	66	70	69	272	26,400
4T	Curtis Strange	68	66	70	68	272	26,400
6T	Larry Mize	68	69	69	67	273	20,100
6T	Ben Crenshaw	67	69	65	72	273	20,100
6T	Jeff Sluman	68	69	68	68	273	20,100
9T	Tom Byrum	67	69	67	71	274	16,200
9T	Doug Tewell	68	66	68	72	274	16,200
9T	Scott Hoch	68	68	71	67	274	16,200
12T	Mark Lye	69	66	68	72	275	11,400
12T	Bobby Wadkins	67	69	73	66	275	11,400
12T	Chip Beck	66	67	71	71	275	11,400
12T	Dave Barr	68	70	70	67	275	11,400
12T	Bob Tway	68	70	70	67	275	11,400
12T	Bruce Lietzke	69	67	69	70	275	11,400
18T	Nick Price	70	68	71	67	276	8,400
18T	Gary Hallberg	70	68	67	71	276	8,400
18T	Fred Wadsworth	69	69	70	68	276	8,400
21T	Steve Elkington	70	63	71	73	277	6,480
21T	Tom Kite	69	69	69	70	277	6,480
21T	Lon Hinkle	68	68	70	71	277	6,480
21T	Barry Jaeckel	70	67	71	69	277	6,480
25T	Paul Azinger	70	66	70	72	278	4,680
25T	Corey Pavin	70	70	68	70	278	4,680
25T	Jack Renner	70	68	70	70	278	4,680
25T	David Frost	69	69	69	71	278	4,680
25T	Howard Twitty	69	69	69	71	278	4,680
30T	Mike Hulbert	72	67	69	71	279	3,566
30T	John Mahaffey	69	68	72	70	279	3,566
30T	Jim Colbert	69	70	69	71	279	3,566
30T	Mike Reid	68	71	68	72	279	3,566
30T	Bill Glasson	69	69	70	71	279	3,566
30T	Brad Fabel	74	64	69	72	279	3,566
30T	Bill Rogers	65	69	75	70	279	3,566
37T	Ed Fiori	69	68	71	72	280	2,760
37T	Gene Sauers	69	68	72	71	280	2,760
37T	Bill Sander	66	72	70	72	280	2,760
37T	Steve Pate	71	69	71	69	280	2,760
41T	Mark Brooks	67	71	72	71	281	2,220
41T	Peter Jacobsen	68	68	74	71	281	2,220
41T	Dan Forsman	67	72	69	73	281	2,220
41T	Hale Irwin	70	70	72	69	281	2,220
41T	Mark Hayes	68	70	72	71	281	2,220
46T	Tony Sills	68	70	77	67	282	1,701
46T	D. A. Weibring	70	69	71	72	282	1,701
46T	*Tray Tyner*	69	70	74	69	282	
46T	Joey Sindelar	70	70	69	73	282	1,701
46T	Bob Gilder	68	68	73	73	282	1,701
51T	Buddy Gardner	69	70	72	72	283	1,436
51T	Curt Byrum	71	68	73	71	283	1,436
51T	Roger Maltbie	73	67	71	72	283	1,436
51T	Blaine McCallister	68	71	73	71	283	1,436
51T	Mark Calcavecchia	69	67	73	74	283	1,436
51T	Mark Wiebe	71	67	71	74	283	1,436
57	Larry Rinker	68	72	73	72	285	1,368
58T	Clarence Rose	66	74	73	73	286	1,338
58T	Pat McGowan	74	65	72	75	286	1,338
58T	David Edwards	68	70	76	72	286	1,338
58T	Dave Rummells	72	67	75	72	286	1,338
62	Jodie Mudd	70	70	73	74	287	1,303
63	Charles Coody	69	70	73	77	289	1,296

DID NOT MAKE CUT

141 Ron Streck, Tom Purtzer, Brian Claar, Gil Morgan
Payne Stewart, Kenny Knox, Larry Nelson, John Cook
Kenny Perry
142 Sam Randolph, Scott Verplank, Fred Couples, Lee Trevino
Jay Haas, Andy Bean
143 David Ogrin, Ronnie Black, Mac O'Grady, Lennie Clements
Dannny Edwards, Tom Watson
144 David Graham, Hal Sutton, Rick Fehr, Donnie Hammond
Phil Blackmar, *Billy Mayfair*
145 Al Geiberger, Rod Curl, John Inman
146 Tim Simpson, Gary Koch
147 Willie Wood, Homero Blancas
148 Andy North
149 Steve Jones, Ernie Gonzalez, Denis Watson
153 Mike Sullivan
74-wd Dave Stockton
77-wd Mark McCumber
80-wd Mark O'Meara

1988
May 19-22

RANK	PLAYER	1R	2R	3R	4R	TOTAL	MONEY
1	Lanny Wadkins	67	68	70	65	270	$135,000
2T	Ben Crenshaw	69	67	68	67	271	56,000
2T	Mark Calcavecchia	68	69	68	66	271	56,000
2T	Joey Sindelar	71	65	67	68	271	56,000
5	Clarence Rose	67	68	65	74	274	30,000
6T	Mark Wiebe	72	67	69	67	275	25,125
6T	David Graham	71	66	70	68	275	25,125
6T	Scott Hoch	67	68	71	69	275	25,125
9T	Chip Beck	71	70	69	67	277	21,000
9T	David Frost	74	66	69	68	277	21,000
11T	Russ Cochran	71	69	72	66	278	15,900
11T	Ken Green	72	67	68	71	278	15,900
11T	Mark Lye	72	71	63	72	278	15,900
11T	John Inman	67	72	67	72	278	15,900
11T	John Mahaffey	69	71	66	72	278	15,900
16T	D.A. Weibring	71	67	72	69	279	10,875
16T	Mark O'Meara	71	71	68	69	279	10,875
16T	Tom Purtzer	74	68	68	69	279	10,875
16T	Mac O'Grady	70	70	69	70	279	10,875
16T	Paul Azinger	70	68	70	71	279	10,875
16T	Steve Pate	69	67	71	72	279	10,875
22T	Mike Hulbert	69	68	75	68	280	6,417
22T	Mike Donald	72	71	69	68	280	6,417
22T	John Cook	77	65	69	69	280	6,417
22T	Dave Rummells	71	66	73	70	280	6,417
22T	Bob Tway	70	70	70	70	280	6,417
22T	Bobby Wadkins	71	71	67	71	280	6,417
22T	Payne Stewart	75	65	68	72	280	6,417
22T	Lee Trevino	69	71	68	72	280	6,417
22T	John Huston	70	67	69	74	280	6,417
31T	Ed Fiori	68	75	69	69	281	4,547
31T	Scott Verplank	72	69	69	71	281	4,547
31T	Doug Tewell	70	70	69	72	281	4,547
31T	Mark Brooks	70	73	64	74	281	4,547
35T	Tom Kite	75	70	67	70	282	3,955
35T	Dave Stockton	73	69	70	70	282	3,955
37T	Scott Simpson	73	68	71	71	283	3,525
37T	Jodie Mudd	67	72	72	72	283	3,525
37T	Gil Morgan	70	69	68	76	283	3,525
40T	David Canipe	71	74	68	71	284	3,075
40T	Jeff Sluman	75	66	73	70	284	3,075
40T	Ronnie Black	69	74	69	72	284	3,075
43T	Kenny Knox	76	68	69	72	285	2,475
43T	Bob Lohr	76	69	67	73	285	2,475
43T	Jim Carter	70	72	70	73	285	2,475
43T	Tommy Nakajima	70	72	69	74	285	2,475
43T	Rick Fehr	70	69	70	76	285	2,475
48T	Lennie Clements	72	72	71	71	286	1,818
48T	*Billy Mayfair*	73	71	72	70	286	
48T	David Ogrin	77	68	69	72	286	1,818
48T	Ray Floyd	72	70	73	71	286	1,818
48T	Fuzzy Zoeller	76	68	69	73	286	1,818
48T	Andrew Magee	72	72	69	73	286	1,818
48T	Buddy Gardner	68	72	73	73	286	1,818
48T	Bill Glasson	73	68	72	73	286	1,818
48T	Corey Pavin	74	68	71	73	286	1,818
48T	Larry Rinker	70	72	70	74	286	1,818
48T	Robert Wrenn	72	67	71	76	286	1,818
59T	Bruce Lietzke	70	71	73	73	287	1,672
59T	Danny Edwards	69	71	72	75	287	1,672
61T	Mike Reid	71	74	75	68	288	1,635
61T	Sam Randolph	72	73	72	71	288	1,635
61T	Richard Zokol	73	71	73	71	288	1,635
64T	Denis Watson	71	72	74	72	289	1,590
64T	Curt Byrum	71	72	71	75	289	1,590
64T	Dan Pohl	73	69	71	76	289	1,590
67T	Donnie Hammond	72	73	74	72	291	1,552
67T	Bill Sander	74	70	73	74	291	1,552
69T	Howard Twitty	71	72	76	73	292	1,515
69T	Nick Price	76	68	74	74	292	1,515
69T	Rod Curl	74	71	71	76	292	1,515
72T	J.C. Snead	73	71	74	75	293	1,477
72T	Jim Thorpe	74	71	72	76	293	1,477
74	Bob Murphy	70	74	74	76	294	1,455

DID NOT MAKE CUT

146	Chris Perry, Tom Watson, Keith Clearwater, Hal Sutton Steve Jones
147	Steve Elkington, Andy North, Larry Mize, Jim Hallet Tom Byrum, Aki Ohmachi, Morris Hatalsky Gene Sauers, Dave Barr
148	Bill Rogers, David Edwards
149	Peter Jacobsen, Hale Irwin, Davis Love III, Mike Tschetter
150	Fulton Allem, Gary Hallberg, *Chip Carter*
151	Andy Bean
152	Roger Maltbie, Brian Tennyson
154	Jerry Pate
157	Willie Wood

1989
May 18-21

RANK	PLAYER	1R	2R	3R	4R	TOTAL	MONEY
1	Ian Baker-Finch	65	70	65	70	270	$180,000
2	David Edwards	72	69	68	65	274	108,000
3T	David Frost	70	66	71	69	276	58,000
3T	Tim Simpson	71	71	66	68	276	58,000
5T	Curtis Strange	74	71	66	66	277	36,500
5T	Lon Hinkle	74	69	66	68	277	36,500
5T	Nick Price	70	66	68	73	277	36,500
8T	Paul Azinger	70	74	69	65	278	28,000
8T	Payne Stewart	70	70	70	68	278	28,000
8T	Scott Simpson	71	67	70	70	278	28,000
8T	Isao Aoki	66	74	66	72	278	28,000
12T	Mike Donald	70	74	69	66	279	19,600
12T	Chip Beck	74	72	66	67	279	19,600
12T	Doug Tewell	71	71	68	69	279	19,600
12T	David Ogrin	72	69	68	70	279	19,600
12T	Fulton Allem	66	73	69	71	279	19,600
17T	Davis Love III	73	72	66	69	280	13,533
17T	Mike Sullivan	67	70	74	69	280	13,533
17T	Joey Sindelar	72	68	71	69	280	13,533
17T	Mark Calcavecchia	68	72	71	69	280	13,533
17T	Mike Hulbert	70	69	71	70	280	13,533
17T	Clarence Rose	67	71	69	73	280	13,533
23T	Steve Pate	71	70	72	68	281	9,600
23T	Nick Faldo	72	72	68	69	281	9,600
23T	Billy Mayfair	71	73	67	70	281	9,600
26T	Chris Perry	71	74	70	67	282	7,400
26T	Steve Elkington	70	70	73	69	282	7,400
26T	Gil Morgan	70	68	74	70	282	7,400
26T	Tom Purtzer	76	70	66	70	282	7,400
26T	Brad Faxon	72	68	70	72	282	7,400
31T	Andy North	70	75	71	67	283	5,800
31T	Robert Wrenn	73	71	68	71	283	5,800
31T	Mark O'Meara	73	68	70	72	283	5,800
31T	Morris Hatalsky	69	74	68	72	283	5,800
31T	Keith Clearwater	68	72	70	73	283	5,800
31T	Dave Barr	74	69	66	74	283	5,800
37T	Loren Roberts	71	72	71	70	284	4,800
37T	Tom Byrum	73	69	70	72	284	4,800
39T	D.A. Weibring	69	77	70	69	285	4,100
39T	Mark Wiebe	70	71	75	69	285	4,100
39T	Bruce Lietzke	75	69	70	71	285	4,100
39T	Jim Carter	75	69	69	72	285	4,100
39T	Corey Pavin	70	73	68	74	285	4,100
44T	Mark Brooks	72	70	75	69	286	3,023
44T	Donnie Hammond	71	70	73	72	286	3,023
44T	Ben Crenshaw	71	73	69	73	286	3,023
44T	Buddy Gardner	71	73	69	73	286	3,023
44T	Andy Bean	69	72	71	74	286	3,023
44T	Mike Reid	72	71	69	74	286	3,023
50T	Peter Jacobsen	71	73	73	70	287	2,490
50T	Tom Kite	72	69	73	73	287	2,490
52T	John Mahaffey	71	74	71	72	288	2,345
52T	Ed Fiori	70	70	74	74	288	2,345
52T	Brad Bryant	73	73	67	75	288	2,345
52T	Sam Randolph	71	70	72	75	288	2,345
56T	Russ Cochran	69	72	78	70	289	2,270
56T	Billy Andrade	77	69	70	73	289	2,270
58T	Bill Glasson	71	74	77	68	290	2,230
58T	Scott Verplank	71	74	74	71	290	2,230
60T	Rod Curl	76	69	77	69	291	2,180
60T	Larry Mize	71	74	70	76	291	2,180
60T	Jim Gallagher	72	72	71	76	291	2,180
63T	Hale Irwin	72	72	77	71	292	2,100
63T	Larry Rinker	73	72	73	74	292	2,100
63T	Jerry Pate	72	70	74	76	292	2,100
63T	Gary Hallberg	70	74	72	76	292	2,100
63T	David Graham	74	70	70	78	292	2,100
63T	Dan Pohl	72	72	76	73	292	2,030
68T	Dave Stockton	71	73	75	74	293	2,030
70	Andrew Magee	70	76	74	74	294	2,000
71	Ray Floyd	73	73	78	73	297	1,980

DID NOT MAKE CUT

147	Bobby Wadkins, Jim Hallet, Dave Rummells, Dave Eichelberger John Inman, Lee Trevino, Bob Tway, Fred Couples
148	Mark Hayes, Phil Blackmar, Dan Forsman Mac O'Grady, Lanny Wadkins
149	Tom Sieckmann, Mark Lye, John Cook
150	Curt Byrum, Ted Schulz
151	Greg Twiggs
152	Kenny Knox, Willie Wood, Jay Haas, Bob Lohr
153	John Huston, Jim Booros
154	Denis Watson
156	*Ralph Howe III*
80-wd	Tommy Armour
dq	Blaine McCallister, Billy Ray Brown, Bill Rogers, *Mark Pfingston*

*Names in italics designate amateurs.

119

THE 1990s

SPINE-TINGLING FINISHES AMID PGA TOUR'S BOOM

The 10 tournaments played in the 90s are some of the most exciting in all of Colonial's 60 years. Four in a row all came down to the very last putt, including two sudden-death playoffs.

In 1990, windy conditions kept the field tight each day. The cut fell at seven over par, and two players scored a 10 on one hole. Still, by Saturday the cream had risen to the top. Leading were 1977 champ Ben Crenshaw and two-time U.S. Open champ Curtis Strange, by one shot over Nick Price and another former champ, Corey Pavin. Those four players were collectively eight-under-par on Sunday, but Crenshaw was hot and accounted for half of those strokes himself. His front nine 30 left all others in his wake, despite losing the lead on the first hole with a par. Epitomized by his dramatic, patented birdie from the trees and rough left of the seventh hole, Crenshaw closed out the nine with three straight birdies. From there he put the finishing touches on a 66 and a three-shot win. This despite hitting his infamous tee shot on #17 into the creek right, from where he managed to save bogey.

ABOVE:
Tom Purtzer won the 1991 Colonial championship.
FACING PAGE:
Ben Crenshaw grabbed his second Colonial title in 1990; pictured with Colonial President Wally Schmuck.

FACING PAGE:
Tom Purtzer's improbable putt for birdie from a greenside bunker on #13 propelled him to the title.

"It's been so long since I've won (two years) I don't know how to act," an elated Crenshaw said. "But I played like a new man this week. I was just more determined, and my swing was good enough to hold up."

In 1991, perfect scoring conditions sent the field on a major birdie binge. Steve Elkington tied the course record of 62 and Keith Clearwater tied the front nine record of 29. Tom Watson scored the only eagle on the 10th hole in tournament history. The man with the "perfect swing," Tom Purtzer, could muster only an opening 70 for 44th place. He climbed to 20th after a Friday 66. By Sunday's start he was tied for 15th place, four shots back of the leaders.

Purtzer shot a 64 Sunday, but the tournament was very much in doubt as he stood in the back sand trap on #13. Staring at

him was a bone-chilling, delicate chip shot toward water. Before he could second-guess himself, Purtzer grabbed his putter and putted the ball out of the bunker and into the hole for an incredible birdie. He went on to win by three, and continued with his best year ever on Tour. No other Colonial champ has surpassed so many competitors (14) on the final day.

Just seven weeks later, the dedicated Colonial Tournament Committee helped stage the 1991 U.S. Women's Open Championship, celebrating the 50th anniversary of its 1941 men's Open. Veteran star Pat Bradley led for three rounds, with 29-time winner Amy Alcott on her heels. But the recently-voted LPGA's "most popular player," Meg Mallon, fired a final-round 67 to overtake the leaders and claim her second straight major victory. The course played as a par 71, with the long third hole a par five.

The 1992 event required sudden-death for the first time in six years. Davis Love III and Billy Mayfair set the early pace with opening 65s. 1985 champ Corey Pavin took over after two rounds. 1980 winner Bruce Lietzke fired a third-round 64, passing them all, including Fort Worth's Mark Brooks. The two former champs from the '80s battled it out on Sunday, with Lietzke eagling the first hole and the scrappy Pavin tying him with a birdie on #17. Lietzke then drained a 12-foot birdie putt on the first extra hole to win. Four former Colonial champs in all finished in the top 10, a Colonial record. (The next year's champ was in there, too.) Brooks tied for fourth place, at 10 under par, his best Colonial finish.

"This is really extra special," Lietzke gushed about his second Colonial win. "I have grown to appreciate this tournament more and more. Even being a young champion in 1980, I knew what this golf tournament meant to me. But in the years since, coming to the Champions Dinner, seeing Mr. Hogan every year, seeing my name on the Wall, you can't help but have the

emotions and traditions build. The golf tournament builds inside you. This without a doubt is one of the dearest to my heart."

It was the foreigners' time to shine again in 1993. Drawing the most attention on day one was 1989 champ Ian Baker-Finch, who doffed his shoes, socks and trousers on #13 in order to step in the lake to hit his second shot. A nationwide cable TV audience got a close-up view of his boxers, and later the PGA Tour sent out a quiet memo to players about keeping their pants on during tournaments. (The next year, Colonial presented him with a pair of plaid boxer shorts.)

Fast fairways and no wind led to more records in '93, as the 36-, 54- and 72-hole scoring marks fell. Keith Clearwater and Lee Janzen both shot nine-under 61s to lower the 18-hole mark, as well. Clearwater's included a back-nine record 28, and Wayne Levi matched that score on the more difficult front nine. On Sunday, a thrilling two-man race between Greg Norman and Fulton Allem went down to the wire. Starting even, they traded the lead twice on the outward nine, only to be tied again at the turn, thanks to an incredible par save at the ninth by Allem. Norman's clutch 15-foot birdie on 18 left Allem with a knee-knocking five-footer for par and the win. He made it, for a new record of 16 under par.

TOP:
Bruce Lietzke won at Colonial for the second time in 1992; pictured with Tournament Chairman M.C. Hamilton Jr.
MIDDLE
Greg Norman birdied #18 Sunday to finish second in 1993.
BOTTOM:
1993 champion Fulton Allem answered Norman's putt to claim the title.

ABOVE:
Nick Price won his first Colonial title in 1994 after a dramatic final-round rally; pictured with Tournament Chairman Floyd Wade.

ABOVE:
Tom Lehman birdied the final two holes to win the 1995 Colonial title by a shot.

The 1994 event started out battling the weather, and then turned into a battle between U.S. Open champions, with Hale Irwin and Scott Simpson trading the lead for two days. Soon the world's hottest player, Nick Price, joined the fray. Staging the greatest come-from-behind victory in Colonial history, Price came from seven shots back to tie Simpson and force a playoff. A five-birdie string on the back nine was interrupted by a night's sleep as two rain delays prevented final-round completion on Sunday.

Simpson's lead was down to one over Irwin and two over Price at the halt of play. Simpson was putting on #12, and both Irwin and Price were playing #14. Price birdied his last three holes prior to the delay. Monday morning he birdied his first two, and then the first playoff hole to top Simpson. It was the first time since 1965 the tournament extended past Sunday.

Irwin also charged Sunday, but finished third, one shot out of the playoff.

"I've been awfully close here a couple of times," Price said. "I just love this golf course. This is a ball-striker's golf course, a very demanding driving course. I'm very proud to have my name up there with Hogan and all the others. I'm just so excited to win here." Price went on to win the British Open and PGA Championship that summer, as well as PGA Player of the Year honors, in his finest year ever.

The two Champions' Choices that year were Guy Boros and Dave Stockton Jr. Showing their quality genes, both champions' sons finished in the top 30 on their first visit to Colonial.

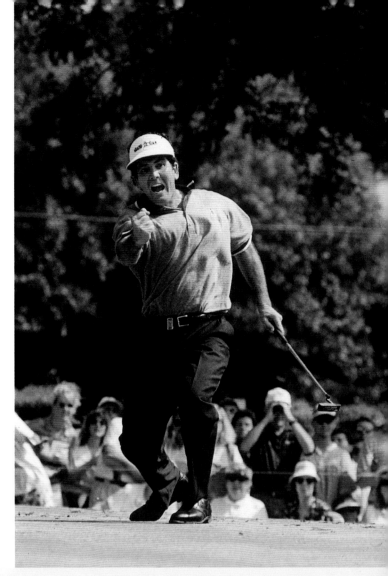

ABOVE:
Corey Pavin captured his second Colonial championship in 1996.

ABOVE:
1997 champion David Frost came from behind on Sunday to win his Colonial title.

In 1995, Colonial dedicated a large statue of Hogan beside its clubhouse, overlooking the 18th hole to launch tournament festivities. Australian Craig Parry took control at nine under par after two rounds. But that's as low as he got. That's as low as anyone got. Parry still led at nine under after three rounds, but 10 players lurked within six shots. Parry led by one, at eight under, with two holes to play. A dramatic birdie-birdie finish by Tom Lehman nabbed a one-shot victory at nine under par. He was the first Colonial champion to birdie the tournament's difficult, final two holes on Sunday. That compares to 1980 when Lietzke birdied two of the last three holes to win, and 1965 when Bruce Crampton birdied four of the last six holes for the title.

"When I'm playing well, I'm capable of winning any tournament," Lehman said. "I can be a great putter at times or an average putter, but when I play my game, I'm not afraid of anything." It was Lehman's second Tour win, and he added the British Open and Tour Championship to it the following year.

The 1996 50th anniversary championship wracked the players with gusty winds and dry fairways, and welcomed a new title sponsor in MasterCard International. Fittingly, it fell to a gritty, well-known shotmaker to triumph. The kitty was a record $1.5 million, and purse levels would shoot even higher over the next several years throughout the Tour. Reigning U.S. Open champ Corey Pavin sat one shot off the lead of Rocco Mediate after 54 holes, followed by Fred Couples, 1988 PGA champion Jeff Sluman and David Duval. Pavin emerged from the battle victorious with the highest winning score at Colonial in 13 years -- eight under par. Sluman finished second, two shots back. Only 11 players finished under par for the tournament as Pavin collected his second Colonial title. Combining his mastery of the

Riviera Country Club, where he also won twice, comparisons of Pavin to Hogan abounded.

"I don't know how many lead changes there were Sunday," Pavin wondered (there were five). "It was like a basketball game. It was hard mentally; and emotionally you just have to stay in there. The course was playing as hard as I've ever seen it play."

Colonial hosted its first sellout crowd ever in 1997, as 'Tiger mania' swept the nation and Fort Worth. Calm weather early in the day sent scores down to their lowest level in tournament history -- a record -- tying cut of even par. Tour phenom Tiger Woods improved his score daily through Saturday and found himself one stroke off the lead of Texan David Ogrin heading into the final round.

Woods was fresh from his first Masters victory, as well as a win in Dallas the week before. He stood at 14 under, Ogrin at 15 under, and the event's 16-under record seemed destined to fall in Sunday's fireworks. But South African David Frost overtook them both on a windy Sunday, and sewed up the title with a dramatic birdie on the 17th hole and a closing 67. "I would like to dedicate this victory to Ben Hogan, who has been a big inspiration to my golf game," Frost said of his 10th American victory. "He's been a big influence on me since I came to America."

Ironically, late that summer, the great Hogan died at age 84. His spirit lives on in many places, but none more so than Colonial.

In 1998, young stars David Duval and Jim Furyk battled Tour rookie Harrison Frazar to the top of the leaderboard. Legendary veteran Tom Watson, at age 48, entered the mix on the weekend, along with Jeff Sluman and Mark Calcavecchia. Shooting 65-66 in his last two rounds, Watson overtook the young guns and captured his first Colonial championship. The critical shot was an incredible 8-iron from a fairway bunker on the 9th hole Sunday. With an awkward stance and lie in the hillside bunker, Watson muscled the shot over water to within 10 feet of the hole and made birdie. Like Nicklaus before him, Watson had finally conquered Colonial.

After the round, Watson compared the shot to his historic shots at the U.S. Open and British Open. "Ben Hogan is an icon here, and to put my name up on that Wall of Champions with the likes of Hogan and all the great players - Snead, Palmer, Nicklaus, well, it's like the Masters, the people who have won this championship. It's a great honor."

To close the decade, the 1999 tournament became the most hotly contested ever. Windy conditions kept the field close and the scores high. Several top Tour winners and major champions rose to the occasion. Lee Janzen, Corey Pavin, Vijay Singh, Phil Mickelson, Jeff Sluman and others all challenged for the lead for three rounds. But it was journeyman Greg Kraft who fired a record-tying 61 to share the 54-hole lead at seven under par.

Numerous players charged and fell back Sunday as the course proved its toughness in the tricky wind. Olin Browne, who only took up the game at age 19 and was a 1998 Champions' Choice, eagled both par fives for a 66 to claim a one-shot win. A birdie on #15 made the difference and avoided a six-man playoff, as he watched 12 players finish after him, unable to tie. The absence of a playoff was remarkable, as 19 players finished within three shots of Browne, and five players tied for second -- the most crowded final leaderboard in Colonial history.

FACING PAGE TOP:
Tom Watson captured his Colonial title in 1998.
MIDDLE:
LPGA star Meg Mallon won the 1991 U.S. Women's Open championship at Colonial.
BOTTOM:
Jim Furyk finished second in 1998 and has three other top 10 Colonial finishes.

TOP:
1999 champion Olin Browne emerged from a crowded leaderboard for his Colonial title.
MIDDLE:
Lanny Wadkins, Valerie Hogan and Ben Crenshaw helped dedicate Colonial's statue of Ben Hogan in 1995.
BOTTOM:
Tiger Woods found himself in contention for the 1997 Colonial title on his first visit, but placed fourth.

1990
May 17-20

Rank	Player	R1	R2	R3	R4	Total	Money
1	Ben Crenshaw	69	65	72	66	272	$180,000
2T	John Mahaffey	67	72	70	66	275	74,667
2T	Nick Price	72	68	67	68	275	74,667
2T	Corey Pavin	66	71	70	68	275	74,667
5T	Curtis Strange	68	69	69	70	276	38,000
5T	Mike Hulbert	71	70	72	63	276	38,000
7T	Payne Stewart	70	72	68	67	277	30,125
7T	Gene Sauers	72	74	69	62	277	30,125
7T	Andrew Magee	71	71	69	66	277	30,125
7T	Brian Tennyson	73	68	70	66	277	30,125
11T	John Huston	69	67	72	70	278	22,000
11T	Russ Cochran	65	69	73	71	278	22,000
11T	Kenny Perry	69	71	71	67	278	22,000
11T	Rocco Mediate	73	72	68	65	278	22,000
15T	Ian Baker-Finch	73	71	71	64	279	16,000
15T	Tom Purtzer	67	70	73	69	279	16,000
15T	Scott Verplank	78	68	68	65	279	16,000
15T	Billy Mayfair	67	68	74	70	279	16,000
15T	Stan Utley	68	72	69	70	279	16,000
20T	Gil Morgan	72	67	75	66	280	11,240
20T	Tom Byrum	71	71	72	66	280	11,240
20T	Billy Andrade	72	68	73	67	280	11,240
20T	Tim Simpson	70	70	69	71	280	11,240
20T	Loren Roberts	69	74	69	68	280	11,240
25T	Peter Jacobsen	67	72	70	72	281	7,975
25T	Tom Watson	71	72	68	70	281	7,975
25T	David Frost	72	70	68	71	281	7,975
25T	Hale Irwin	73	71	69	68	281	7,975
29T	Scott Simpson	70	72	72	68	282	6,358
29T	Hal Sutton	71	72	70	69	282	6,358
29T	Curt Byrum	68	69	74	71	282	6,358
29T	Dan Forsman	70	71	73	68	282	6,358
29T	Mike Donald	70	73	68	71	282	6,358
29T	Scott Hoch	67	73	68	74	282	6,358
35T	Larry Mize	73	70	68	72	283	4,930
35T	Davis Love III	71	70	72	70	283	4,930
35T	Kenny Knox	70	74	71	68	283	4,930
35T	Dave Rummells	71	76	71	65	283	4,930
35T	David Peoples	74	73	68	68	283	4,930
40T	Bruce Lietzke	70	73	69	72	284	4,100
40T	Clark Dennis	69	70	72	73	284	4,100
40T	Richard Zokol	67	71	76	70	284	4,100
43T	Robert Gamez	70	74	72	69	285	3,300
43T	Jay Haas	76	68	70	71	285	3,300
43T	Blaine McCallister	69	76	72	68	285	3,300
43T	Joe Ozaki	72	75	70	68	285	3,300
43T	P.H. Horgan III	73	72	71	69	285	3,300
48T	Bobby Wadkins	72	73	71	70	286	2,620
48T	Jay Delsing	74	74	73	69	286	2,620
48T	Robert Wrenn	73	69	69	75	286	2,620
51T	Fuzzy Zoeller	72	73	71	71	287	2,353
51T	Bob Estes	73	69	71	74	287	2,353
51T	Billy Ray Brown	70	72	70	75	287	2,353
51T	Ronnie Black	69	71	76	71	287	2,353
51T	Bill Sander	73	70	74	70	287	2,353
51T	Denis Watson	72	73	71	71	287	2,353
57T	Lanny Wadkins	72	74	68	74	288	2,220
57T	Steve Elkington	70	75	72	71	288	2,220
57T	Jim Thorpe	73	74	72	69	288	2,220
57T	Mike Sullivan	74	72	64	68	288	2,220
57T	Bob Eastwood	72	70	78	68	288	2,220
62T	Paul Azinger	71	72	74	72	289	2,120
62T	Joey Sindelar	75	71	71	72	289	2,120
62T	Ray Floyd	74	69	73	73	289	2,120
62T	David Edwards	77	67	68	77	289	2,120
62T	Mark Wiebe	69	73	77	70	289	2,120
67T	Jerry Pate	72	72	77	69	290	2,050
67T	Fulton Allem	71	76	75	69	290	2,050
69	Keith Clearwater	71	75	76	70	292	2,220
70T	Jodie Mudd	78	69	74	72	293	1,990
70T	Doug Tewell	75	67	78	73	293	1,990
72	Tom Kite	73	74	77	70	294	1,960
73T	Duffy Waldorf	72	70	78	75	295	1,920
73T	Jim Gallagher Jr.	75	72	74	74	295	1,920
73T	Tommy Armour III	70	75	79	71	295	1,920
76	Leonard Thompson	73	74	74	75	296	1,880
77	Tom Sieckmann	73	74	76	75	298	1,860

DID NOT MAKE CUT

148 Bill Britton, Peter Persons, Jay Don Blake, Jeff Sluman, Steve Pate
149 Mark O'Meara, Mark Brooks, Chip Beck, Jim Carter, Rod Curl
150 Andy North, Mark Calcavecchia, Bob Tway, Bob Gilder, D.A. Weibring, Tom Weiskopf
151 Chris Perry
152 Dave Stockton
153 Dow Finsterwald Jr., Bobby Gee
154 Clarence Rose, Brad Faxon, David Graham, *Chris Patton*
155 David Ogrin, Roger Maltbie
156 Joel Edwards
70-wd Ed Fiori
72-wd Bill Glasson
79-wd Mark Lye

1991
May 23-26

Rank	Player	R1	R2	R3	R4	Total	Money
1	Tom Purtzer	70	66	67	64	267	$216,000
2T	Scott Hoch	67	67	70	66	270	89,600
2T	David Edwards	66	68	68	68	270	89,600
2T	Bob Lohr	68	68	63	71	270	89,600
5T	Mark Calcavecchia	65	68	68	70	271	45,600
5T	Fred Funk	65	68	68	70	271	45,600
7T	Ian Baker-Finch	70	65	71	66	272	36,150
7T	Tom Watson	68	66	69	69	272	36,150
7T	Wayne Grady	68	67	67	70	272	36,150
7T	Stan Utley	68	64	69	71	272	36,150
11T	Scott Simpson	70	67	67	69	273	27,600
11T	Keith Clearwater	68	64	69	72	273	27,600
11T	Jim Hallet	66	72	64	71	273	27,600
14T	Chip Beck	71	68	69	66	274	21,000
14T	Jeff Sluman	68	66	68	72	274	21,000
14T	Bobby Wadkins	70	67	67	70	274	21,000
14T	Russ Cochran	71	66	68	69	274	21,000
18T	Bruce Lietzke	66	69	70	70	275	15,648
18T	Doug Tewell	70	70	65	70	275	15,648
18T	Mike Hulbert	67	70	65	73	275	15,648
18T	Gene Sauers	66	66	68	75	275	15,648
18T	Nolan Henke	68	69	65	73	275	15,648
23T	Dan Pohl	71	67	70	68	276	10,380
23T	Steve Elkington	73	69	62	72	276	10,380
23T	Blaine McCallister	68	69	68	71	276	10,380
23T	Wayne Levi	67	65	73	71	276	10,380
23T	Chris Perry	66	65	70	75	276	10,380
23T	Clark Dennis	69	70	70	67	276	10,380
29T	Dan Forsman	71	70	72	64	277	7,980
29T	Loren Roberts	67	66	69	75	277	7,980
29T	Peter Persons	65	72	70	70	277	7,980
29T	Ed Dougherty	68	68	70	71	277	7,980
33T	Corey Pavin	71	66	71	70	278	6,206
33T	Bob Tway	73	69	68	68	278	6,206
33T	Mike Reid	69	72	68	69	278	6,206
33T	Phil Blackmar	69	72	71	66	278	6,206
33T	Dan Halldorson	67	69	71	71	278	6,206
33T	David Peoples	70	65	69	74	278	6,206
33T	Dave Barr	68	72	68	70	278	6,206
40T	Curtis Strange	70	70	67	72	279	4,800
40T	Larry Mize	67	68	71	73	279	4,800
40T	Steve Pate	68	71	68	72	279	4,800
40T	Buddy Gardner	73	64	70	72	279	4,800
44T	Davis Love III	71	69	70	70	280	3,628
44T	John Huston	69	72	66	73	280	3,628
44T	Robert Gamez	70	68	71	71	280	3,628
44T	Jim Gallagher Jr.	68	70	70	72	280	3,628
44T	Brad Faxon	69	68	70	73	280	3,628
44T	Duffy Waldorf	68	71	71	70	280	3,628
50T	Tom Kite	69	71	69	72	281	2,853
50T	Rocco Mediate	75	67	66	73	281	2,853
50T	Billy Mayfair	67	68	72	74	281	2,853
50T	Ken Green	69	70	70	72	281	2,853
50T	Kenny Knox	74	65	70	72	281	2,853
50T	Robert Wrenn	72	67	69	73	281	2,853
50T	Kirk Triplett	69	70	72	70	281	2,853
57T	Lanny Wadkins	70	69	73	70	282	2,652
57T	Nick Price	72	69	67	74	282	2,652
57T	Billy Andrade	70	72	71	69	282	2,652
57T	Dave Rummells	72	67	69	74	282	2,652
57T	Mark Lye	66	75	73	68	282	2,652
57T	Brian Tennyson	70	70	67	75	282	2,652
63T	Kenny Perry	73	69	70	71	283	2,556
63T	Mike Smith	70	71	70	72	283	2,556
65T	Tim Simpson	71	71	74	68	284	2,484
65T	Ray Floyd	69	69	74	72	284	2,484
65T	Jerry Pate	71	71	74	68	284	2,484
65T	Mark Wiebe	69	72	69	74	284	2,484
69T	Tom Byrum	68	71	75	72	286	2,412
69T	John Mahaffey	68	70	74	74	286	2,412
71	Bob Wolcott	73	69	71	74	287	2,376
72T	Joey Sindelar	74	68	75	71	288	2,340
72T	Denis Watson	70	72	71	75	288	2,340
74	Tommy Armour III	73	68	74	78	293	2,304
75	Mike Donald	69	73	76	77	295	2,280
	Mike Springer	71	71	69	wd	x	(2,256)

DID NOT MAKE CUT

143 Brian Claar, D.A. Weibring, Dave Stockton, Payne Stewart, Gil Morgan, Ryoken Kawagishi, Tom Sieckmann, Jerry Haas
144 Peter Jacobsen, David Graham, Jay Delsing, Jay Don Blake
145 Ben Crenshaw, Mark O'Meara
146 Roger Maltbie, Jeff Maggert, Billy Ray Brown, Craig Stadler, Andrew Magee, David Frost, Bob Estes, Lindy Miller
147 Curt Byrum, Jim Thorpe, Andy North, Mark Brooks, John Daly
149 Dow Finsterwald Jr., Larry Silveira
150 Scott Verplank
151 Sam Randolph
154 Rod Curl

1992
May 21-24

Rank	Player	R1	R2	R3	R4	Total	Money
1	Bruce Lietzke	69	68	64	66	267*	$234,000
2	Corey Pavin	68	64	70	65	267*	140,400
3	Jim Gallagher	70	68	63	68	269	88,400
4T	Mark Brooks	69	66	68	67	270	57,200
4T	Rick Fehr	69	68	69	64	270	57,200
6T	Greg Norman	70	68	69	65	272	42,087
6T	Keith Clearwater	66	69	69	68	272	42,087
6T	John Cook	69	71	67	65	272	42,087
6T	Dillard Pruitt	67	68	69	68	272	42,087
10T	Ben Crenshaw	70	67	70	66	273	28,817
10T	Craig Stadler	66	67	71	69	273	28,817
10T	Mark Calcavecchia	69	66	68	70	273	28,817
10T	Jeff Sluman	72	65	68	68	273	28,817
10T	Bruce Fleisher	68	69	70	66	273	28,817
10T	Fulton Allem	69	65	71	68	273	28,817
16T	Lanny Wadkins	72	68	68	66	274	17,073
16T	Ray Floyd	70	65	72	67	274	17,073
16T	Davis Love III	65	69	68	72	274	17,073
16T	Wayne Grady	71	69	65	69	274	17,073
16T	Larry Mize	71	68	65	70	274	17,073
16T	Gil Morgan	68	71	70	65	274	17,073
16T	Nolan Henke	70	68	68	68	274	17,073
16T	Richard Zokol	70	67	71	66	274	17,073
16T	Brian Claar	67	69	70	68	274	17,073
25T	Tom Watson	72	70	66	67	275	10,140
25T	Hale Irwin	71	65	71	68	275	10,140
25T	Gene Sauers	68	70	71	66	275	10,140
25T	Lee Janzen	71	68	71	65	275	10,140
25T	Ed Dougherty	72	68	67	68	275	10,140
30T	Ian Baker-Finch	71	67	69	69	276	8,255
30T	Billy Mayfair	65	71	73	67	276	8,255
30T	Jeff Maggert	71	71	69	65	276	8,255
30T	Clark Dennis	68	71	69	68	276	8,255
34T	Payne Stewart	70	68	71	68	277	6,565
34T	Mike Reid	68	71	71	67	277	6,565
34T	D.A. Weibring	69	70	71	67	277	6,565
34T	Fred Funk	74	66	70	67	277	6,565
34T	Tom Byrum	70	69	67	71	277	6,565
34T	Neal Lancaster	76	64	73	64	277	6,565
40T	Tom Kite	70	66	72	70	278	4,556
40T	Peter Jacobsen	72	68	67	71	278	4,556
40T	Steve Elkington	68	70	70	70	278	4,556
40T	Steve Pate	70	67	69	72	278	4,556
40T	Jay Haas	68	67	73	70	278	4,556
40T	Dan Forsman	70	69	66	73	278	4,556
40T	Bill Britton	69	73	70	66	278	4,556
40T	Jim Hallet	71	68	68	71	278	4,556
40T	Larry Rinker	70	72	66	70	278	4,556
49T	Fuzzy Zoeller	73	66	71	69	279	3,176
49T	Chip Beck	70	71	69	69	279	3,176
49T	Tom Weiskopf	72	70	69	68	279	3,176
49T	Joey Sindelar	72	69	65	73	279	3,176
49T	Blaine McCallister	67	67	70	75	279	3,176
49T	Scott Gump	74	67	67	71	279	3,176
55T	Nick Price	71	67	71	71	280	2,951
55T	Tim Simpson	73	65	71	71	280	2,951
55T	John Huston	71	69	70	70	280	2,951
55T	Jim Thorpe	72	70	68	70	280	2,951
59T	Kenny Perry	70	72	71	68	281	2,847
59T	Rocco Mediate	70	69	71	71	281	2,847
59T	Mike Standly	67	68	73	73	281	2,847
59T	Kirk Triplett	67	70	69	75	281	2,847
63T	Scott Hoch	69	72	69	72	282	2,756
63T	Russ Cochran	72	68	69	73	282	2,756
63T	Ronnie Black	75	66	67	74	282	2,756
66T	Roger Maltbie	70	71	71	72	284	2,678
66T	Gary Hallberg	68	70	74	72	284	2,678
66T	Hal Sutton	72	69	71	72	284	2,678
69T	Ken Green	73	69	72	71	285	2,561
69T	Jodie Mudd	69	71	74	71	285	2,561
69T	David Edwards	68	72	73	72	285	2,561
69T	Bob Lohr	72	70	71	72	285	2,561
69T	Mike Hulbert	72	69	70	74	285	2,561
69T	Bob Gilder	70	72	70	73	285	2,561
75	Brad Faxon	74	68	74	71	287	2,470
76	Robert Gamez	70	72	74	73	289	2,444
77	Denis Watson	70	72	78	70	290	2,418

DID NOT MAKE CUT

139-wd Wayne Levi
143 Duffy Waldorf, Tom Sieckmann, Scott Simpson, Bruce Zabriski Howard Twitty, Bob Estes, Mark Wiebe, Mike Donald, Stan Utley, Bob Tway
144 Buddy Gardner, Tom Purtzer, Kenny Knox, Andrew Magee
145 Dave Rummells, Billy Ray Brown, David Frost, Loren Roberts, Tom Lehman
146 Phil Blackmar, Jim Woodward
147 Doug Tewell
148 David Peoples
149 Dan Pohl, Ed Humenik, *Mitch Voges*
150 Billy Andrade, Ted Schulz
151 Scott Verplank, Rod Curl, John Daly
153 Chris Tucker
155 Dow Finsterwald Jr.

1993
May 27-30

Rank	Player	R1	R2	R3	R4	Total	Money
1	Fulton Allem	66	63	68	67	264	$234,000
2	Greg Norman	69	64	64	68	265	140,400
3	Jeff Maggert	65	68	68	66	267	88,400
4T	Duffy Waldorf	65	69	69	65	268	57,200
4T	Loren Roberts	66	70	66	66	268	57,200
6T	Tom Watson	69	64	71	65	269	43,550
6T	John Huston	66	70	66	67	269	43,550
6T	David Edwards	69	67	63	70	269	43,550
9T	Corey Pavin	70	65	67	68	270	36,400
9T	Keith Clearwater	71	61	69	69	270	36,400
11T	Lee Janzen	70	65	75	61	271	26,650
11T	Mark Calcavecchia	69	64	69	69	271	26,650
11T	Hale Irwin	68	66	69	68	271	26,650
11T	Gil Morgan	67	69	69	66	271	26,650
11T	Tom Lehman	72	65	65	69	271	26,650
11T	D.A. Weibring	66	68	68	69	271	26,650
17	David Frost	68	66	71	67	272	20,800
18T	Rick Fehr	68	71	66	68	273	18,850
18T	Wayne Levi	71	68	71	63	273	18,850
20T	Mark Brooks	72	66	68	68	274	16,250
20T	Russ Cochran	66	67	77	64	274	16,250
22T	Dan Forsman	68	69	67	71	275	12,480
22T	Billy Mayfair	71	68	67	69	275	12,480
22T	Jim Thorpe	73	68	67	67	275	12,480
22T	Dick Mast	64	66	69	76	275	12,480
22T	Kirk Triplett	71	68	67	69	275	12,480
27T	Craig Stadler	69	68	70	69	276	9,035
27T	Mike Hulbert	68	73	72	63	276	9,035
27T	Craig Parry	69	69	70	68	276	9,035
27T	Fred Funk	70	71	71	64	276	9,035
27T	Bill Glasson	67	70	74	65	276	9,035
27T	Massy Kuramoto	73	67	65	71	276	9,035
33T	Bruce Lietzke	69	72	70	66	277	6,034
33T	Ian Baker-Finch	74	67	68	68	277	6,034
33T	Ben Crenshaw	72	69	68	68	277	6,034
33T	Fuzzy Zoeller	69	68	70	70	277	6,034
33T	Mark Wiebe	68	71	70	68	277	6,034
33T	Roger Maltbie	68	68	73	68	277	6,034
33T	Dudley Hart	71	69	71	66	277	6,034
33T	Jay Don Blake	71	71	69	66	277	6,034
33T	Bruce Fleisher	71	71	65	70	277	6,034
33T	Greg Kraft	71	66	68	72	277	6,034
33T	Bill Britton	70	66	72	69	277	6,034
33T	Kenny Perry	70	70	66	71	277	6,034
45T	Nick Price	69	70	68	71	278	3,578
45T	Steve Elkington	70	68	74	66	278	3,578
45T	Larry Mize	68	71	69	70	278	3,578
45T	Gene Sauers	68	69	69	72	278	3,578
45T	Michael Allen	74	68	68	68	278	3,578
45T	Jodie Mudd	72	68	68	70	278	3,578
45T	Ted Schulz	71	69	70	68	278	3,578
45T	Clark Dennis	70	67	68	73	278	3,578
53T	Blaine McCallister	70	70	69	70	279	2,995
53T	Brad Faxon	69	73	68	69	279	2,995
53T	Russell Beiersdorf	72	68	69	70	279	2,995
53T	Brian Claar	69	68	71	71	279	2,995
53T	Brad Fabel	73	69	69	68	279	2,995
58	Tom Kite	72	66	71	71	280	2,912
59T	Stan Utley	72	69	69	71	281	2,873
59T	Greg Twiggs	72	69	69	71	281	2,873
61T	Phil Blackmar	68	74	72	68	282	2,795
61T	Steve Pate	67	72	76	67	282	2,795
61T	Jim McGovern	72	70	70	70	282	2,795
61T	Gary Hallberg	71	70	70	71	282	2,795
65T	Davis Love III	72	70	72	69	283	2,678
65T	Brett Ogle	70	71	70	72	283	2,678
65T	Ed Dougherty	75	67	71	70	283	2,678
65T	Dave Barr	68	72	73	70	283	2,678
65T	Tom Byrum	72	70	72	69	283	2,678
70	Wayne Grady	73	69	69	73	284	2,600
71T	Mark O'Meara	69	71	73	73	286	2,561
71T	Steve Lowery	73	68	70	75	286	2,561
71T	*Justin Leonard*	73	69	72	72	286	
74	Jim Gallagher	71	68	73	75	287	2,522
75	Tad Rhyan	70	71	72	75	288	2,496
76	Mark Hayes	69	72	72	77	290	2,470

DID NOT MAKE CUT

139-wd Doug Tewell
143 Scott Hoch, Kelly Gibson, Chip Beck, Rocco Mediate Mike Standly, Dillard Pruitt, Dave Rummells
144 Tom Purtzer, Joey Sindelar, Denis Watson
145 Dan Pohl, Ed Humenik, Billy Andrade, Howard Twitty Mark Carnevale, Joe Ozaki
146 John Flannery, Bob Estes, Peter Persons
147 Bobby Clampett
148 Andrew Magee, Hal Sutton, Richard Zokol, Bob Tway
149 Bobby Wadkins, Joel Edwards
150 Trevor Dodds, Phil Mickelson
151 John Mahaffey, Jeff Sluman, Robert Gamez
152 Rod Curl
153 Billy Ray Brown
69-dq Payne Stewart
73-wd David Peoples
76-wd Peter Jacobsen

1994
May 26-30

Rank	Player	R1	R2	R3	R4	Total	Money
1	Nick Price	65	70	67	64	266*	$252,000
2	Scott Simpson	66	65	64	71	266*	151,200
3	Hale Irwin	64	70	68	65	267	95,200
4	Peter Jordan	68	70	66	66	270	67,200
5T	Tom Lehman	66	66	69	70	271	51,100
5T	Brad Faxon	70	66	67	68	271	51,100
5T	Gary Hallberg	67	67	65	72	271	51,100
8	Phil Mickelson	68	68	71	65	272	43,400
9T	Corey Pavin	68	67	69	70	274	37,800
9T	John Cook	66	71	67	70	274	37,800
9T	Mark McCumber	68	69	67	70	274	37,800
12T	Mark Calcavecchia	68	69	71	67	275	29,400
12T	Ben Crenshaw	69	69	69	68	275	29,400
12T	Fuzzy Zoeller	68	70	68	69	275	29,400
15T	David Edwards	72	67	68	69	276	23,800
15T	Clark Dennis	69	69	67	71	276	23,800
15T	David Frost	65	68	75	68	276	23,800
18T	Kenny Perry	73	67	69	68	277	18,900
18T	Ken Green	67	68	69	75	277	18,900
18T	Kirk Triplett	71	68	69	69	277	18,900
18T	Joe Ozaki	70	69	71	67	277	18,900
22T	John Huston	70	68	65	75	278	14,560
22T	Bob Estes	67	71	71	69	278	14,560
22T	Guy Boros	70	63	71	74	278	14,560
25T	Tom Purtzer	71	69	70	69	279	10,920
25T	Steve Pate	69	64	74	72	279	10,920
25T	Wayne Grady	71	65	68	75	279	10,920
25T	Lennie Clements	70	68	67	74	279	10,920
25T	David Ogrin	70	68	68	73	279	10,920
30T	Lee Janzen	70	70	71	69	280	7,478
30T	Bruce Lietzke	67	72	69	72	280	7,478
30T	Loren Roberts	70	65	71	74	280	7,478
30T	Dave Stockton Jr.	69	68	68	75	280	7,478
30T	D.A. Weibring	69	70	68	73	280	7,478
30T	Andrew Magee	67	73	71	69	280	7,478
30T	Scott Hoch	68	70	69	73	280	7,478
30T	Mike Reid	67	66	71	76	280	7,478
30T	Roger Maltbie	69	67	72	72	280	7,478
30T	Mike Heinen	70	70	68	72	280	7,478
30T	Glen Day	69	68	71	72	280	7,478
30T	Mike Springer	67	71	73	69	280	7,478
42T	Davis Love III	72	69	71	69	281	4,900
42T	Mark Brooks	68	67	72	74	281	4,900
42T	Brett Ogle	72	70	67	72	281	4,900
42T	Joey Sindelar	71	70	72	68	281	4,900
42T	Steve Stricker	71	67	67	76	281	4,900
47T	Dave Stockton	70	68	71	73	282	3,845
47T	Mike Hulbert	70	67	71	74	282	3,845
47T	Steve Lowery	71	71	71	69	282	3,845
50T	Keith Clearwater	70	68	67	78	283	3,409
50T	Tom Byrum	72	69	71	69	283	3,409
50T	Jodie Mudd	70	71	72	70	283	3,409
50T	Donnie Hammond	68	70	69	76	283	3,409
50T	*John Harris*	69	72	71	71	283	
55	Brian Henninger	69	71	70	74	284	3,248
56T	Greg Norman	70	69	71	75	285	3,136
56T	Jeff Maggert	71	66	75	73	285	3,136
56T	Howard Twitty	70	68	73	74	285	3,136
56T	David Feherty	67	72	68	78	285	3,136
56T	Dave Barr	71	71	69	74	285	3,136
56T	Bruce Fleisher	71	70	71	73	285	3,136
56T	Jay Don Blake	69	65	74	77	285	3,136
63T	Jeff Sluman	73	68	74	71	286	2,996
63T	Mark Carnevale	69	73	67	77	286	2,996
63T	Hajime Meshiai	66	74	72	74	286	2,996
66T	Hal Sutton	72	70	70	75	287	2,912
66T	Fred Funk	68	71	70	78	287	2,912
66T	John Inman	68	72	74	73	287	2,912
69	Billy Mayfair	71	71	72	74	288	2,856
70	Michael Allen	69	73	72	76	290	2,828
71T	Doug Tewell	68	70	75	78	291	2,786
71T	Paul Goydos	70	72	75	74	291	2,786
73	Rick Fehr	71	70	77	75	293	2,744

DID NOT MAKE CUT

143 Jim Thorpe, Larry Rinker, Bob Tway, Curtis Strange, Nolan Henke, Duffy Waldorf, Blaine McCallister
144 Fulton Allem, Jim Gallagher Jr., Ted Tryba, Jeff Woodland, Craig Parry, Bob Lohr, Greg Kraft, Grant Waite, John Morse, Russell Beiersdorf
145 Bob Gilder, Ian Baker-Finch, Mark O'Meara, John Adams, Chip Beck
146 Dave Rummells, Lanny Wadkins, Dan Pohl
147 Richard Zokol
148 Gil Morgan, Jesper Parnevik
149 Brandel Chamblee, Denis Watson
150 Russ Cochran
151 Dow Finsterwald Jr.
78-dq Robert Gamez
79-wd Mike Standly

Names in italics designate amateurs.

1990s

1995
May 25-28

Rank	Player	R1	R2	R3	R4	Total	Money
1	Tom Lehman	67	68	68	68	271	$252,000
2	Craig Parry	66	65	70	71	272	151,200
3	D.A. Weibring	66	72	69	67	274	95,200
4	Woody Austin	67	69	66	73	275	67,200
5T	Justin Leonard	68	72	68	68	276	51,100
5T	Brad Faxon	67	70	75	64	276	51,100
5T	Mark McCumber	67	73	68	68	276	51,100
8T	Mark Calcavecchia	70	67	68	72	277	39,200
8T	Jeff Maggert	66	68	74	69	277	39,200
8T	Billy Mayfair	68	71	67	71	277	39,200
8T	Rocco Mediate	69	68	70	70	277	39,200
12T	Nick Price	73	69	70	66	278	29,400
12T	Scott Verplank	69	68	70	71	278	29,400
12T	David Duval	67	71	76	64	278	29,400
15T	Lanny Wadkins	69	73	67	70	279	20,335
15T	Larry Mize	72	70	69	68	279	20,335
15T	David Frost	69	72	70	68	279	20,335
15T	Steve Elkington	68	68	77	66	279	20,335
15T	Brett Ogle	67	72	72	68	279	20,335
15T	Billy Andrade	65	71	72	71	279	20,335
15T	Mike Hulbert	66	70	68	75	279	20,335
15T	Jay Don Blake	70	72	73	64	279	20,335
23T	Tom Kite	70	68	71	71	280	12,110
23T	Peter Jacobsen	69	71	69	71	280	12,110
23T	Jeff Sluman	69	67	76	68	280	12,110
23T	Lennie Clements	64	69	74	73	280	12,110
23T	Dave Barr	68	72	71	69	280	12,110
23T	Brad Bryant	67	74	72	67	280	12,110
29T	Bruce Lietzke	67	70	74	70	281	9,310
29T	Gil Morgan	73	68	70	70	281	9,310
29T	Bob Tway	70	69	70	72	281	9,310
29T	Mike Standly	70	72	71	68	281	9,310
33T	Phil Mickelson	69	71	73	69	282	7,087
33T	Scott Simpson	74	68	70	70	282	7,087
33T	Kenny Perry	73	68	74	67	282	7,087
33T	Steve Lowery	73	69	71	69	282	7,087
33T	Fred Funk	69	71	71	71	282	7,087
33T	Kirk Triplett	69	72	71	70	282	7,087
33T	Neal Lancaster	71	71	70	70	282	7,087
33T	Glen Day	70	72	69	71	282	7,087
41T	Tom Watson	68	69	70	76	283	5,180
41T	Fuzzy Zoeller	66	72	74	71	283	5,180
41T	David Edwards	67	71	75	70	283	5,180
41T	Robin Freeman	72	69	68	74	283	5,180
41T	Mike Sullivan	70	71	72	70	283	5,180
46T	Dan Pohl	68	72	75	69	284	3,808
46T	Steve Pate	72	69	70	73	284	3,808
46T	Loren Roberts	70	70	71	73	284	3,808
46T	Jim McGovern	67	75	77	65	284	3,808
46T	John Mahaffey	69	72	71	72	284	3,808
46T	Keith Fergus	69	70	76	69	284	3,808
52T	Payne Stewart	66	72	74	73	285	3,248
52T	Clark Dennis	64	74	76	71	285	3,248
52T	Guy Boros	73	69	75	68	285	3,248
52T	Scott Hoch	69	70	74	72	285	3,248
52T	Tray Tyner	68	70	74	73	285	3,248
52T	Robert Gamez	68	69	75	73	285	3,248
58T	Curtis Strange	66	72	71	77	286	3,108
58T	Davis Love III	70	68	74	74	286	3,108
58T	Charlie Rymer	72	70	75	69	286	3,108
61T	Bob Lohr	68	74	73	72	287	3,038
61T	Paul Goydos	69	68	73	77	287	3,038
63T	Jerry Pate	67	73	76	72	288	2,968
63T	Gary Hallberg	70	71	74	73	288	2,968
63T	Joe Ozaki	68	74	73	73	288	2,968
66T	Joey Sindelar	67	72	76	75	289	2,884
66T	Chip Beck	68	71	77	74	289	2,884
66T	Paul Stankowski	70	71	74	75	289	2,884
69	Michael Bradley	68	70	75	80	290	2,828
70	Mike Reid	68	73	80	73	291	2,800
71	John Huston	71	71	76	x	wd	

DID NOT MAKE CUT

143	Ernie Els, Corey Pavin, Mark O'Meara, Blaine McCallister, Mark McNulty, Bill Glasson, Greg Kraft, Kelly Gibson, Duffy Waldorf
144	Hale Irwin, Mark Brooks, Fulton Allem, Jim Gallagher Jr., Jodie Mudd Dave Stockton Jr., Brian Claar, Jim Furyk, Pete Jordan
145	Brian Henninger, Dicky Pride, Brandel Chamblee, Mike Heinen, Keith Clearwater, Donnie Hammond, Gene Sauers, Ted Tryba
146	Larry Nelson, Nolan Henke, Wayne Grady, Dillard Pruitt, John Cook
147	Tom Purtzer, Lee Janzen, Andy North, *Trip Kuehne*
148	John Daly, Andrew Magee, Tommy Tolles, Dan Forsman
149	*Anthony Rodriguez*
150	Ben Crenshaw
152	Bob Estes, Ian Baker-Finch
154	Rod Curl
wd	Mike Springer

1996
May 16-19

Rank	Player	R1	R2	R3	R4	Total	Money
1	Corey Pavin	69	67	67	69	272	$270,000
2	Jeff Sluman	69	67	70	68	274	162,000
3	Rocco Mediate	68	66	68	73	275	102,000
4	Fred Couples	70	67	68	71	276	72,000
5	Davis Love III	72	70	68	67	277	60,000
6T	Ben Crenshaw	71	71	70	66	278	48,562
6T	Payne Stewart	69	69	72	68	278	48,562
6T	Tommy Tolles	72	64	75	67	278	48,562
6T	Steve Jones	67	76	68	67	278	48,562
10T	Justin Leonard	73	69	66	71	279	39,000
10T	Jeff Gallagher	66	70	71	72	279	39,000
12T	David Duval	69	70	69	68	74	280	30,375
12T	Bob Tway	70	70	72	68	280	30,375
12T	David Edwards	70	69	69	72	280	30,375
12T	Joe Ozaki	71	70	69	71	280	30,375
16T	Woody Austin	74	66	70	71	281	23,250
16T	Scott Hoch	71	70	69	71	281	23,250
16T	John Morse	70	79	70	72	281	23,250
16T	Emlyn Aubrey	67	69	71	74	281	23,250
20T	Brad Faxon	72	70	72	68	282	14,683
20T	Billy Mayfair	70	69	73	70	282	14,683
20T	Larry Nelson	76	67	69	70	282	14,683
20T	Bruce Lietzke	71	71	68	72	282	14,683
20T	Craig Stadler	68	68	73	73	282	14,683
20T	Jim Gallagher Jr.	70	69	72	71	282	14,683
20T	Tom Purtzer	69	69	71	73	282	14,683
20T	Mark McCumber	68	69	71	74	282	14,683
20T	Gil Morgan	70	67	70	75	282	14,683
29T	Tom Kite	68	70	75	70	283	10,200
29T	Curtis Strange	70	67	72	74	283	10,200
29T	Vijay Singh	74	70	71	68	283	10,200
32T	Peter Jacobsen	71	73	67	73	284	8,300
32T	Craig Parry	70	69	75	70	284	8,300
32T	Roger Maltbie	70	70	71	73	284	8,300
32T	Brett Ogle	68	72	67	77	284	8,300
32T	David Ogrin	70	67	74	73	284	8,300
32T	Franklin Langham	72	72	69	71	284	8,300
38T	Steve Elkington	70	73	71	71	285	6,000
38T	Gene Sauers	70	73	73	69	285	6,000
38T	Wayne Levi	66	68	74	77	285	6,000
38T	Omar Uresti	66	69	75	75	285	6,000
38T	Jim Furyk	68	73	70	74	285	6,000
38T	Scott Verplank	70	66	73	76	285	6,000
38T	Mike Heinen	69	71	69	76	285	6,000
38T	Phil Blackmar	74	66	77	68	285	6,000
46T	Tom Watson	73	69	69	75	286	3,900
46T	Mark Brooks	71	67	75	73	286	3,900
46T	John Huston	69	71	70	76	286	3,900
46T	Mike Hulbert	71	70	66	79	286	3,900
46T	Lennie Clements	73	71	71	71	286	3,900
46T	Allen Doyle	70	74	75	67	286	3,900
46T	Bob Lohr	70	70	76	70	286	3,900
46T	Neal Lancaster	72	71	70	73	286	3,900
46T	Doug Martin	70	72	70	74	286	3,900
55	Fred Funk	72	71	70	74	287	3,450
56T	Nick Price	69	70	72	77	288	3,345
56T	Fuzzy Zoeller	69	75	70	74	288	3,345
56T	Mike Reid	73	69	72	74	288	3,345
56T	Don Pooley	70	73	71	74	288	3,345
56T	Steve Lowery	73	70	72	73	288	3,345
56T	Glen Day	73	70	76	69	288	3,345
62T	Lanny Wadkins	70	68	73	78	289	3,225
62T	Sean Murphy	76	68	67	78	289	3,225
64T	Nolan Henke	68	72	78	72	290	3,150
64T	Andrew Magee	70	68	77	75	290	3,150
64T	Billy Andrade	72	69	73	76	290	3,150
67T	Ernie Els	75	69	71	76	291	3,075
67T	Brian Claar	75	68	72	76	291	3,075
69T	Dave Stockton Jr.	74	70	74	74	292	3,015
69T	Kirk Triplett	68	74	72	78	292	3,015
71T	Keith Clearwater	70	73	75	75	293	2,925
71T	Duffy Waldorf	74	69	75	75	293	2,925
71T	Marco Dawson	72	68	76	77	293	2,925
71T	Jerry Kelly	68	74	74	77	293	2,925
75	Dan Pohl	72	71	73	78	294	2,850
76	Steve Stricker	72	71	73	79	295	2,820
	Grant Waite	71	70	72	dq		

DID NOT MAKE CUT

145	Tom Lehman, Clark Dennis, Larry Mize, Wayne Grady Joel Edwards, Dave Barr, Hugh Royer III
146	Guy Boros, Bobby Wadkins, Ted Tryba, Jay Don Blake Patrick Burke, Brad Bryant
147	David Frost, Kenny Perry, Blaine McCallister, Brandel Chamblee
148	Bob Estes, Mark Wiebe, Paul Goydos, Tim Herron Fulton Allem, Jay Delsing
149	Loren Roberts, Chip Beck, Steve Schneiter
150	Robin Freeman, D.A. Weibring
151	Jeff Maggert
153	Mark Calcavecchia
154	Paul Stankowski
157	Rod Curl
159	Lee Rinker
84-wd	John Adams
wd	Ian Baker-Finch

1997
May 22-25

Rank	Player	R1	R2	R3	R4	Total	Money
1	David Frost	66	63	69	67	265	$288,000
2T	Brad Faxon	63	66	70	68	267	140,800
2T	David Ogrin	66	67	62	72	267	140,800
4T	Tiger Woods	67	65	64	72	268	70,400
4T	Paul Goydos	64	65	68	71	268	70,400
6T	Bob Tway	65	66	69	69	269	55,600
6T	Dudley Hart	68	66	68	67	269	55,600
8	Jim Furyk	64	67	67	72	270	49,600
9	John Huston	67	67	67	70	271	46,400
10T	Loren Roberts	67	68	66	71	272	40,000
10T	Steve Pate	69	66	64	73	272	40,000
10T	Glen Day	69	70	65	68	272	40,000
13T	Jeff Sluman	66	69	68	70	273	32,000
13T	Justin Leonard	64	67	68	74	273	32,000
15T	Jeff Maggert	71	67	68	68	274	25,600
15T	Kirk Triplett	69	64	67	74	274	25,600
15T	Stewart Cink	69	66	67	72	274	25,600
15T	Greg Kraft	67	68	69	70	274	25,600
15T	Shigeki Maruyama	69	68	68	69	274	25,600
20T	Bill Glasson	67	69	70	69	275	20,000
20T	Billy Andrade	67	70	68	70	275	20,000
22T	Steve Elkington	69	71	65	71	276	13,047
22T	Phil Mickelson	70	64	70	72	276	13,047
22T	Bruce Lietzke	69	68	68	71	276	13,047
22T	Mark Brooks	68	69	69	70	276	13,047
22T	Craig Stadler	73	66	67	70	276	13,047
22T	Lee Janzen	71	68	67	70	276	13,047
22T	Patrick Burke	68	70	68	70	276	13,047
22T	Emlyn Aubrey	69	67	76	64	276	13,047
22T	Russ Cochran	71	67	71	67	276	13,047
22T	Billy Ray Brown	68	67	70	71	276	13,047
22T	Kazuhiko Hosokawa	71	69	66	70	276	13,047
33T	Fuzzy Zoeller	71	65	70	71	277	8,100
33T	Lanny Wadkins	66	70	71	70	277	8,100
33T	Larry Nelson	68	69	70	70	277	8,100
33T	Fulton Allem	67	69	67	74	277	8,100
33T	Tommy Tolles	66	70	71	70	277	8,100
33T	Scott Hoch	70	70	69	68	277	8,100
33T	Brent Geiberger	69	65	68	75	277	8,100
33T	Phil Blackmar	70	66	68	73	277	8,100
41T	David Duval	65	70	66	77	278	5,600
41T	D.A. Weibring	68	66	69	75	278	5,600
41T	Mike Standly	69	67	72	70	278	5,600
41T	Bob Estes	71	69	67	71	278	5,600
41T	Mike Brisky	72	68	71	67	278	5,600
41T	Kevin Sutherland	69	69	72	68	278	5,600
41T	Grant Waite	70	70	65	73	278	5,600
48T	Mike Hulbert	69	70	71	69	279	4,021
48T	Tom Kite	70	67	69	73	279	4,021
48T	Payne Stewart	68	66	68	77	279	4,021
48T	Len Mattiace	73	67	67	72	279	4,021
48T	John Morse	71	67	70	71	279	4,021
48T	Larry Rinker	66	73	65	75	279	4,021
54T	Corey Pavin	71	68	71	70	280	3,584
54T	Peter Jacobsen	67	71	70	72	280	3,584
54T	Billy Mayfair	68	72	73	67	280	3,584
54T	Scott Simpson	68	72	71	69	280	3,584
54T	Brian Henninger	65	74	73	68	280	3,584
54T	Willie Wood	70	70	70	70	280	3,584
54T	Doug Martin	72	67	70	71	280	3,584
54T	Robert Damron	71	68	67	74	280	3,584
54T	Joe Ozaki	72	68	69	71	280	3,584
63T	Joey Sindelar	68	69	73	71	281	3,376
63T	Tim Herron	67	73	71	70	281	3,376
63T	Jeff Gallagher	67	72	67	75	281	3,376
63T	Marco Dawson	72	70	67	74	281	3,376
67	Craig Parry	70	67	74	71	282	3,296
68T	Blaine McCallister	70	68	73	73	284	3,248
68T	Ed Fiori	67	71	70	76	284	3,248
70T	Davis Love III	70	70	74	71	285	3,184
70T	Kelly Gibson	70	66	72	77	285	3,184
72	Mark Calcavecchia	67	70	76	74	287	3,136
73	Duffy Waldorf	69	71	72	76	288	3,104
	Fred Funk	67	65	71	wd		

DID NOT MAKE CUT

141	Woody Austin, Steve Lowery, Rocco Mediate, Steve Jones Paul Stankowski, Andrew Magee, Tom Lehman, Stuart Appleby
142	Clarence Rose, David Edwards, Robert Gamez Omar Uresti, Phil Tataurangi
143	Tom Purtzer, Ben Crenshaw, Joe Durant, Lennie Clements
144	Tom Watson, Guy Boros
145	Nolan Henke, Keith Clearwater, Scott Gump
146	*Alberto Ochoa*
147	Mike Reid, Jim Gallagher Jr., Dave Stockton Jr.
148	Chip Beck
149	Jerry Kelly, Sandy Lyle
156	Rod Curl
73-wd	Jay Don Blake

1998
May 21-24

Rank	Player	R1	R2	R3	R4	Total	Money
1	Tom Watson	68	66	65	66	265	$414,000
2	Jim Furyk	66	67	66	68	267	248,400
3	Jeff Sluman	67	67	66	69	269	156,400
4	Harrison Frazar	64	67	68	71	270	110,400
5	John Cook	68	66	69	68	271	92,000
6T	Jim Gallagher Jr.	69	69	68	66	272	79,925
6T	Kenny Perry	68	65	69	70	272	79,925
8T	Justin Leonard	70	70	67	66	273	69,000
8T	Brian Henninger	70	66	68	69	273	69,000
10T	Dan Forsman	69	67	71	67	274	55,200
10T	Craig Parry	68	69	69	68	274	55,200
10T	Stuart Appleby	68	69	69	68	274	55,200
10T	Steve Flesch	68	66	72	68	274	55,200
14T	David Frost	68	69	69	69	275	40,250
14T	David Duval	66	70	68	71	275	40,250
14T	Clark Dennis	68	68	68	71	275	40,250
14T	Mike Brisky	70	70	66	69	275	40,250
18T	Fred Couples	72	69	67	68	276	24,485
18T	Lanny Wadkins	66	71	70	69	276	24,485
18T	Payne Stewart	68	72	66	70	276	24,485
18T	Jeff Maggert	69	72	67	68	276	24,485
18T	John Huston	70	69	66	71	276	24,485
18T	Scott Hoch	67	73	66	70	276	24,485
18T	Rocco Mediate	67	68	67	74	276	24,485
18T	Scott McCarron	70	67	67	72	276	24,485
18T	Kirk Triplett	69	68	68	71	276	24,485
18T	Doug Martin	67	69	70	69	276	24,485
18T	Skip Kendall	68	71	69	68	276	24,485
29T	Nick Faldo	72	69	70	66	277	15,295
29T	Bruce Lietzke	67	69	67	74	277	15,295
29T	Fred Funk	75	65	68	69	277	15,295
29T	Tommy Armour III	70	65	72	70	277	15,295
33T	Frank Nobilo	69	68	73	68	278	13,283
33T	Jerry Kelly	67	69	71	71	278	13,283
35T	Nick Price	71	69	68	71	279	11,098
35T	Bob Tway	67	71	72	69	279	11,098
35T	Steve Jones	69	69	72	69	279	11,098
35T	Len Mattiace	71	69	70	69	279	11,098
35T	Phil Blackmar	66	68	72	73	279	11,098
35T	Scott Verplank	70	69	71	69	279	11,098
41T	Corey Pavin	73	66	69	72	280	7,626
41T	Mark Calcavecchia	68	65	70	77	280	7,626
41T	David Edwards	72	69	68	71	280	7,626
41T	Joey Sindelar	69	70	74	67	280	7,626
41T	Brent Geiberger	70	69	67	74	280	7,626
41T	Glen Day	72	66	71	71	280	7,626
41T	Mark Wiebe	71	70	71	68	280	7,626
41T	David Ogrin	71	64	71	74	280	7,626
41T	Stewart Cink	68	72	67	73	280	7,626
50T	Peter Jacobsen	69	70	71	71	281	5,658
50T	Rick Fehr	70	69	70	72	281	5,658
50T	Dudley Hart	68	72	69	72	281	5,658
53T	Fulton Allem	69	69	72	72	282	5,156
53T	Dan Pohl	70	66	77	69	282	5,156
53T	Mark Brooks	71	70	70	71	282	5,156
53T	Guy Boros	68	73	71	70	282	5,156
53T	Blaine McCallister	69	71	71	71	282	5,156
53T	Brandel Chamblee	68	69	75	70	282	5,156
53T	Kevin Sutherland	69	71	73	69	282	5,156
53T	Jay Don Blake	72	69	71	70	282	5,156
53T	Gabriel Hjertstedt	70	69	73	70	282	5,156
53T	Lee Rinker	69	68	74	71	282	5,156
53T	Brad Fabel	67	68	71	76	282	5,156
64T	Tom Kite	69	70	74	70	283	4,830
64T	Jim Carter	67	72	69	75	283	4,830
64T	Grant Waite	70	70	67	76	283	4,830
67	Dave Stockton Jr.	71	69	75	69	284	4,738
68	R.W. Eaks	67	73	74	71	285	4,692
69T	Craig Stadler	71	70	71	74	286	4,600
69T	Steve Lowery	70	69	75	72	286	4,600
69T	Robert Damron	74	66	70	76	286	4,600
72	David Toms	71	69	76	71	287	4,508
73T	Billy Andrade	71	69	77	71	288	4,439
73T	Neal Lancaster	69	71	73	75	288	4,439

DID NOT MAKE CUT

142	Bob Estes, Paul Stankowski, Billy Mayfair, Brett Quigley, Brad Faxon, Loren Roberts, Lee Janzen, Frank Lickliter, Russ Cochran, Jeff Gallagher, Hajime Meshiai
143	Paul Goydos, Scott Simpson, Mike Hulbert
144	Duffy Waldorf, D.A. Weibring, Greg Kraft
145	Steve Pate, Tom Byrum, Olin Browne, Esteban Toledo, Mike Standly
146	Ben Crenshaw, Tommy Tolles, Mike Reid, Vijay Singh, Wayne Grady, Dave Stockton
147	Omar Uresti
148	Billy Ray Brown, David Sutherland, Brad Elder
149	Keith Clearwater
150	Phil Mickelson
152	Trevor Dodds
156	Rod Curl
74-wd	Bill Glasson

1999
May 20-23

Rank	Player	R1	R2	R3	R4	Total	Money
1	Olin Browne	73	67	66	66	272	$504,000
2T	Jeff Sluman	67	71	69	66	273	168,000
2T	Fred Funk	68	68	69	68	273	168,000
2T	Paul Goydos	70	68	69	66	273	168,000
2T	Tim Herron	68	69	67	69	273	168,000
2T	Greg Kraft	75	67	61	70	273	168,000
7T	John Huston	72	65	71	66	274	84,350
7T	Billy Mayfair	67	68	71	68	274	84,350
7T	Craig Parry	72	68	68	66	274	84,350
7T	Bob Estes	70	68	68	68	274	84,350
11T	Phil Mickelson	72	63	70	70	275	50,680
11T	John Cook	68	66	70	71	275	50,680
11T	Davis Love III	72	66	68	69	275	50,680
11T	Len Mattiace	70	69	67	69	275	50,680
11T	Corey Pavin	69	64	74	68	275	50,680
11T	Vijay Singh	67	72	66	70	275	50,680
11T	Stuart Appleby	71	67	68	69	275	50,680
11T	Jim Carter	71	70	68	66	275	50,680
11T	Duffy Waldorf	73	67	68	67	275	50,680
11T	Brian Watts	71	66	70	68	275	50,680
21T	Lee Janzen	71	69	65	71	276	29,120
21T	Stewart Cink	70	72	70	64	276	29,120
21T	Dan Forsman	69	72	66	69	276	29,120
21T	Kirk Triplett	72	66	70	68	276	29,120
21T	Scott Verplank	72	65	66	73	276	29,120
26T	Tom Lehman	71	71	64	71	277	21,140
26T	Mark Calcavecchia	69	67	72	69	277	21,140
26T	Billy Andrade	73	68	69	67	277	21,140
26T	Scott Hoch	69	66	70	72	277	21,140
30T	Tommy Armour III	73	70	67	68	278	18,200
30T	Joe Durant	69	66	70	73	278	18,200
30T	Skip Kendall	71	67	72	68	278	18,200
33T	Chris Perry	70	73	70	66	279	14,793
33T	Kenny Perry	73	66	73	67	279	14,793
33T	Brandel Chamblee	73	69	70	67	279	14,793
33T	Franklin Langham	68	72	67	72	279	14,793
33T	Tom Pernice, Jr.	73	71	66	69	279	14,793
33T	Mark Wiebe	70	66	74	69	279	14,793
39T	Fred Couples	72	71	68	69	280	10,640
39T	Justin Leonard	73	66	69	72	280	10,640
39T	Steve Elkington	68	68	75	69	280	10,640
39T	Tom Watson	74	70	66	70	280	10,640
39T	Robert Damron	73	66	73	68	280	10,640
39T	Clark Dennis	72	67	69	72	280	10,640
39T	Brent Geiberger	71	70	68	71	280	10,640
39T	Andrew Magee	74	70	66	70	280	10,640
47T	Tom Kite	73	68	71	69	281	7,532
47T	Steve Flesch	66	74	66	75	281	7,532
47T	Scott McCarron	72	69	72	68	281	7,532
47T	Kevin Sutherland	73	70	68	70	281	7,532
51T	Glen Day	74	69	73	66	282	6,678
51T	Jim Gallagher, Jr.	71	72	66	73	282	6,678
51T	Bob Friend	70	70	69	73	282	6,678
51T	Loren Roberts	74	69	66	73	282	6,678
55T	Jim Furyk	74	69	70	70	283	6,272
55T	Mike Hulbert	70	70	73	70	283	6,272
55T	Steve Lowery	72	66	75	70	283	6,272
55T	Frank Nobilo	72	70	72	69	283	6,272
55T	Steve Pate	72	69	68	74	283	6,272
55T	Mike Brisky	72	72	74	65	283	6,272
55T	Dennis Paulson	74	68	69	72	283	6,272
62T	Jonathan Kaye	75	69	69	71	284	5,992
62T	Rocco Mediate	71	71	70	72	284	5,992
62T	Dan Pohl	70	69	77	68	284	5,992
65T	Mark Brooks	71	71	70	73	285	5,768
65T	Harrison Frazar	73	68	72	72	285	5,768
65T	Brian Henninger	78	66	72	69	285	5,768
65T	Bradley Hughes	73	71	71	70	285	5,768
65T	D.A. Weibring	72	69	72	72	285	5,768
70T	Jay Haas	70	71	73	72	286	5,572
70T	Willie Wood	69	71	75	71	286	5,572
72T	Omar Uresti	72	68	71	76	287	5,460
72T	Mike Weir	71	69	78	69	287	5,460
74	David Frost	73	71	72	72	288	5,376
75T	Fulton Allem	72	72	73	72	289	5,292
75T	Dave Stockton, Jr.	71	71	73	74	289	5,292
77T	Eric Booker	71	71	75	73	290	5,152
77T	Bill Glasson	71	73	73	73	290	5,152
77T	Fuzzy Zoeller	71	70	73	76	290	5,152

DID NOT MAKE CUT

145	Robert Allenby, Blaine McCallister, Larry Mize, Chris Riley, Joey Sindelar
146	Notah Begay III, Alan Bratton, Billy Ray Brown, Keith Clearwater, Jerry Kelly, Frank Lickliter, Mike Reid, Craig Stadler, Esteban Toledo, Bob Tway
147	Gabriel Hjertstedt, David Ogrin, Tom Purtzer, David Toms, Lanny Wadkins
148	Ben Crenshaw, Bruce Lietzke
149	Doug Dunakey
150	J.P. Hayes, Nolan Henke
151	Peter Jacobsen, Paul Stankowski, Dave Stockton
152	Rod Curl
153	Jay Don Blake
70-dq	Neal Lancaster
77-dq	Dudley Hart
80-wd	John Daly

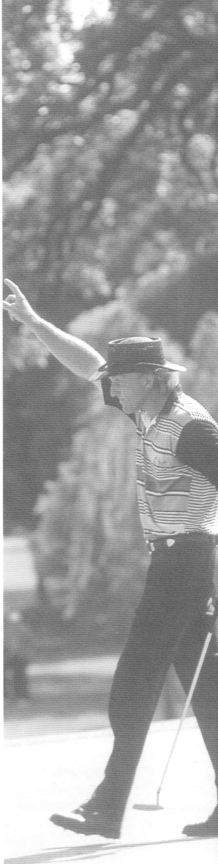

Names in italics designate amateurs.

THE 2000s

NEW MILLENNIUM, NEW GENERATION OF CHAMPIONS

A new century brought continued growth and excitement to Colonial and professional golf. A young generation of players, in the shadow of Tiger Woods, began establishing themselves on Tour.

In 2000, challenging weather kept players close until Saturday. Stewart Cink, fresh off his second career win, followed his opening 70 with 64-65 to stake a three-shot lead. Veterans Davis Love III and Fred Couples appeared to be the most likely to have a chance at reeling him in on Sunday. Then Cink rattled off three early birdies to seem in complete control.

Lefty Phil Mickelson, fresh off his 15th Tour victory but six shots back, had other ideas. He followed up his front side 33 with three consecutive birdies on holes #10-12. He then delivered the body blow with more birdies at #15 and 18, for a two-shot win. Cink finished second, tied with Love. Mickelson's remarkable 63 was the only one recorded by the entire field that week, and it remains the lowest round ever fired by a Colonial champion on Sunday.

ABOVE:
Phil Mickelson won the 2000 Colonial title with a closing 63.
FACING PAGE:
Nick Price won his second Colonial championship in 2002.

"To have won this tournament is an amazing feeling," Mickelson said. "I can't explain how good it feels to have won this championship and to have shot a low round to do it."

In 200, Mickelson returned to try to become the only back-to-back Colonial champ since Ben Hogan, and he almost did it. Leading after the first and third rounds, he appeared well suited to stave off the many good players nipping at his heels.

Young Spanish superstar Sergio Garcia was playing well in his Colonial debut, and started the Sunday round five shots behind the defending champion. He then gave Mickelson a taste of his own medicine. A sizzling 29 on the front side set the pace for Garcia's own 63, overtaking all challengers and besting Mickelson by two shots. His first American victory at age 21 made him the youngest player ever, and the first European, to win at Colonial.

I'm glad I was able to win, finally, on the toughest Tour in the world," Garcia commented. "Doing it on Ben Hogan's course, it will always be special. To be able to win at his course, where he played almost his whole life, it makes me feel prouder."

The 2002 tournament saw experience ultimately win the day. 1994 champion Nick Price used a 65 on Friday to take the lead, and at 54 holes his closest pursuer was five shots back. Although he hadn't won in four years, he was never seriously threatened on Sunday, and his five-shot win was the tournament's largest victory margin since 1968. Price thus became the eighth two-time winner at Colonial, and he was the only player to reach double figures under par. The victory re-invigorated the world's best player from the mid-1990s, who went on to his best year in nearly a decade.

LEFT:
Sergio Garcia captured the 2001 Colonial championship.

"I couldn't be happier to have won here," he remarked. "To have won here twice, well, I didn't think this day was going to come. I proved I could do it again. This golf course has stood the test of time. All the players have come here with all the new equipment, but this golf course still beats everyone. It's a great, great golf course."

Bank of America became title sponsor in 2003, the purse reached $5 million, and the eyes of the entire world watched Colonial as the world's best female player, and a global media circus, crashed the party. Annika Sorenstam tested her game, trying to accomplish something not done since Babe Zaharias in 1945 -- making a cut against the men. Zaharias also had won the Texas Women's Open at Colonial in 1940.

Four-time winner Kenny Perry, who quietly placed second the year before, returned on a mission of his own. Rain-softened greens and no wind set the stage for birdies and scoring records. While Sorenstam hung tough but missed the cut, Perry staked out a lead of eight under par for 36 holes. He then blistered the field Saturday with a 61, setting a new 54-hole record of 17 under par that surpassed the old *72-hole* mark. He coasted on Sunday for a six-shot win over Texan Justin Leonard, whose own 61 never threatened. Perry's 19-under par total is the current 72-hole record.

The course and Mother Nature fought back some in 2004. Birdies could be had, but the 36-hole cut of three over par was the highest on Tour so far. Justin Leonard led at six under par after Friday, but trailed three players by four shots Saturday -- fellow Texan Chad Campbell, lefty Steve Flesch and Brian Gay. The hot Campbell fired a 61 in the third round with *two bogeys* on the front nine. None of those players had ever missed the cut at Colonial, and Gay finished second in 2001.

TOP:
LPGA superstar Annika Sorenstam drew the world's attention with her entry at Colonial in 2003.
BOTTOM:
Phil Mickelson came oh-so-close to winning back-to-back Colonial titles.

Flesch, however, worked the ball flawlessly in Sunday's wind to post a 67 and clip Campbell by a shot. "I take pride in the fact that I am a good ball-striker, and I think that really helped me around here," Flesch noted. "Having my name on that Wall with that group of champions is unbelievable. I remember playing my rookie year, looking at those names and thinking, 'every good player that has ever played golf has run through this place.' That's important to me."

In 2005, the wind laid down for the second time in three years, and the record book was re-written once more. Kenny Perry found the zone again, and the birdies came in buckets. Record hot temperatures baked spectators while Perry dusted the field. He held a three-shot lead after two rounds and a seven shot lead after 54 holes. Over his four rounds, Perry carded only one bogey, and then one double-bogey on the 71st hole after the tournament was well in hand.

In becoming Colonial's ninth two-time champion, Perry established new 36-hole and 54-hole scoring marks, and tied his own record of 19 under par for 72 holes. He holds or shares the scoring mark for all four rounds. "I'm so in love with this place, I just played hard for the men in the plaid jackets," Perry commented. "I can't say enough about the men and women that work this tournament. They have a lot of passion and love for this tournament. I love the history here. I'm ecstatic. It was a great week. I know this is Hogan's Alley and all that, but maybe somewhere down in the corner they can put 'Perry's Place.'"

TOP:
Steve Flesch captured the Colonial championship in 2004.
BOTTOM:
Kenny Perry won his first Colonial title in 2003 with a record 72-hole score. Then he tied it in 2005 for his second win.

Over the event's first 60 years, it's been proven that no one type of player has a distinct advantage at Colonial. Long hitters, short hitters, scramblers, etc. -- they've all won at Hogan's Alley when able to put their whole game together. And while experience is considered a key to winning at Colonial, a young player with confidence and a well-rounded game can still claim the title. The one constant through them all, though, is the great Ben Hogan -- his actual presence or his everlasting spirit. Always has been, always will be.

TOP:
Chad Campbell used a course record-tying 61 to place second in 2004.
MIDDLE:
Sergio Garcia was Colonial's first European champion.
BOTTOM:
Justin Leonard fired a course record-tying 61 to place second in 2003.

results

2000
May 18-21

Rank	Player	R1	R2	R3	R4	Total	Money
1	Phil Mickelson	67	68	70	63	268	$594,000
2T	Stewart Cink	70	64	65	71	270	290,400
2T	Davis Love III	67	66	69	68	270	290,400
4T	Rocco Mediate	68	67	69	68	272	145,200
4T	David Toms	67	66	72	67	272	145,200
6T	Greg Kraft	67	68	71	67	273	114,675
6T	Bob Estes	69	72	66	66	273	114,675
8T	Jim Furyk	69	66	72	67	274	89,100
8T	Mark Calcavecchia	72	67	67	68	274	89,100
8T	John Cook	66	70	70	68	274	89,100
8T	Len Mattiace	67	72	67	68	274	89,100
8T	Mike Weir	67	68	69	70	274	89,100
13T	Jeff Sluman	69	68	67	71	275	56,571
13T	Tim Herron	70	66	69	70	275	56,571
13T	Fred Funk	70	67	69	69	275	56,571
13T	Kirk Triplett	72	66	71	66	275	56,571
13T	Skip Kendall	69	67	70	69	275	56,571
13T	Joel Edwards	68	72	65	70	275	56,571
13T	Shigeki Maruyama	69	70	70	66	275	56,571
20T	John Huston	70	71	68	67	276	38,445
20T	Scott Verplank	69	72	67	68	276	38,445
20T	Kevin Sutherland	71	68	68	69	276	38,445
20T	Jay Don Blake	71	72	67	66	276	38,445
24T	Fred Couples	70	66	68	73	277	26,117
24T	Bill Glasson	70	67	72	68	277	26,117
24T	Brent Geiberger	75	66	68	68	277	26,117
24T	Billy Andrade	70	66	75	66	277	26,117
24T	Mike Reid	75	66	70	66	277	26,117
24T	Russ Cochran	75	66	68	68	277	26,117
24T	Carl Paulson	69	73	71	64	277	26,117
31T	Steve Flesch	71	67	70	70	278	20,955
31T	Charles Raulerson	70	70	71	67	278	20,955
33T	David Frost	67	69	69	74	279	19,057
33T	J.L. Lewis	73	68	69	69	279	19,057
35T	Peter Jacobsen	73	69	68	70	280	15,922
35T	Stuart Appleby	71	71	69	69	280	15,922
35T	Frank Nobilo	68	70	73	69	280	15,922
35T	Greg Chalmers	73	69	68	70	280	15,922
35T	Scott Dunlap	68	68	67	77	280	15,922
35T	Robin Freeman	70	69	69	72	280	15,922
41T	Vijay Singh	73	67	72	69	281	12,210
41T	Mark O'Meara	73	66	68	74	281	12,210
41T	Jay Haas	69	70	70	72	281	12,210
41T	Kenny Perry	70	71	70	70	281	12,210
41T	Brian Gay	70	70	70	71	281	12,210
46T	Keith Clearwater	67	71	73	71	282	9,355
46T	Loren Roberts	77	66	71	68	282	9,355
46T	Steve Pate	70	69	71	72	282	9,355
46T	Brian Watts	69	68	69	76	282	9,355
50T	Tom Kite	69	72	73	69	283	7,959
50T	Jerry Kelly	75	68	70	70	283	7,959
50T	Tom Byrum	71	71	72	69	283	7,959
50T	Jimmy Green	69	71	74	69	283	7,959
50T	Robert Damron	71	72	69	71	283	7,959
55T	Glen Day	70	70	75	69	284	7,491
55T	Tom Pernice Jr.	72	70	70	72	284	7,491
55T	J.P. Hayes	70	70	67	77	284	7,491
55T	Kaname Yokoo	72	69	72	71	284	7,491
59	Duffy Waldorf	73	69	70	73	285	7,326
60	Paul Goydos	74	68	69	75	286	7,260
61	Justin Leonard	73	70	74	70	287	7,194
62T	Steve Elkington	71	70	73	74	288	6,996
62T	Robert Allenby	71	68	77	72	288	6,996
62T	Brandt Jobe	73	69	75	71	288	6,996
62T	Casey Martin	74	69	71	74	288	6,996
62T	Kazuhiko Hosokawa	72	71	74	71	288	6,996
67	Neal Lancaster	72	70	71	76	289	6,798
68T	Nick Faldo	71	70	75	74	290	6,699
68T	Jim Carter	72	70	77	71	290	6,699
70	Rory Sabbatini	68	70	79	74	291	6,600

DID NOT MAKE CUT

144	Olin Browne, Billy Mayfair, Scott Gump, Franklin Langham
145	Craig Parry, Notah Begay III, Brian Henninger, Chris DiMarco, Dennis Paulson, Esteban Toledo
146	Lee Janzen, Tom Purtzer, Mark Brooks, Joey Sindelar, Harrison Frazar
147	Tommy Armour III, Mike Hulbert, Gary Nicklaus, Carlos Franco, Joe Ozaki
148	Scott Hoch, Bruce Lietzke, Bob Tway, Edward Fryatt
149	Corey Pavin, Omar Uresti, *Hunter Haas*
150	Ben Crenshaw, Rich Beem, Matt Gogel
151	Blaine McCallister, Robert Gamez, Stephen Ames, Bradley Hughes
152	Brad Elder
74-wd	Rod Curl, Ted Tryba
75-wd	Jonathan Kaye
77-wd	Fulton Allem
79-wd	Dan Pohl

2001
May 17-20

Rank	Player	R1	R2	R3	R4	Total	Money
1	Sergio Garcia	69	69	66	63	267	$720,000
2T	Phil Mickelson	65	68	66	70	269	352,000
2T	Brian Gay	66	69	69	65	269	352,000
4	Glen Day	68	72	64	66	270	192,000
5T	Justin Leonard	69	67	70	66	272	146,000
5T	Shigeki Maruyama	72	65	65	70	272	146,000
5T	Brett Quigley	69	64	66	73	272	146,000
8T	Corey Pavin	68	64	73	68	273	116,000
8T	Rocco Mediate	72	62	69	70	273	116,000
8T	David Toms	67	70	66	70	273	116,000
11T	Vijay Singh	69	68	69	68	274	88,000
11T	Jesper Parnevik	70	69	67	68	274	88,000
11T	Per-Ulrik Johansson	69	68	68	69	274	88,000
11T	Mike Sposa	71	66	67	70	274	88,000
15T	Tom Lehman	67	68	68	72	275	64,000
15T	Jeff Sluman	71	64	69	71	275	64,000
15T	Robert Allenby	72	68	65	70	275	64,000
15T	Kirk Triplett	68	67	70	70	275	64,000
15T	Greg Chalmers	71	69	67	68	275	64,000
20T	Billy Mayfair	71	68	69	68	276	50,000
20T	Fred Funk	70	68	67	71	276	50,000
22T	Jim Furyk	65	71	69	72	277	40,000
22T	Blaine McCallister	71	64	71	71	277	40,000
22T	Scott McCarron	68	67	72	70	277	40,000
22T	Jim Carter	73	67	68	69	277	40,000
26T	Fulton Allem	68	73	67	70	278	27,800
26T	Stewart Cink	71	70	67	70	278	27,800
26T	Rich Beem	70	68	71	69	278	27,800
26T	Brent Geiberger	68	69	72	69	278	27,800
26T	Stephen Ames	68	71	66	73	278	27,800
26T	Brad Elder	70	71	67	70	278	27,800
26T	Bob Estes	68	73	64	73	278	27,800
26T	Kenny Perry	72	67	70	69	278	27,800
34T	Tom Kite	68	71	69	71	279	20,200
34T	John Cook	71	71	70	67	279	20,200
34T	Jose Coceres	70	67	70	72	279	20,200
34T	Joe Ogilvie	75	66	68	70	279	20,200
34T	Jonathan Kaye	71	65	70	73	279	20,200
34T	Geoff Ogilvy	70	70	68	71	279	20,200
40T	Hal Sutton	73	69	66	72	280	15,200
40T	Frank Nobilo	70	68	72	70	280	15,200
40T	Joey Sindelar	74	67	72	67	280	15,200
40T	Brandel Chamblee	71	66	73	70	280	15,200
40T	Chris DiMarco	71	71	66	72	280	15,200
40T	J.L. Lewis	71	67	69	73	280	15,200
46T	David Duval	69	68	73	71	281	10,880
46T	Bob Tway	75	67	66	73	281	10,880
46T	Steve Flesch	69	69	69	74	281	10,880
46T	Brandt Jobe	71	70	68	72	281	10,880
46T	Greg Kraft	69	69	71	72	281	10,880
46T	Skip Kendall	69	68	73	71	281	10,880
52T	David Frost	73	69	70	70	282	9,520
52T	Bob May	70	72	69	71	282	9,520
54T	Harrison Frazar	73	65	69	76	283	9,160
54T	Len Mattiace	74	68	70	71	283	9,160
54T	Craig Barlow	72	69	69	72	283	9,160
54T	Scott Dunlap	69	71	68	75	283	9,160
58T	Bruce Lietzke	71	71	69	73	284	8,840
58T	Mike Weir	70	71	68	75	284	8,840
58T	Robert Damron	70	71	73	70	284	8,840
58T	J.P. Hayes	73	67	68	76	284	8,840
62T	Steve Pate	70	70	69	76	285	8,520
62T	Mark Brooks	67	72	72	74	285	8,520
62T	Briny Baird	72	68	71	74	285	8,520
62T	Brian Wilson	70	70	74	71	285	8,520
66	Keith Clearwater	72	70	68	76	286	8,320
67	D. A. Weibring	69	71	72	75	287	8,240
68	Ronnie Black	69	70	74	75	288	8,160
69	Tim Herron	70	71	75	74	290	8,080
70	Tom Purtzer	70	69	73	79	291	8,000
71	Dave Stockton Jr.	70	71	77	76	294	7,920

DID NOT MAKE CUT

143	Olin Browne, Nick Price, Fred Couples, Franklin Langham, Esteban Toledo, Edward Fryatt
144	Chris Smith, Lee Janzen, Brad Faxon, Brian Watts, Chris Perry, Billy Andrade, Steve Jones, Kazuhiko Hosokawa
145	Fuzzy Zoeller, Stuart Appleby, Matt Gogel, Joe Durant, Joel Edwards
146	Duffy Waldorf, Jeff Maggert, Michael Clark II, Andrew Magee, Spike McRoy
147	Ben Crenshaw, Kaname Yokoo
148	Tom Pernice Jr., Mike Hulbert
149	Dave Stockton
150	Jerry Kelly
151	Greg Norman, Dan Pohl, Dennis Paulson, Ian Baker-Finch
152	Chris Riley, Rod Curl
153	Carl Paulson, Mark Calcavecchia
154	Hunter Haas
71-wd	Dudley Hart
74-wd	Scott Verplank
76-wd	Carlos Franco
77-wd	David Berganio Jr.
79-wd	Rory Sabbatini

2002
May 16-19

Rank	Player	R1	R2	R3	R4	Total	Money
1	Nick Price	69	65	66	67	267	$774,000
2T	David Toms	71	71	64	66	272	378,400
2T	Kenny Perry	70	66	69	67	272	378,400
4	Dudley Hart	73	65	70	65	273	206,400
5T	Davis Love III	70	70	67	67	274	163,400
5T	Phil Tataurangi	70	69	66	69	274	163,400
7	Tom Watson	68	72	66	69	275	144,050
8T	Stuart Appleby	70	71	71	64	276	120,400
8T	Esteban Toledo	67	67	72	70	276	120,400
8T	Steve Flesch	68	67	70	71	276	120,400
8T	Jonathan Byrd	73	67	68	68	276	120,400
12T	Vijay Singh	70	69	67	68	277	79,243
12T	Hal Sutton	69	68	71	69	277	79,243
12T	Olin Browne	71	66	67	70	277	79,243
12T	Frank Lickliter II	67	68	68	72	277	79,243
12T	Billy Andrade	71	64	69	71	277	79,243
12T	Joel Edwards	72	68	65	70	277	79,243
12T	Bob Tway	68	67	70	70	277	79,243
19T	Justin Leonard	70	68	69	71	278	53,965
19T	Shigeki Maruyama	72	67	69	70	278	53,965
19T	Scott Verplank	67	70	72	69	278	53,965
19T	Cameron Beckman	71	69	70	68	278	53,965
23T	Phil Mickelson	73	70	69	67	279	38,270
23T	Tom Lehman	71	67	71	70	279	38,270
23T	Peter Jacobsen	72	68	69	70	279	38,270
23T	John Huston	70	70	71	68	279	38,270
23T	Bob Estes	65	72	72	70	279	38,270
28T	Corey Pavin	68	71	69	72	280	29,240
28T	Jesper Parnevik	69	72	70	69	280	29,240
28T	Jerry Kelly	69	71	72	68	280	29,240
28T	Scott McCarron	70	70	69	71	280	29,240
28T	Chad Campbell	72	68	71	69	280	29,240
33T	Stewart Cink	72	69	69	71	281	24,295
33T	Bob Burns	68	68	72	73	281	24,295
33T	Briny Baird	71	71	70	67	281	24,295
36T	Steve Jones	67	73	70	72	282	20,694
36T	Mike Weir	71	68	73	70	282	20,694
36T	Matt Gogel	69	71	73	69	282	20,694
36T	Peter Lonard	68	70	69	75	282	20,694
40T	Steve Elkington	74	68	72	69	283	15,480
40T	Loren Roberts	70	73	67	73	283	15,480
40T	Jay Haas	69	74	72	68	283	15,480
40T	Chris DiMarco	72	71	71	69	283	15,480
40T	Mark Brooks	68	71	73	71	283	15,480
40T	Steve Lowery	67	75	72	69	283	15,480
40T	Brandt Jobe	67	72	69	75	283	15,480
40T	David Peoples	72	71	71	69	283	15,480
48T	Lee Janzen	69	72	74	69	284	10,589
48T	David Frost	72	67	73	72	284	10,589
48T	Jeff Maggert	68	74	72	70	284	10,589
48T	David Gossett	74	69	71	70	284	10,589
48T	Per-Ulrik Johansson	68	73	73	70	284	10,589
48T	Joey Sindelar	68	71	74	71	284	10,589
48T	John Rollins	70	73	69	72	284	10,589
48T	Luke Donald	73	69	69	73	284	10,589
56T	Brent Geiberger	72	68	76	69	285	9,675
56T	Carl Paulson	68	72	74	71	285	9,675
56T	Skip Kendall	68	71	74	72	285	9,675
56T	Pat Perez	72	66	74	73	285	9,675
60	Tom Pernice Jr.	72	69	72	74	287	9,460
61T	Billy Mayfair	70	73	71	74	288	9,245
61T	Brandel Chamblee	69	73	72	74	288	9,245
61T	Jose Coceres	70	68	73	77	288	9,245
61T	Ian Leggatt	70	69	74	75	288	9,245
65	Glen Day	69	67	77	77	290	9,030
66T	K.J. Choi	69	72	69	81	291	8,901
66T	Rod Pampling	72	71	73	75	291	8,901
68T	J.J. Henry	72	71	75	74	292	8,729
68T	Brian Gay	70	66	78	78	292	8,729
70T	Duffy Waldorf	71	71	74	78	294	8,557
70T	Paul Stankowski	72	69	74	79	294	8,557
72	Neal Lancaster	71	72	77	76	296	8,428

DID NOT MAKE CUT

144	Jim Furyk, Jeff Sluman, Robert Allenby, Brad Faxon, Kirk Triplett, Craig Parry, Greg Kraft, Mike Sposa, Brian Watts, Brett Quigley, Chris Riley
145	David Duval, Mark O'Meara, John Cook, Tim Herron, Craig Perks, Bob May, Greg Chalmers, Jonathan Kaye
146	Ben Crenshaw, Steve Pate, Frank Nobilo, Charles Howell III, Joe Durant, Jay Don Blake
147	J.L. Lewis, Dan Pohl, Notah Begay III, Geoff Ogilvy, Craig Stadler, Kevin Sutherland, Chris Smith
148	Fulton Allem, Jim Carter, Dennis Paulson, Len Mattiace
149	Harrison Frazar, Kaname Yokoo
150	Steve Stricker, Sergio Garcia, David Berganio Jr.
151	Rory Sabbatini
152	Heath Slocum, Mathew Goggin, Tom Kite
72-wd	Rocco Mediate
73-dq	Garrett Willis
77-wd	Keith Clearwater, Robert Damron, Fred Funk
78-wd	Rich Beem
83-wd	Rod Curl

2003
May 22-25

Rank	Player	R1	R2	R3	R4	Total	Money
1	Kenny Perry	68	64	61	68	261	$900,000
2	Justin Leonard	68	72	66	61	267	540,000
3	Jeff Sluman	68	68	67	65	268	340,000
4	Brandt Jobe	67	70	68	64	269	240,000
5T	Jim Furyk	68	65	69	68	270	175,625
5T	Hal Sutton	71	67	65	67	270	175,625
5T	Pat Bates	69	66	69	66	270	175,625
5T	Rory Sabbatini	64	70	67	69	270	175,625
9T	Fred Funk	70	67	69	66	272	130,000
9T	Harrison Frazar	69	69	66	68	272	130,000
9T	Dan Forsman	66	66	73	67	272	130,000
9T	Esteban Toledo	68	68	69	67	272	130,000
13T	Phil Mickelson	67	70	68	68	273	91,000
13T	Loren Roberts	67	69	70	67	273	91,000
13T	Stewart Cink	67	70	66	70	273	91,000
13T	Marco Dawson	68	70	71	64	273	91,000
13T	Steve Flesch	69	66	69	69	273	91,000
18T	Olin Browne	67	71	68	68	274	70,000
18T	Lee Janzen	71	67	70	66	274	70,000
18T	Jay Haas	69	70	67	68	274	70,000
21T	Nick Price	70	70	65	70	275	48,357
21T	Billy Mayfair	69	70	68	68	275	48,357
21T	Dean Wilson	71	67	69	68	275	48,357
21T	Briny Baird	70	68	68	69	275	48,357
21T	John Senden	71	70	68	66	275	48,357
21T	Tim Petrovc	68	66	72	69	275	48,357
21T	Brandel Chamblee	70	69	70	66	275	48,357
28T	Corey Pavin	68	70	69	69	276	32,536
28T	Shigeki Maruyama	70	68	70	68	276	32,536
28T	Frank Lickliter II	68	66	70	72	276	32,536
28T	Gene Sauers	69	68	70	69	276	32,536
28T	Patrick Sheehan	65	72	68	71	276	32,536
28T	Jay WIlliamson	67	67	73	69	276	32,536
28T	Carl Pettersson	71	69	68	68	276	32,536
35T	Dudley Hart	70	71	68	68	277	24,650
35T	Jesper Parnevik	66	68	73	70	277	24,650
35T	Billy Andrade	68	68	71	70	277	24,650
35T	Alex Cejka	70	70	65	72	277	24,650
35T	Bob Burns	69	70	70	68	277	24,650
40T	Kirk Triplett	69	71	70	68	278	19,500
40T	Tim Herron	71	68	69	70	278	19,500
40T	Chad Campbell	67	67	74	70	278	19,500
40T	Glen Day	67	70	75	66	278	19,500
40T	Spike McRoy	67	70	75	66	278	19,500
45T	Rocco Mediate	68	72	68	71	279	14,014
45T	Brian Gay	68	69	76	66	279	14,014
45T	Brett Quigley	67	73	68	71	279	14,014
45T	Stephen Ames	67	72	74	66	279	14,014
45T	Woody Austin	70	67	72	70	279	14,014
45T	Shaun Micheel	71	69	72	67	279	14,014
45T	J.L. Lewis	72	69	70	68	279	14,014
52T	Craig Parry	67	70	72	71	280	11,725
52T	Bob Tway	69	70	73	68	280	11,725
52T	Joe Durant	70	70	71	69	280	11,725
52T	J.P. Hayes	70	71	71	68	280	11,725
56T	Mark Calcavecchia	65	75	72	69	281	11,200
56T	Duffy Waldorf	67	70	71	73	281	11,200
56T	Brian Watts	67	71	72	71	281	11,200
56T	Greg Chalmers	68	71	72	70	281	11,200
56T	Mike Sposa	67	69	74	71	281	11,200
61	Len Mattiace	69	69	75	69	282	10,900
62T	David Frost	69	71	75	68	283	10,650
62T	Scott Verplank	69	69	71	74	283	10,650
62T	Brian Henninger	70	69	71	73	283	10,650
62T	Brenden Pappas	70	68	74	71	283	10,650
66T	Peter Jacobsen	72	68	71	73	284	10,200
66T	Joey Sindelar	69	71	71	73	284	10,200
66T	Steve Elkington	72	68	70	74	284	10,200
66T	Rich Beem	68	69	76	71	284	10,200
66T	Jonathan Kaye	73	67	72	72	284	10,200
71T	Brent Geiberger	71	70	72	72	285	9,800
71T	Luke Donald	68	71	73	73	285	9,800
71T	Cliff Kresge	68	70	73	74	285	9,800
74T	Jeff Brehaut	68	70	74	74	286	9,550
74T	Tom Byrum	70	71	72	73	286	9,550
76	Fulton Allem	75	66	74	78	293	9,400

DID NOT MAKE CUT

142	Tom Lehman, Tom Pernice Jr., J.J. Henry, Rod Pampling, Paul Goydos, Ian Leggatt, Cameron Beckman, Jonathan Byrd
143	Sergio Garcia, Stuart Appleby, Skip Kendall, David Peoples John Rollins, Matt Gogel, Peter Lonard, Chris Smith
144	Scott Simpson, Robert Gamez, Per-Ulrik Johansson
145	Carl Paulson, Tim Clark, Heath Slocum, Arron Oberholser, Annika Sorenstam
146	Mark Brooks, Joel Edwards, Aaron Barber
147	Bob Estes, Geoff Ogilvy, Dan Pohl
148	Kevin Sutherland, James McLean
150	Craig Perks, Scott McCarron
154	Rod Curl
wd	Pat Perez, David Toms
dq	Keith Clearwater

2004
May 19-23

Rank	Player	R1	R2	R3	R4	Total	Money
1	Steve Flesch	66	69	67	67	269	$954,000
2	Chad Campbell	70	71	61	68	270	572,400
3	Stephen Ames	70	69	68	64	271	360,400
4	Craig Perks	64	71	70	68	273	254,400
5T	Skip Kendall	68	71	68	67	274	186,162
5T	Robert Gamez	71	64	71	68	274	186,162
5T	Bo Van Pelt	68	69	72	65	274	186,162
5T	Tim Petrovic	66	71	69	68	274	186,162
9T	Jeff Maggert	66	69	73	67	275	143,100
9T	Mark Brooks	71	68	67	69	275	143,100
9T	John Senden	66	74	70	65	275	143,100
12T	Kenny Perry	67	71	70	68	276	116,600
12T	Loren Roberts	68	70	71	67	276	116,600
14T	Justin Leonard	70	64	72	71	277	72,433
14T	Stewart Cink	66	70	71	70	277	72,433
14T	Lee Janzen	70	66	71	70	277	72,433
14T	Jesper Parnevik	65	72	68	72	277	72,433
14T	Kirk Triplett	69	69	71	68	277	72,433
14T	Chris Riley	67	71	69	70	277	72,433
14T	Zach Johnson	71	65	68	73	277	72,433
14T	Brian Gay	70	67	65	75	277	72,433
14T	Tom Byrum	68	69	71	69	277	72,433
14T	Tim Clark	68	70	69	70	277	72,433
14T	Joe Ogilvie	71	70	68	68	277	72,433
14T	Brian Bateman	69	69	68	71	277	72,433
26	Fred Funk	70	72	65	71	278	42,400
27T	Bob Tway	70	69	68	72	279	38,425
27T	J.L. Lewis	68	66	75	70	279	38,425
27T	Peter Lonard	71	72	67	70	279	38,425
27T	Stephen Leaney	70	68	71	70	279	38,425
31T	Corey Pavin	70	70	72	68	280	32,536
31T	Dennis Paulson	67	70	71	72	280	32,536
31T	Rory Sabbatini	72	69	67	72	280	32,536
31T	Glen Day	72	71	67	70	280	32,536
35T	Phil Mickelson	71	66	70	74	281	25,572
35T	Sergio Garcia	72	67	73	69	281	25,572
35T	Davis Love III	74	67	72	68	281	25,572
35T	Scott Verplank	72	68	67	74	281	25,572
35T	Joe Durant	70	73	69	69	281	25,572
35T	Brett Quigley	70	68	68	75	281	25,572
41T	Hal Sutton	71	67	73	71	282	20,670
41T	Joey Sindelar	71	69	72	70	282	20,670
41T	Dudley Hart	67	70	75	66	282	20,670
44T	David Toms	72	70	68	73	283	16,024
44T	Chris DiMarco	69	71	72	71	283	16,024
44T	Todd Hamilton	72	71	70	70	283	16,024
44T	Rod Pampling	72	71	69	71	283	16,024
44T	Frank Lickliter II	68	70	68	77	283	16,024
44T	Tommy Armour III	69	74	71	69	283	16,024
50T	Brad Faxon	70	68	75	71	284	12,905
50T	Aaron Baddeley	68	71	74	71	284	12,905
50T	Kent Jones	70	69	73	72	284	12,905
50T	Briny Baird	71	69	71	73	284	12,905
54T	Robert Allenby	67	76	73	69	285	11,978
54T	Steve Elkington	71	71	73	70	285	11,978
54T	Rocco Mediate	72	71	71	71	285	11,978
54T	Mathias Gronberg	70	74	71	66	285	11,978
54T	Matt Gogel	70	73	76	66	285	11,978
54T	Neal Lancaster	73	70	70	72	285	11,978
54T	Carl Petterson	67	74	73	71	285	11,978
61T	Mike Weir	68	73	71	74	286	11,501
61T	Scott Hend	69	74	72	71	286	11,501
63T	Tim Herron	69	72	72	74	287	11,130
63T	Luke Donald	69	74	73	71	287	11,130
63T	Geoff Ogilvy	74	69	69	75	287	11,130
63T	Hunter Mahan	70	71	71	75	287	11,130
63T	Patrick Sheehan	71	70	69	77	287	11,130
68T	Jeff Sluman	72	70	74	72	288	10,706
68T	Dan Pohl	71	72	72	73	288	10,706
68T	Steve Lowery	69	74	75	70	288	10,706
71T	Len Mattiace	71	71	74	73	289	10,441
71T	Brenden Pappas	73	70	72	74	289	10,441
73	Mark Calcavecchia	72	68	75	75	290	10,282
74	Bob Estes	68	74	72	77	291	10,176

DID NOT MAKE CUT

144	Pat Bates, J.J. Henry, Stuart Appleby, Olin Browne, Fulton Allem, Tripp Isenhour, D.J. Brigman, Dan Forsman, Heath Slocum, Woody Austin
145	Shigeki Maruyama, Bob Burns, John Rollins, John Huston, Jonathan Kaye, Ted Purdy, Harrison Frazar, Danny Ellis
146	Billy Mayfair, Brent Geiberger, Jonathan Byrd, Ryan Palmer
147	Duffy Waldorf
148	Keith Clearwater, Lucas Glover,
149	Esteban Toledo, Hank Kuehne, Jay Williamson
150	David Frost, Craig Bowden
151	Dean Wilson, Mark Hensby
153	Notah Begay III
154	Bill Glasson
160	Rod Curl
71-wd	Rich Beem
74-wd	Hidemichi Tanaka
75-wd	John Riegger
77-wd	Ben Crane
wd	Kevin Na

*Names in italics designate amateurs.

2005
May 16-21

Rank	Player	R1	R2	R3	R4	Total	Money
1	Kenny Perry	65	63	64	69	261	$1,008,000
2	Billy Mayfair	67	66	66	69	268	604,800
3T	David Toms	69	66	68	66	269	291,200
3T	Joe Durant	71	63	69	66	269	291,200
3T	Peter Lonard	69	66	65	69	269	291,200
6T	Bernhard Langer	68	69	66	67	270	163,600
6T	Aaron Baddeley	69	66	67	68	270	163,600
6T	Scott Hend	68	67	68	67	270	163,600
6T	Brandt Jobe	65	69	67	69	270	163,600
6T	Rod Pampling	66	68	69	67	270	163,600
6T	Tim Petrovic	71	69	66	64	270	163,600
6T	Rory Sabbatini	67	69	68	66	270	163,600
13T	Ted Purdy	66	65	71	69	271	108,266
13T	Justin Rose	68	68	71	64	271	108,266
13T	Steve Stricker	68	65	66	72	271	108,266
16	Fredrik Jacobson	68	69	65	70	272	95,200
17T	Ben Crane	69	66	70	68	273	81,200
17T	Kevin Na	65	71	71	66	273	81,200
17T	Kirk Triplett	66	66	72	69	273	81,200
17T	Bo Van Pelt	70	67	68	68	273	81,200
21T	K.J. Choi	69	66	70	69	274	58,240
21T	Tim Clark	71	64	69	70	274	58,240
21T	Arron Oberholser	68	67	70	69	274	58,240
21T	Tom Purtzer	71	70	69	64	274	58,240
21T	Bob Tway	67	69	69	69	274	58,240
26T	Phil Mickelson	71	69	68	67	275	40,600
26T	Jim Furyk	69	68	67	71	275	40,600
26T	Corey Pavin	70	66	68	71	275	40,600
26T	Stuart Appleby	68	69	71	67	275	40,600
26T	Zach Johnson	71	68	70	66	275	40,600
26T	Justin Leonard	67	69	69	70	275	40,600
32T	Shigeki Maruyama	69	70	69	68	276	30,987
32T	Loren Roberts	68	67	73	68	276	30,987
32T	Heath Slocum	68	72	69	67	276	30,987
32T	Scott Verplank	71	69	68	68	276	30,987
32T	Jeff Maggert	73	66	67	70	276	30,987
32T	Jeff Sluman	68	70	68	70	276	30,987
38T	Stephen Ames	73	68	68	68	277	23,520
38T	Arjun Atwal	70	65	69	73	277	23,520
38T	Brian Bateman	64	72	74	67	277	23,520
38T	Geoff Ogilvy	71	67	64	75	277	23,520
38T	John Senden	70	68	66	73	277	23,520
38T	D.J. Trahan	64	67	71	75	277	23,520
44T	Tom Lehman	72	68	70	68	278	16,528
44T	Harrison Frazar	66	70	70	72	278	16,528
44T	Hunter Haas	73	67	67	71	278	16,528
44T	Steve Jones	69	68	71	70	278	16,528
44T	Stephen Leaney	66	69	71	72	278	16,528
44T	Hunter Mahan	72	67	70	69	278	16,528
44T	Pat Perez	71	67	69	71	278	16,528
51T	Mark Brooks	71	67	71	70	279	13,179
51T	Jonathan Byrd	67	71	73	68	279	13,179
51T	Joe Ogilvie	71	68	74	66	279	13,179
51T	Jesper Parnevik	69	72	71	67	279	13,179
51T	Jason Allred	69	72	67	71	279	13,179
51T	Skip Kendall	67	70	72	70	279	13,179
57T	Bart Bryant	70	71	67	72	280	12,432
57T	Daniel Chopra	73	67	71	69	280	12,432
57T	Stewart Cink	72	67	69	72	280	12,432
57T	Brian Gay	71	70	70	69	280	12,432
57T	Hank Kuehne	71	70	71	68	280	12,432
62T	Bob Estes	71	68	71	71	281	11,984
62T	Jonathan Kaye	73	67	72	69	281	11,984
62T	Kevin Sutherland	70	69	70	72	281	11,984
65T	Briny Baird	69	65	75	73	282	11,704
65T	Craig Perks	73	67	72	70	282	11,704
67T	Fred Funk	71	69	73	70	283	11,480
67T	Andrew Magee	70	71	66	76	283	11,480
69T	Robert Gamez	71	70	71	72	284	11,256
69T	Ryan Palmer	70	70	72	72	284	11,256
71T	Frank Lickliter II	70	70	73	72	285	11,032
71T	Patrick Sheehan	62	72	75	76	285	11,032

DID NOT MAKE CUT

142	Fulton Allem, Tommy Armour III, Tom Byrum, Chris DiMarco, Steve Elkington, Sergio Garcia, Lucas Glover, Mathias Gronberg, Davis Love III, Joey Sindelar, Hal Sutton, Nick Watney
143	Olin Browne, Glen Day, Tim Herron, Peter Jacobsen, J.L. Lewis, Carl Pettersson, Brett Quigley, Duffy Waldorf, Charles Warren, Jay Williamson
144	Woody Austin, Rich Beem, Alex Cejka, Keith Clearwater, J.J. Henry, Casey Wittenberg
145	Chad Campbell, Todd Hamilton, D.A. Points
146	Andre Stolz
147	Shaun Micheel, Kevin Stadler, Mike Weir
150	Steve Flesch, Rocco Mediate
151	Joey Snyder III
160	David Frost
161	Rod Curl
72-wd	Vaughn Taylor
74-wd	Dudley Hart

GIVING BACK

GOLF AND CHARITY GO TOGETHER

The sport and business of golf are unique in many ways. That's why they are so successful, especially in today's world. One of its unique attributes is golf's connection and commitment to charity. More than any other sport or sports organization, professional golf ties itself more directly to charity and with significantly greater impact in terms of dollars and support.

In late 2005, the PGA Tour tournaments collectively reached the astonishing level of $1 billion generated for charity in the last 70 years. Projections indicate another billion dollars for charity could be achieved in just 10 more years. Phenomenal.

And what about golf and charity outside the PGA Tour? Could that be another billion dollars? Think of all the things golfers, professional or otherwise, do for charity on their own. Think of all the fund-raising golf tournaments held throughout the year in cities and towns across America. Golfers are so passionate about their sport that they love to use it to help the less fortunate and better their communities.

Colonial Country Club and its annual tournament's connection to charity go all the way back to its beginning more than 60 years ago. When club founder Marvin Leonard successfully enticed the USGA to bring the 1941 U.S. Open to Fort Worth, he knew he needed a significant community organization for a partner. That partner was the Fort Worth Golf Association, which not only helped stage the event, but also received a portion of the revenue in order to carry forward its mission of growing the game and teaching its values. That few thousand dollars for one organization in 1941 stands in contrast to the $1.6 million generated by Colonial in 2005 for six dozen charities.

For more perspective, remember that back in the 1940s and 1950s, the Colonial National Invitation was lucky if it broke even on expenses. In the past 20 years, PGA Tour events have become multi-million dollar affairs. This has allowed tournaments to start touching more and more organizations with ever-increasing dollars. Colonial has generated more than $13 million for over 125 organizations in the last 10 years.

"We are very proud to give back to the Fort Worth community through so many terrific organizations," said 2006 Colonial President Bill Bowers, who has also served as Tournament Chairman. "This is a very giving community, and we are pleased to be such a big part of it each year."

Since 1996, the event's primary beneficiary has been Cook Children's Medical Center, helping ensure that no child is denied medical care because of inability to pay. Cook philanthropy partner Jewel Charity, a well-known organization in Fort Worth, has helped Colonial and Cook make this happen.

"Colonial has provided more than five million dollars to Cook Children's Medical Center during the last decade. This amazing generosity has allowed many sick and needy children to receive much-needed medical care," shared Russell K. Tolman, president and chief executive officer of Cook Children's Health Care System. "Just as great legends have been made on the golf course, today's winning partnership between Colonial and Cook Children's follows the vision of great Fort Worth philanthropists by supporting high-quality pediatric care for low-income families."

A pre-natal screening for Kelly Molinaro turned into a referral to a pediatric cardiologist and the Cook Children's Heart Center. Her unborn son, Nicholas, had a congenital anomaly, Tetralogy of Fallot, a combination of four heart defects. The anomaly includes pulmonary stenosis, a narrowing of the pulmonary artery; plus a displaced aorta, enlarged ventricle and a hole in the septum, the wall that separates the heart's two chambers. Despite its intimidating and complex definition, Tetralogy of Fallot can be repaired.

The Molinaro family, in consultation with pediatric cardiologists, cardiothoracic surgeons and Heart Center staff, made plans for Nicholas' surgery and follow-up care before he was born. Shortly after birth, Nicholas underwent surgery, and was hospitalized in the medical center's intensive care unit.

Now, almost two years later, the toddler is a busy little boy whose mom is happy to note that "he can do anything his heart desires."

Colonial provides important support to dozens of other charities each year in addition to Cook. Furthermore, many of Colonial's members volunteer their own time and money for these organizations, and serve as leaders on their Boards.

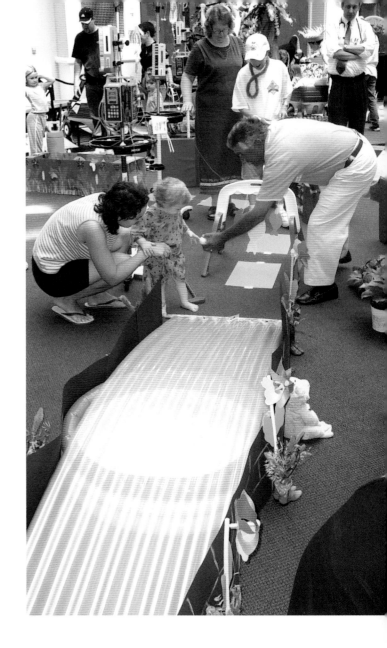

More important than the dollar amounts tallied for charity is the work that is being done, and the lives that are changed. The donations focus on youth and support a variety of programs, including camp scholarships for disabled, special needs or low-income children, residency programs/services for abused, neglected and at-risk children, cultural programs/field trips for underserved students, college scholarships, educational mentoring programs, medical diagnostic and treatment services for disabled and low-income children, after-school programs, support services for homeless families, and more.

Many recipients of the tournament's largesse are organizations that are widely known in the community, but some are not as high profile. Big Brothers and Big Sisters, Boys & Girls Clubs, Lena Pope Home, Edna Gladney Home, Camp Fire, Junior

Achievement, Texas Boys Choir, Texas Girls Choir, and Ronald McDonald House all have received Colonial support. So have Child Advocates of Tarrant County, The Women's Shelter, All Church Home for Children, H.O.P.E Farm Inc., Camp Summit, Happy Hill Farm, Union Gospel Mission, Youth Orchestra of Greater Fort Worth, and many, many more.

"Support from Colonial has been incredibly important to Buckner Children and Family Services and our See the Difference program," noted Development Officer Jill Lewis. "It has helped validate the relatively new program, which empowers children and youth to make healthy choices and build a solid foundation for success in life."

Through Tarrant County Cancer Care Services, Colonial helps support families with a child battling cancer. With Cornerstone Assistance Network, poor families move from dependence on society to being independent, contributing members of society.

H.O.P.E. Farm targets inner-city youth from single-parent homes who lack a positive male influence in their lives. Founded by former police officer Gary Randle and public safety officer Noble Crawford, H.O.P.E. (Helping Other People Excel) provides values training, academic help, and a program of accountability every day after school and all day in the summer.

"A young boy named Johnny had been kept in a closet and starved by his own father," Randle explained. "He came to H.O.P.E. at age four. His self-esteem and self-worth began to heighten through consistent love, structure and mutual concern. When eventually adopted, he changed his name to Richard as part of a disassociation with his former life.

"Richard is thriving, having gone from a starved child to an A-B average student with no discipline problems in school," Randle continued. "With Colonial's help, we can continue to grow at-risk boys like Richard into tomorrow's leaders."

Child Advocates (CATC), provides a volunteer, court-appointed advocate to help abused and at-risk children who have been removed from their homes. These dedicated volunteers stay personally involved with the children and their cases until they finally have a safe and permanent home. What the volunteers see is heart-breaking. What they do is life-changing.

CATC Executive Director Nancy Fisher relates this story of seven-year-old Sarah: "She was in her fourth foster placement in the span of three weeks. When it was time to get ready for bed, her new foster mom asked what school she attended so she could make plans for taking her in the morning. Sarah's eyes welled up with tears, because she could only remember her teacher's name and her best friend, but not the name of her school.

She then remembered meeting a nice lady only the day before who had given her a business card and told her to call if she ever was scared, lonely or confused. It was her volunteer advocate. The foster mom called Sarah's advocate, who happily told her that she had been at Sarah's school the day before, meeting with her teach and counselor. In Sarah's ever-changing world, being able to go back to the only normalcy she knew at the time was astronomical!"

Lee Ann Embry, Director of Community Resources for the Presbyterian Night Shelter pointed out, "Because of Colonial's support, we are able to feed and care for 35 families on any given night, including mothers and babies who have been turned a way from every shelter in the Metroplex, lost hope and ended up on the streets of Fort Worth."

Program Director Becca Glaser of Reata Rehabilitation utilizes Colonial support in a summer camp for kids with autism. "These children participated in activities interacting with horses and other farm animals. This is a highly therapeutic experience for children who have significant difficulty interacting with other humans. The connections that were made between the children and horses were amazing."

Among all these many causes and missions, of course, Colonial supports junior golf through The First Tee, North Texas Junior Golf Foundation, and others. These young people will grow up to be the golfers of tomorrow, and they will run the golf tournaments and fund-raisers of tomorrow. And they will continue the great tradition of giving back to their communities.

It is the legacy of Marvin Leonard. It is the legacy of golf.

Fort Worth Sister Cities uses Colonial support to operate its International Leadership Academy, designed to help youth become global leaders. The program brings youngsters from Fort Worth and seven sister cities together under one roof to discuss the world's issues and conflicts from a variety of perspectives and cultures.

Lena Pope founded her home primarily as an orphanage 75 years ago. This home now serves 20,000 youth and families with therapeutic foster care, alternative education, counseling services and family preservation programs. "Colonial has been a longtime supporter and friend of Lena Pope Home," observed Associate Director of Development Angie Gofredo. "This funding has helped us create a future of hope for children and families."

CHARITIES RECEIVING DONATIONS IN THE LAST 15 YEARS

All Church Home for Children
Alliance for Children
American Cancer Society
American Heart Association
Arlington Pregnancy Center
American Red Cross
Ballet Concerto
Bart Granger Memorial Fund
Bass Performance Hall
Bentgrass Research Inc.
Big Brothers & Sisters of Tarrant County
Boys & Girls Clubs of Fort Worth
Boy Scouts of America
Bobby Bragan Youth Foundation
Brooks House Fndtn./Teen Crisis Center
Buckner Children and Family Services
Byron Nelson Scholarship Fund (Abilene Christian Univ.)
Camp Carter YMCA
Camp Fire USA First Texas Council
Camp Sanguinity
Camp Summit
Casa Manana
Celebration Shop
Child Advocates of Tarrant County
Child Study Center
Children's Closet
Children's Medical Center of Dallas
Christ's Haven for Children
Clayton Child Care
Communities in Schools
Community Foundation of North Texas
Cook Children's Medical Center
Cornerstone Assistance Network
Crime Prevention Resource Center
Ekklesia Christian School
Epilepsy Assoc. of Tarrant County
EXPANCO
Fellowship of Christian Athletes
First Orlando Foundation (Payne Stewart)
First Tee of Fort Worth
Fort Worth Hebrew Day School
Fort Worth Youth Golf Association
Fort Worth Museum of Science & History
Fort Worth Opera Association
Fort Worth Sister Cities International
Fort Worth Streams & Valleys
Fort Worth Symphony Orchestra
Raymond Gafford Scholarship Fund
Gill Children's Services
Girl Scout Council
Gladney Center for Adoption
Goodfellow Fund
Goodrich Center for the Deaf
Goodwill Industries
Habitat for Humanity
Happy Hill Farm
Harris Methodist Health Foundation
Hill School
Historic Fort Worth
H.O.P.E. Farm Inc.
I Have a Dream Foundation
Jim Bob Norman Scholarship Fund
Junior Achievement

Kids Who Care
KinderFrog School - TCU
The Learning Center of North Texas
Lena Pope Home
Liberation Community Inc.
Lighthouse for the Blind
Log Cabin Village
Meals on Wheels
Mental Health Connection of Tarrant County
Mental Health Housing Development Corp.
Mercy Med+Flight
National Jewish Medical Center
National Multiple Sclerosis Society
North TX Golf Course Superintendents Assoc.
North Texas PGA
The Parenting Center
Performing Arts Fort Worth – Children's Fund
Performing Arts High School
Gary Player Foundation
Playgrounds Unlimited
Presbyterian Night Shelter
Prevent Blindness Texas
Roaring Lambs Junior Golf Academy
Ronald McDonald House
Salesmanship Club of Dallas
Salvation Army
Schola Cantorum
Score A Goal in the Classroom
Sickle Cell Foundation
SIDS Alliance of North Texas
Southwestern Exposition & Livestock Show
Special Olympics Texas
Spirit of Christmas
Susan G. Komen Breast Cancer Foundation
Tarrant Area Food Bank
Tarrant Council Alcoholism & Drug Abuse
Tarrant County Cancer Care Services
Tarrant County Challenge/Because We Care
Tarrant County Interfaith AIDS Network
Tarrant County MHMR
El Tesoro de Vida
Texas Boys' Choir
Texas Christian University
Texas Girls' Choir
Texas Golden Gloves
Texas Golf Hall of Fame
Texas Trail of Fame
Texas Wesleyan University
Union Gospel Mission
United Cerebral Palsy of Tarrant County
United Community Centers
United Negro College Fund
United Way of Tarrant County
Volunteers of America
The WARM Place
Wings of Hope Equitherapy
Women's Center of Tarrant County
Women's Haven of Tarrant County
The Women's Shelter
World Golf Foundation
YMCA of Metropolitan Fort Worth
YWCA Child Care Center
YoungLife Urban
Youth Orchestra of Greater Fort Worth

The above organizations have received direct donations from the tournament. Numerous other organizations benefit annually from the tournament through contributions related to services provided, such as staffing concessions stands, etc.

COLONIAL VOLUNTEERS
LABOR, LAUGHTER, AND LOVE

I t brings to mind famous pairs like Tracy and Hepburn, Newman and Woodward, Bogie and Bacall.

It's a bond. A deep bond.

It's the passionate relationship between Colonial and its golf tournament volunteers, many of whose tenure spans four decades and, in some cases, generations within the same family. Some are members of Colonial Country Club; many are not.

Staying with the Tinseltown allusions, it also has the scale of a Cecil B. DeMille epic. The corps of volunteers that has conducted Colonial's annual PGA Tour event for 60 years encompasses a cast of thousands, individuals linked by a common cause.

ABOVE:
Volunteers are essential to Colonial's PGA Tour event, making up four dozen committees. Some are very visible on-course, while others are just as important behind the scenes.
FACING PAGE:
Volunteers usually work in well-trained and invaluable teams.

Whereas the inaugural Colonial NIT in 1946 was overseen by a three-man tournament committee -- Marvin Leonard, Johnny Ballard and F.M. "Max" Highfill, the latter serving as chairman -- the organizational chart for the 2006 Bank of America Colonial lists forty-one separate committees. Those committees operate within six general categories: Sponsors, Players, Operations, Special Events, Administration, and Advisory. It takes about 1,000 volunteers total to stage the event each year.

And whereas ramping up for the first few iterations of the Colonial NIT might conceivably have been accomplished over several lunch or dinner meetings, today's tournament requires year-round planning and execution. No sooner does a new Colonial champion slip on the stylish Stewart plaid sports jacket, and pose for cameramen with the Leonard Trophy, than gears begin grinding and wheels are set in motion toward another Sunday afternoon 365 days out.

Benefits derived from serving on the tournament committee are numerous and varied, among them forming lasting friendships, maintaining Colonial's long-established standards of excellence and having an opportunity to interact with golf celebrities, some of whom become more than mere casual acquaintances.

Then there's the not-insignificant matter of providing tangible benefits to the citizens of Fort Worth through worldwide exposure and charitable donations. Notes Elliott Garsek, the current tournament chairman, "The work we do is not only beneficial to Colonial but to our community, and to numerous worthy charitable organizations. Specifically, as a result of our tournament, we have been able to provide charity funding in excess of $13 million over the last 10 years."

Some Colonial volunteers have worked the tournament since those bygone days when the elite Colonial field included five-time NIT champion Ben Hogan. Dick McHargue, with 46 years of service, heads the active seniority list. Juanita Waddell (41 years) and O.W. Hildebrand, Jr. (40) follow, while both Phil Thomas (39) and Henry J. Britt (38) are closing in on a major milestone. The big four-oh.

To recognize contributions of its long-term tournament volunteers, Colonial in 1986 created an honorary committee, the Pride of the Plaid. Its initial inductees included tournament pioneers -- Marvin Leonard, Max Highfill, S.M. "Bing" Bingham, Johnny Ballard, Jim Bryon, Allen Connor, Ray Finley, Jim Fuller, Berl Godfrey, Curtis Thomas, and Al Welsh. All former tournament chairmen are automatically inducted.

Since 1987, an additional three dozen men and women have been inducted into this "Hall of Fame" of Colonial volunteers. "It's a big honor," said Donna Thomason, who was inducted in 1996 and whose tenure with the Scoring Committee spanned 40 years. "It's big because everyone who is a member did their job very well, and they did it for a long time."

F. M. "Max" Highfill (1946-51)

S. M. "Bing" Bingham (1952-63)

Frank Rogers (1964-66, 1969-70)

Foist Motheral (1967-68)

The Colonial Tournament Committee poses with 2005 champion Kenny Perry in the traditional "Toast to the Champion" on Sunday evening.

Echoed Jim Hunt, a 1998 Pride of the Plaid inductee who has served on the Caddies Committee for 30 years, "It means a lot because there are not that many people who have been inducted, and there are not going to be that many more. The best reward, though, has been being involved with so many great people."

Floyd Wade became a volunteer in 1971. During the next two decades, Wade chaired several committees before ascending to Tournament Chairman in the mid-1990s. "I got to know more people at the club in the first six months that I worked on the golf tournament than in the previous four years of my membership," he said. "Once I started going to the meetings, I immediately wanted to be involved as much as I possibly could. The tournament gets to be part of you."

Bill Bowers, currently Colonial's president and the tournament chairman from 1989-91, during which time Southwestern Bell became the first title sponsor, worked on the Parking Committee in the early 1960s, while attending TCU. After joining Colonial roughly a decade later, Bowers became a tournament volunteer.

| Byron L. "Pete" Davis (1971-73) | Joe Cauker (1974-76) | William W. Spears (1977-79) | Rodney Johnston (1980-82) |

Paul D. Cato, Jr. (1983-85)

H. Wallace Schmuck (1986-88)

Bill Bowers (1989-91)

M. C. Hamilton, Jr. (1992-93)

Floyd R. Wade (1994-96)

Sam R. Day (1997)

Phil Thomas (1998-2001)

Dee Finley (2002-04)

Elliott S. Garsek (2005 - present)

once becoming a club member," he said. "The satisfaction you get from volunteering is to be part of a successful team, where individuals from all walks of life, and from not only our local community, but from around the country, come together to make the week of Colonial special for so many."

While Colonial's recent tournament chairmen have been a mix of lawyers, dentists, insurance executives, and small business owners, and while some earned their stripes in tournament Sales or Operations or Player Relations, there's no one specific path to the top of the organization chart. "The essential attribute for a tournament chairman is to love this city and this club," said Dee Finley, an attorney who served in that capacity from 2002-04. "It certainly meant a lot to me that we were able to return significant dollars to our community and support some 70 charities, large and small. They are very appreciative, and we are blessed to be able to do that."

Charity is just one reason Colonial volunteers return so enthusiastically to their duty stations. (Keep in mind that "volunteer" comes from the French word voluntaire, which refers to someone who willingly puts in long hours and hard work without compensation. It's sort of like indentured servitude, only with a better collection of polo shirts.) Or as Joe Cauker, tournament chairman from 1974-76, noted: "I went to my first tournament meeting at lunch and got out of it after 6 o'clock. If I hadn't had such a good and forgiving business partner, I never could have done the job."

Another perk for volunteers is getting to interact with golf's immortals. Floyd Henk, for example, was asked several years back as a marshal to escort Byron and Peggy Nelson to the 8th green. "They wanted to see the golfers," Henk said. "I spent over a memorable hour with them until the last group came through." And volunteer marshal Doug Attaway was walking between the fourth fairway and driving range when Arnold Palmer approached him. "He came up and said how much he thought of all the volunteers and thanked me for being one," Attaway said.

Like Nelson and Palmer, the late Payne Stewart was a fan favorite in Fort Worth. Platt Allen III, during his tenure with the Parking Committee, enjoyed interacting with Stewart and other players at the end of the day. "We would look forward to seeing and visiting with the players after their rounds, while they waited for their cars," Allen said. "Payne was a popular player and attracted a lot of attention. He would sit in a folding chair with his ankles crossed and talk to anyone that came by. One day a young boy walked up and asked for Payne's autograph. Payne signed his hat but the boy looked disappointed. Payne asked what was the matter, and the boy replied, `I thought you were Peter Jacobsen.' Payne laughed, and gave the boy his hat. He said, `Peter will be out in a minute. Get him to sign this one.'"

One cherished Payne Stewart autograph belongs to Taylor Burnette, the 10-year-old grandson of long-time volunteer Bill Lonon. "Taylor was only five months old when my wife, Verne, and I took him to the tournament," Lonon recalled. "Verne purchased a Colonial cap from the pro shop as a remembrance of his first professional golf tournament. She wanted to get autographs, which was difficult in the crowds with baby and stroller. I was marshaling the tournament. When I finished my Saturday round and joined them, I could see the disappointment of no autographs.

"I took the cap and went to the practice green. One pro was just beginning to practice. I asked him if he would sign my grandson's cap. He said, `Sure, be glad to.' Payne Stewart signed his name across the bill of the cap very legibly. It was, and still is, the only autograph on Taylor's cap. What a thrill to have that keepsake."

FOND MEMORIES

Many memories that tournament volunteers treasure most have a humorous twist. Bill Serrault, a club member and 35-year volunteer whose stellar work on the sales committee has earned him top-producer recognition, recalls being paired in the pro-am with Lionel Hebert, who informed Serrault he was teeing the ball too high. Serrault heeded Hebert's advice and faithfully spent the next 12 months teeing his ball lower.

Serrault's pro-am partner the following year turned out to be none other than Jack Nicklaus. After observing his partner

TOP:
Volunteer marshals provide important help with gallery control.
BOTTOM:
Volunteers on the SHOTLink Committee support the PGA Tour statistics program and television broadcast by recording every shot by every player.

for several holes, Nicklaus offered Serrault some constructive criticism: "You would hit your driver better if you teed the ball higher."

Marshal James Archer, with 36 years of tournament service, once was working the 18th green when a paddling of ducks decided to take a stroll on the putting surface just as players in the fairway prepared to hit their approach shots. "While the golfers waited, I walked on to the green to chase the ducks back into the lake," he recalled. "The crowd was laughing and rooting for the ducks. I was yelling `Quack, quack, quack' at the ducks and getting closer to them. As I did so, the ducks turned on me and chased me off the green! The crowd loved it."

Archer's memories as a marshal include being thwarted by Gary Player and Dave Stockton while trying to quench his thirst. "Player and Stockton had just teed off on number 10 and were walking toward their balls," Archer noted. "It was extremely hot that year, and I ran over to a lemonade stand on the side of the 10th fairway and bought a drink. I had just returned to the inside of the ropes when Gary said, `Marshal, could you please get me lemonade?' I walked over to him and handed him my drink. He thanked me and at that moment Dave said, `Are you playing favorites? Where is my lemonade?' I said, `Of course not. I'll be right back.' So I ran all the way back to the drink stand and got Dave's lemonade. I ran back and gave it to him. By this time, I was hot and exhausted. I think they were appreciative, but I never got my lemonade."

Merlene Niedermayer, another 30-year volunteer, was working the 11th green when Fuzzy Zoeller's approach shot landed on the fringe, right next to her. "He was not playing very well," she recalls. "Fuzzy handed me his putter and said to the crowd, `She can probably do better than I am doing.' My husband [Jim] was also marshaling that day and was watching from across the green as I pretended to address Fuzzy's ball. Jim was thinking I was going to hit the ball -- he about died. Ever since then, Jim has referred to Fuzzy as my "boyfriend."

Zoeller, the 1981 Colonial champion, nearly won a second title in 1983, but ultimately lost to Jim Colbert in a tournament record six-hole playoff. Volunteer Jim "Corky" Dawson still chuckles at the memory of overhearing Zoeller say to Colbert on the 16th tee: "Hurry up and hit your ball. I don't want to miss 60 Minutes."

Sam Day, tournament chairman in 1997, recalls that Colbert's arduous victory in 1983 launched a new and lasting tradition. "Colbert said right after the trophy presentation, `I don't want this to end, I'm having too much fun. Can I buy everybody here a drink?' At that time of day, late on Sunday after a long week, everyone was ready to pack up and get home. But while Colbert was talking to the media, we quickly set up in the ballroom. Then he came down and joined us. He made a toast to the tournament committee, and we toasted him. It was something special that has been carried forward."

Another enduring Colonial tradition from the same era, a quail breakfast on Thursday morning immediately preceding tournament play, evolved from parties M.C. Hamilton, tournament chairman in 1992-93, hosted at his home. "M.C. liked to entertain his friends from Abilene, people associated with the LaJet Classic (later Southwest Classic), which back then was another event on the PGA Tour," explained Dr. Wally Schmuck, Colonial chairman from 1986-88. "Then M.C. began inviting members of the tournament committee and sponsors. It finally became be so big that M.C. said he was sorry, but he just couldn't do it any more. The solution was to move the Quail Breakfast over to the club, which we did."

UNFORGETTABLE MOMENTS

Volunteer David Richardson was serving on the communications team when he witnessed one of the most talked-about incidents in tournament history. "I was walking with Ian Baker-Finch's group the year he hit his tee shot short on the par-3 13th hole," Richardson recalled. "The ball was lying in about one inch of water. Baker-Finch removed his shoes and socks and very gracefully removed his trousers. He played the ball onto the green, then redressed. The gallery went wild. For the remainder of the round, the ladies were shouting at him `Hit it in the water.'"

Baker-Finch figured in another amusing anecdote that Bill Bowers shared: "My first year as chairman [1989], we extended Ian a sponsor's exemption. He was playing his first year in the United States. On Saturday night as I left the club, I saw him waiting for his car. He introduced me to his wife, Jenny, and we had a nice visit. He was leading the tournament and I told them we would be very pleased if he won (he did).

"At the presentation, he was given an oversized check for $180,000. Ian was then off to Detroit for a corporate outing, while Jenny was off to their new residence in Florida.

"The next day I dropped by the Tournament Office around 8 a.m. The phone rang shortly after that, and it was Jenny calling from Florida. She was at their bank, trying to deposit the oversized check, which was not signed. I told her the check she had was only for purposes of the presentation, that the PGA Tour wire transfers the money to each winner's bank and she would have the transfer that day. This began a good friendship with the Baker-Finches that has lasted over the years."

During his first year as tournament chairman in 1980, Rodney Johnston had the privilege to play in the Wednesday pro-am with former U.S. President Gerald Ford, who after leaving the Oval Office spent much of his free time on the links. Johnston enlisted his son Carter to be his caddie. "My wife [Gale] was taking photographs," he said. "On the first two holes, she kept motioning to us from behind the gallery ropes, shouting, `Carter, get in the picture. Carter, get in the picture.' Finally on the third hole, one of the spectators came over to Gale and said, "Lady, that is President Ford, not President Carter."

Johnston, like other tournament chairmen before and since, is grateful to have been handed the reins. "Colonial has been very important to me and my family. I could never repay all that it has meant to me," he said. "Volunteering gives you the opportunity to support the game of golf and to work with some really fine people. Sharing time with them is special."

Thomas, who began volunteering as a teenager and whose father, Curtis, was on the Colonial NIT committee, encourages club members, especially new ones, to become part of the tournament team. "It's all for the benefit of your club and your community, and you need to take part," said Thomas, who served as chairman from 1998-2001. "Of course, if you do get involved, there are lots of hours and the pay is really low. But it's fun, and when the day is over, you can see what's been accomplished. As long as someone doesn't expect to come in and start at the top, we welcome new volunteers. There's always plenty of work to be done."

Perhaps Colonial member Don Gerik, who's worked 30-plus years on the tournament, aptly summed up the prevailing sentiment among volunteers: "I have offered my services and participated in many activities of this club through the years, but my most satisfying accomplishment has been working with the other members and outside volunteers to make Colonial a first-class event.

"No matter what the job is, you can count on it being done with a great deal of pride and sincerity and in a professional way. This team of dedicated volunteers has always worked together in making sure everything goes as smoothly as possible. I am very proud to be a small part of this team."

TOP:
Lady scorers gather in the Volunteer Headquarters with other committees and volunteers.
MIDDLE:
Volunteers on the Transportation Committee shuttles players and their families around town all hours of the day.
BOTTOM:
Leaderboard volunteers keep track of the tournament leaders.

PRIDE OF THE PLAID

COLONIAL'S VOLUNTEER HALL OF FAME

Marvin Leonard *

F. M. "Max" Highfill *	(Chairman 1946-51)
S. M. "Bing" Bingham *	(Chairman 1952-63)
Frank Rogers *	(Chairman 1964-66, 1969-70)
Foist Motheral	(Chairman 1967-68)
Byron L. "Pete" Davis *	(Chairman 1971-73)
Joe Cauker	(Chairman 1974-76)
William W. Spears *	(Chairman 1977-79)
Rodney Johnston	(Chairman 1980-82)

Paul D. Cato, Jr. *	(Chairman 1983-85)
H. Wallace Schmuck	(Chairman 1986-88)
Bill Bowers	(Chairman 1989-91)
M. C. Hamilton, Jr. *	(Chairman 1992-93)
Floyd R. Wade	(Chairman 1994-96)
Sam R. Day	(Chairman 1997)
Phil Thomas	(Chairman 1998-2001)
Dee Finley	(Chairman 2002-04)

Charter members:

Johnny Ballard *	Jim Fuller
Jim Byron *	Berl Godfrey *
Allen Conner *	Curtis Thomas *
Ray Finley *	Al Welsh *

INDUCTEES: 1987-2006

Joe Bowlin *	James Dacus *	Jim Hunt	Clif Overcash Jr.	J. J. Thomas
Jack Brownfield *	Charles Floyd *	Jordan Jones	Jon Payne	Donna Thomason
Jack Burge *	Don Foard	Howard F. Kane *	Porter Pierce *	Jack Townes
Les Burton *	Jerry Hahn *	Robert Lansford	G. J. Post, Jr	Guy F. "Bud" Woodard
Luther Callaway *	Deanna Hailey	Dick McHargue	Pat Schmuck	
Dede Cauker	E.C. "Trey" Harper III	Mike Moore	Stu Shultz *	
Tim Clark *	Shirley Hayter	Haynes Morris *	Steve Sikes	
Dr. Dewitt Claunch *	R. M. "Dick" Hazlewood *	Melvin Musgrove	Jim Teague	* - Deceased

BEST FINISH, BY PLAYER, 1946 -2005

Name	Tournaments	Best Finish
Tommy Aaron	17	3rd, 1968
Rick Acton	1	Missed Cut, 1974
John Adams	5	Tie 47, 1984
Sam Adams	2	Missed Cut, 1974
Charley Akey	1	28th, 1946
Skip Alexander	6	2nd, 1950
Bob Allard	1	Missed Cut, 1974
Fulton Allem	17	Champion, 1993
Michael Allen	2	Tie 45, 1993
Robert Allenby	5	Tie 15, 2001
Ras Allen	1	Missed Cut, 1974
Bud Allin	9	Tie 11, 1974, 1975
Jason Allred	1	Tie 51, 2005
Stephen Ames	5	3rd, 2004
Billy Andrade	14	Tie 12, 2002
Isao Aoki	1	Tie 8, 1989
Stuart Appleby	9	Tie 8, 2002
George Archer	17	Tie 3, 1967
Tommy Armour III	8	Tie 29, 1998
Wally Armstrong	7	Tie 9, 1977
Arjun Atwal	1	Tie 38, 2005
Emlyn Aubrey	2	Tie 16, 1996
Woody Austin	6	4th, 1995
Paul Azinger	6	Tie 8, 1989
Aaron Baddeley	2	Tie 6, 2005
Briny Baird	5	Tie 33, 2002
Butch Baird	9	Tie 6, 1977
Ian Baker-Finch	10	Champion 1989
Al Balding	6	Tie 23, 1956, 1957
Seve Ballesteros	1	Tie 18, 1984
Bob Barbarossa	1	72nd, 1973
Aaron Barber	1	Missed Cut, 2003
David Barber	1	Tie 61, 1974
Jerry Barber	10	Tie 4, 1953
Miller Barber	20	Tie 6, 1977
Craig Barlow	1	Tie 54, 2001
*Tommy Barnes	1	32nd, 1948
John Barnum	1	30th, 1952
Dave Barr	11	Tie 12, 1987
*Ray Barr	2	Missed Cut, 1980-81
Herman Barron	2	Tie 11, 1946
Brian Bateman	2	Tie 14, 2004
Pat Bates	2	Tie 5, 2003
Rex Baxter, Jr.	6	Tie 26, 1965
George Bayer	12	Tie 4, 1956
Andy Bean	8	6th, 1980
Frank Beard	12	Tie 8, 1967
Chip Beck	16	Tie 9, 1988
Cameron Beckman	2	Tie 19, 2002
Rich Beem	6	Tie 26, 2001
Notah Begay III	4	Missed Cut, 1999-2000, '02, '04
Russell Beiersdorf	2	Tie 53, 1993
Deane Beman	8	Tie 17, 1972
David Berganio Jr.	2	Missed Cut, 2002
Al Besselink	8	Tie 14, 1958
Leo Biagetti	2	Tie 21, 1954
Don Bies	10	Tie 10, 1972
Ronnie Black	8	Tie 9, 1986
Woody Blackburn	5	Tie 20, 1977
Phil Blackmar	10	Tie 33, 1991
Jay Don Blake	11	Tie 15, 1995
Homero Blancas	17	Champion, 1970
Chris Blocker	7	Tie 30, 1968
Martin Bohen	1	Missed Cut, 1974
Charles Bolling	1	Tie 52, 1986
Tommy Bolt	21	Champion, 1958
Paul Bondeson	3	Tie 46, 1967
Eric Booker	1	Tie 77, 1999
Jim Booros	2	Tie 28, 1982
Guy Boros	5	Tie 22, 1994
Julius Boros	27	Champion 1960, 1963
Craig Bowden	1	Missed Cut, 2004
Frank Boynton	2	Tie 37, 1969
Michael Bradley	1	69th, 1995
Mike Brannan	1	Missed Cut, 1980
Alan Bratton	1	Missed Cut, 1999
Jeff Brehaut	1	Tie 74, 2003
Gay Brewer	17	Tie 4, 1964
*Danny Briggs	1	Missed Cut, 1982
D.J. Brigman	1	Missed Cut, 2004
Mike Brisky	3	Tie 14, 1998
Bill Britton	6	Tie 33, 1993
Mark Brooks	20	Tie 4, 1992
Al Brosch	1	Tie 9, 1951
Billy Ray Brown	7	Tied 51, 1990
Ken Brown	1	Tie 72, 1986
Pete Brown	4	Tie 12, 1964
Olin Browne	8	Champion 1999
Bart Bryant	1	Tie 57, 2005
Brad Bryant	9	Tie 23, 1995
Gordon Bryson	1	Tie 35, 1956
Johnny Bulla	5	Tie 7, 1948
Jack Burke, Jr.	15	2nd, 1951
Patrick Burke	2	Tie 22, 1997
Walter Burkemo	1	Tie 15, 1954
Bob Burns	3	Tie 33, 2002
George Burns	7	Tie 15, 1982
Bob Byman	2	Tie 36, 1980
Jonathan Byrd	4	Tie 8, 2002
Curt Byrum	5	Tie 29, 1990
Tom Byrum	14	Tie 9, 1987
George Cadle	6	Tie 20, 1977
Steve Cain	1	Missed Cut, 1974
Mark Calcavecchia	17	Tie 2, 1988
Rex Caldwell	8	Tie 11, 1984
Bil Calfee	1	Missed Cut, 1978, 1980
Chad Campbell	4	2nd, 2004
Joe Campbell	7	Tie 21, 1959
*William Campbell	1	Tie 11, 1952
David Canipe	1	Tie 40, 1988
Mark Carnevale	1	Tie 63, 1994
*Chip Carter	1	Missed Cut, 1988
Jim Carter	8	Tie 11, 1999
Alex Cejka	2	Tie 35, 2003
Billy Casper	17	Champion, 1964, 1968
Antonio Cerda	1	Tie 4, 1955
Ron Cerrudo	8	Tie 24, 1971
Greg Chalmers	4	Tie 15, 2001
Brandel Chamblee	9	Tie 21, 2003
Warren Chancellor	1	Withdrew, 1974
Bob Charles	12	Tie 4, 1969
Don Cherry	6	Tie 28, 1954
K.J. Choi	2	Tie 21, 2005
Daniel Chopra	1	Tie 57, 2005
Stewart Cink	9	Tie 2, 2000
Brian Claar	6	Tie 16, 1992
Bobby Clampett	6	Tie 12, 1983
Jimmy Clark	5	Tie 11, 1952
Michael Clark II	1	Missed Cut, 2001
Tim Clark	3	Tie 14, 2004
Keith Clearwater	19	Champion, 1987
Lennie Clements	9	Tie 5, 1982
Jose Coceres	2	Tie 34, 2001
Bob Cochran	1	27th, 1946
Russ Cochran	12	Tie 11, 1988, 1990
*Charles Coe	7	Tie 10, 1950
Jim Colbert	14	Champion, 1983
Bobby Cole	7	Tie 23, 1978
Bill Collins	6	Tie 17, 1961, 1963
Joe Collins	1	Missed Cut, 1974
Ross Collins	1	Tie 65, 1968
Tim Collins	1	Tie 71, 1975
Byron Comstock	1	Missed Cut, 1974
Frank Conner	7	6th, 1981
Joe Conrad	5	Tie 14, 1956
Charles Coody	25	2nd, 1967
John Cook	18	5th, 1998
Pete Cooper	5	Tie 10, 1950
Fred Couples	12	4th, 1996
Chuck Courtney	11	3rd, 1974
Bruce Crampton	16	Champion, 1965
Ben Crane	2	Tie 17, 2005
*L.M. Crannell, Jr.	1	42nd, 1952
Dick Crawford	7	Tie 14, 1969
Ben Crenshaw	32	Champion, 1977, 1990
Jacky Cupit	11	Tie 17, 1961, 1963
Rod Curl	30	Champion, 1974
John Daly	4	Missed Cut, 1991-92, 1995, 1999
Robert Damron	6	Tie 39, 1999
Sonny Davis	1	Missed Cut, 1974
Marco Dawson	3	Tie 13, 2003
Glen Day	12	4th, 2001
Jay Delsing	3	Tie 48, 1990
Roberto De Vicenzo	8	Champion, 1957
Jimmy Demaret	10	Tie 6, 1956
Clark Dennis	9	Tie 14, 1998
Jim Dent	6	Tie 38, 1974
Bruce Devlin	19	Champion, 1966
Gardner Dickinson	18	Champion, 1969
Bob Dickson	10	Tie 4, 1975
Terry Diehl	7	Tie 35, 1976
Chris DiMarco	5	Tie 40, 2002
Terry Dill	9	Tie 13, 1968
Trevor Dodds	2	Missed Cut, 1993, 1998
Jay Dolan	1	Tie 61, 1967
Mike Donald	11	Tie 11, 1985
Luke Donald	3	Tie 48, 2002
Ed Dougherty	6	Tie 25, 1992
Dave Douglas	2	Tie 18, 1950
Dale Douglass	9	Tie 12, 1970
Bob Duden	1	41st, 1952
Allen Doyle	1	Tie 46, 1996
Ed Dudley	1	24th, 1946
Michael Dugger	1	Missed Cut, 1974
Doug Dunakey	1	Missed Cut, 1999
Scott Dunlap	2	Tie 35, 2000
Joe Durant	7	Tie 3, 2005
David Duval	6	Tie 12, 1995-96
R. W. Eaks	1	68th, 1998
Bob Eastwood	10	Tie 5, 1982
Danny Edwards	12	Tie 9, 1982
David Edwards	20	2nd, 1989, 1991
Jerry Edwards	7	Tie 6, 1963
Joel Edwards	7	Tie 12, 2002
Dave Eichelberger	14	Tie 40, 1977
Brad Elder	3	Tie 26, 2001
Lee Elder	13	4th, 1973
Steve Elkington	18	Tie 15, 1995
Danny Ellis	1	Missed Cut, 2004
Richard Ellis	1	Missed Cut, 1974
Wes Ellis, Jr.	1	Tie 36, 1959
Ernie Els	2	Tie 67, 1996
*Billy Erfurth	1	Tie 39, 1953
Randy Erskine	2	Tie 21, 1975
Bob Estes	16	Tie 6, 2000
Tom Evans	2	Missed Cut, 1974-75
Max Evans	1	49th, 1956
Jack Ewing	2	Tie 11, 1974
Brad Fabel	3	Tie 30, 1987
Nick Faldo	3	Tie 23, 1989
Don Fairfield	6	Tie 28, 1960
Brad Faxon	14	Tie 2, 1997
George Fazio	2	Tie 17, 1947
David Feherty	1	Tie 56, 1994
Rick Fehr	6	Tie 4, 1992
Keith Fergus	12	Tie 14, 1979
Jim Ferree	8	Tie 5, 1962
Jim Ferrier	6	Tie 12, 1951
Mike Fetchick	2	26th, 1957
Forrest Fezler	6	Tie 29, 1976
Dow Finsterwald	13	2nd, 1955
Dow Finsterwald Jr	4	Missed Cut, 1990-92, 94
Ed Fiori	12	Tie 9, 1980
Pat Fitzsimons	2	Tie 38, 1974
John Flannery	1	Missed Cut, 1993
Jack Fleck	7	Tie 10, 1963
Marty Fleckman	6	Tie 21, 1976
Bruce Fleisher	7	Tie 10, 1992
Pete Fleming	1	43rd, 1954
Steve Flesch	8	Champion, 2004
Ray Floyd	26	Tie 7, 1981
Doug Ford	16	Tie 2, 1953
Dan Forsman	13	Tie 10, 1980
John Fought III	4	Tie 16, 1980
Carlos Franco	2	Missed Cut, 2000
Harrison Frazar	8	4th, 1998
Robin Freeman	3	Tie 35, 2000
Bob Friend	1	Tie 51, 1999
David Frost	21	Champion, 1997
Edward Fryatt	2	Missed Cut, 2000-01
Fred Funk	15	Tie 5, 1991
Rod Funseth	9	Tie 17, 1970
Ed Furgol	8	3rd, 1957
Marty Furgol	6	Tie 11, 1953
Jim Furyk	10	2nd, 1998
Raymond Gafford	7	Tie 4, 1952
Jeff Gallagher	3	Tie 10, 1996
Jim Gallagher Jr.	11	3rd, 1992
Robert Gamez	11	Tie 5, 2004
Sergio Garcia	5	Champion, 2001
Buddy Gardner	10	Tie 7, 1985
Bill Garrett	2	70th, 1970
Jimmy Gauntt	1	Tie 36, 1953
Brian Gay	6	Tie 2, 2001
*Bobby Gee	1	Missed Cut, 1990
Al Geiberger	26	Champion, 1975, 1979
Brent Geiberger	8	Tie 24, 2000
Vic Ghezzi	3	Tie 6, 1947
Kelly Gibson	2	Missed Cut, 1993
Gibby Gilbert	12	Tie 17, 1970
Bob Gilder	14	Tie 5, 1976
*Vinnie Giles	1	Missed Cut, 1973
Bill Glasson	13	Tie 20, 1997

Name	Tournaments	Best Finish
Dave Glenz	1	Missed Cut, 1975
Lucas Glover	2	Missed Cut, 2004-05
Randy Glover	4	Tie 13, 1966
Bob Goalby	17	Tie 11, 1967
Bob Goetz	1	Missed Cut, 1974
Matt Gogel	4	Tie 36, 2002
Mathew Goggin	1	Missed Cut, 2002
Joel Goldstrand	1	Tie 35, 1970
Ernie Gonzalez	1	Missed Cut, 1987
J. C. Goosie	1	Tie 36, 1958
David Gossett	1	Tie 48, 2002
Paul Goydos	8	Tie 2, 1999
*John Grace	1	Missed Cut, 1976
Wayne Grady	9	Tie 7, 1991
David Graham	18	Tie 6, 1988
Lou Graham	14	Tie 7, 1974
*John Granger	1	Tie 62, 1973
Thomas Gray	1	Tie 12, 1983
Ken Green	5	Tie 11, 1988
Hubert Green	11	3rd, 1975
Jimmy Green	1	Tie 50, 2000
Bert Greene	7	6th, 1972
Bobby Greenwood	2	Missed Cut, 1970,'75
Gary Groh	2	Missed Cut, 1975-76
Mathias Gronberg	2	Tie 54, 2004
Scott Gump	3	Tie 49, 1992
Fred Haas	14	2nd, 1954
Hunter Haas	3	Tie 44, 2005
Jay Haas	15	Tie 18, 2003
Jerry Haas	1	Missed Cut, 1991
Gary Hallberg	14	Tie 5, 1983
Dan Halldorson	7	Tie 33, 1991
Jim Hallet	4	Tie 11, 1991
Bob Hamilton	3	Tie 5, 1946
Todd Hamilton	2	Tie 44, 2004
Laurie Hammer	1	Tie 41, 1968
Donnie Hammond	8	Tie 35, 1985
Phil Hancock	4	Missed Cut, 1978-79
Chick Harbert	1	Tie 6, 1947
Jack Harden	2	Tie 36, 1953
Paul Harney	6	Tie 9, 1961
Chandler Harper	11	Champion, 1955
Roland Harper	5	Tie 53, 1968
*John Harris	1	Tie 50, 1994
Labron Harris, Jr.	7	Tie 12, 1973
Dutch Harrison	10	Tie 3, 1950
Dudley Hart	9	4th, 2002
Morris Hatalsky	7	Tie 31, 1989
Fred Hawkins	15	2nd, 1959
Dale Hayes	1	Missed Cut, 1977
J.P. Hayes	4	Tie 52, 2003
Mark Hayes	14	Tie 27, 1979
Ted Hayes	2	Tie 50, 1972
Clayton Heafner	4	Champion, 1948
Vance Heafner	2	Tie 11, 1981
Jerry Heard	10	Champion, 1972
Jay Hebert	14	Tie 9, 1960, 1961
Lionel Hebert	20	Tie 5, 1959
Mike Heinen	3	Tie 30, 1994
Scott Hend	2	Tie 6, 2005
Nolan Henke	7	Tie 16, 1992
Harold Henning	5	Tie 6, 1968
Brian Henninger	7	Tie 8, 1998
Bunky Henry	3	Tie 43, 1970
J.J. Henry	4	Tie 68, 2002
Mark Hensby	1	Missed Cut, 2004
Tim Herron	9	Tie 2, 1999
Jeff Hewes	1	Tie 68, 1979
Doug Higgins	1	32nd, 1955
Mike Higgins	1	Withdrew, 1974
Dave Hill	11	Tie 6, 1969
Mike Hill	7	Tie 21, 1975
Jimmy Hines	1	Tie 13, 1946
Lon Hinkle	12	Tie 3, 1983
Larry Hinson	8	Tie 17, 1970
Babe Hiskey	6	Tie 20, 1966
Gabriel Hjertstedt	2	Tie 53, 1998
Scott Hoch	17	Tie 2, 1991
Ben Hogan	21	Champion, 1946, 1947, 1952, 1953, 1959
*Royal Hogan	2	25th, 1946, 1947
Tony Holguin	2	Tie 29, 1953
Mike Holland	2	Missed Cut, 1982-83
Frank (Bud) Holscher	4	Tie 24, 1955
Wilf Homenuik	2	Tie 12, 1971
Herb Hooper	1	Missed Cut, 1972
*Ed Hopkins	1	Tie 50, 1956
P. H. Horgan III	1	Tie 43, 1990
Kazuhiko Hosokawa	3	Tie 22, 1997
*Ralph Howe III	1	Missed Cut, 1989

Name	Tournaments	Best Finish
Charles Howell III	1	Missed Cut, 2002
Bradley Hughes	2	Tie 65, 1999
Mike Hulbert	16	Tie 5, 1990
Ed Humenik	2	Missed Cut, 1992-93
John Huston	15	Tie 6, 1993
Bob Inman	1	Tie 28, 1954
Joe Inman	8	Tie 5, 1982
John Inman	4	Tie 11, 1988
Walker Inman, Jr.	1	40th, 1956
Hale Irwin	22	2nd, 1981
Tripp Isenhour	1	Missed Cut, 2004
Don Iverson	4	Tie 21, 1975
Tony Jacklin	3	Tie 19, 1968
John Jacobs	3	Tie 52, 1972
Tommy Jacobs	9	2nd, 1964
Peter Jacobsen	24	Champion, 1984
Fredrik Jacobson	1	16th, 2005
Barry Jaeckel	11	Tie 12, 1976
Jim Jamieson	4	Tie 42, 1973
Don January	27	Tie 2, 1979
Lee Janzen	12	Tie 11, 1993
Tom Jenkins	7	Tie 21, 1981
Joe Jimenez	1	Tie 34, 1960
Brandt Jobe	5	4th, 2003
Per-Ulrik Johansson	3	Tie 11, 2001
George Johnson	1	Tie 7, 1972
Howie Johnson	6	Tie 9, 1970
Zach Johnson	2	Tie 14, 2004
Al Johnston	4	Tie 22, 1963
Bill Johnston	3	Tie 22, 1958
Ralph Johnston	3	Tie 26, 1972
Grier Jones	11	Tie 8, 1976
Kent Jones	1	Tie 50, 2004
Steve Jones	8	Tie 6, 1996
Peter Jordan	2	4th, 1994
Mike Kallam	1	Missed Cut, 1974
Monty Kaser	1	Tie 31, 1974
Ryoken Kawagishi	1	Missed Cut, 1991
Jack Kay	1	Tie 50, 1956
*Jack Kay, Jr.	1	Missed Cut, 1986
Jonathan Kaye	7	Tie 34, 2001
Herman Keiser	3	Tie 4, 1948
Jerry Kelly	7	Tie 28, 2002
Spike Kelley	1	Tie 55, 1975
Skip Kendall	8	Tie 5, 2004
Bill Kerr	1	Tie 43, 1956
Joe Kirkwood, Jr.	3	Tie 23, 1950
Tom Kite	30	Tie 3, 1981
Charles Klein	4	Tie 15, 1952
Harold Kneece	1	Tie 31, 1964
Dick Knight	1	Tie 30, 1960
Kenny Knox	7	Tie 35, 1990
George Knudson	13	2nd, 1965
Gary Koch	10	Tie 5, 1983
Greg Kraft	9	Tie 2, 1999
Bill Kratzert	8	Tie 19, 1985
Cliff Kresge	2	Tie 71, 2003
Ted Kroll	9	Tie 3, 1958
Hank Kuehne	2	Missed Cut, 2004
*Trip Kuehne	1	Missed Cut, 1995
Massy Kuramoto	1	Tie 27, 1993
Greg Ladehoff	1	Tie 68, 1986
Ky Laffoon	5	17th, 1947
Ralph Landrum	2	Tie 52, 1985
Neal Lancaster	8	Tie 33, 1995
Bernhard Langer	2	Tie 3, 1986
Franklin Langham	4	Tie 32, 1996
Stan Lee	2	Tie 26, 1977
Ian Leggatt	2	Tie 61, 2002
Stephen Leaney	2	Tie 27, 2004
Tom Lehman	11	Champion, 1995
Tony Lema	5	Tie 3, 1965, 1966
Justin Leonard	12	Tie 2, 2003
Stan Leonard	8	Tie 4, 1956
Wayne Levi	6	Tie 8, 1979
J. C. Lewis	6	Tie 27, 2004
Jack Lewis	2	Tie 60, 1971
Frank Lickliter II	6	Tie 12, 2002
Bruce Lietzke	27	Champion, 1980, 1992
Pat Lindsey	1	72nd, 1984
John Lister	4	Tie 15, 1975
Lawson Little	2	Tie 9, 1947
Gene Littler	29	Champion, 1971
Bobby Locke	2	Tie 3, 1947
Bob Lohr	9	Tie 2, 1991
Peter Lonard	4	Tie 3, 2005
Lyn Lott	6	Tie 4, 1977
Dick Lotz	6	Tie 7, 1970
John Lotz	2	Tie 33, 1968

Name	Tournaments	Best Finish
Davis Love III	17	2nd, 1987, 2000
Steve Lowery	8	Tie 33, 1995
Bob Lunn	7	Tie 6, 1969
Mark Lye	14	Tie 11, 1984,1988
Sandy Lyle	1	Missed Cut, 1997
Andrew Magee	13	Tie 7, 1990
Jeff Maggert	12	3rd, 1993
John Mahaffey	22	Tie 2, 1990
Hunter Mahan	2	Tie 44, 2005
Ted Makalena	1	Tie 58, 1967
Bill Mallon	1	68th, 1977
Roger Maltbie	18	Tie 15, 1982
Lloyd Mangrum	15	2nd, 1952
Bob Mann	1	Missed Cut, 1979
Dave Marr	12	Tie 10, 1964
Graham Marsh	1	Tie 48, 1977
Fred Marti	11	2nd, 1972
Casey Martin	1	Tie 62, 2000
Doug Martin	3	Tie 18, 1998
Billy Martindale	5	Tie 10, 1965
Milton Marusic	1	Tie 39, 1953
Shigeki Maruyama	7	Tie 5, 2001
Don Massengale	8	Tie 31, 1966
Rik Massengale	7	Tie 11, 1977
Jim Masserio	4	Tie 17, 1977
Dick Mast	2	Tie 22, 1993
Len Mattiace	8	Tie 8, 2000
Terry Mauney	2	Tie 16, 1980
Bill Mawhinney	1	Tie 35, 1956
Billy Maxwell	19	Tie 3, 1959
Bob May	2	Tie 52, 2001
Dick Mayer	12	2nd, 1957
Billy Mayfair	18	2nd, 2005
Shelley Mayfield	4	Tie 15, 1954
Rives McBee	3	Tie 67,1970
Blaine McCallister	14	Tie 23, 1991
Bob McCallister	3	Tie 40, 1962
Scott McCarron	5	Tie 18, 1998
Gary McCord	7	Tie 7, 1974
Mike McCullough	6	Tie 36, 1983
Mark McCumber	9	Tie 5, 1995
Jerry McGee	9	Tie 7, 1971
Jim McGovern	2	Tie 46, 1995
Jack McGowan	5	Tie 5, 1966
Pat McGowan	6	Tie 47, 1984
James McLean	1	Missed Cut, 2003
B. R. McLendon	8	Tie 11, 1977
John McMullin	1	Tie 21, 1959
Artie McNickle	4	Tie 36, 1980
Mark McNulty	2	Tie 5, 1983
Spike McRoy	2	Tie 40, 2003
Harold McSpaden	1	Tie 11, 1946
Rocco Mediate	16	3rd, 1996
Steve Melnyk	12	Tie 4, 1978
Bob Menne	3	Tie 26, 1974
Dennie Meyer	1	Missed Cut, 1976
Hajime Meshiai	2	Tie 63, 1994
Dick Metz	10	Tie 9, 1946
Shaun Micheel	2	Tie 45, 2003
Phil Mickelson	12	Champion, 2000
Cary Middlecoff	18	Champion, 1951
*Danny Mijovic	1	Missed Cut, 1984
Allen Miller	3	Tie 50, 1975
Johnny Miller	7	Tie 17, 1972
Lindy Miller	6	Tie 8, 1979
Bobby Mitchell	8	Tie 19, 1974
Jeff Mitchell	4	3rd, 1980
Larry Mize	14	6th, 1985
Jack Montgomery	7	Tie 13, 1968
Eric Monti	2	Tie 29, 1955
Orville Moody	9	Tie 3, 1971
Paul Moran	1	Missed Cut, 1974
Gil Morgan	22	3rd, 1984
Mike Morley	7	2nd, 1976
Bobby Morris	1	27th, 1947
John Morse	3	Tie 16, 1996
Larry Mowry	1	Tie 11, 1969
Jodie Mudd	8	Tie 37, 1988
Bob Murphy	18	2nd, 1985
Sean Murphy	1	Tie 62, 1996
Kevin Na	2	Tie 17, 2005
Kel Nagle	11	2nd, 1961
Tommy Nakajima	2	Tie 43, 1988
Bill Nary	5	Tie 11, 1953
Jim Nelford	5	Tie 18, 1983
Byron Nelson	18	Tie 3, 1954
Larry Nelson	15	Tie 15, 1985
Dwight Nevil	4	Tie 62, 1973
Dave Newquist	1	Missed Cut, 1976
Jack Newton	3	Tie 60, 1979

*Names in italics designate amateurs.

CHAPTER FIFTEEN

Name	Tournaments	Best Finish
Bobby Nichols	11	Tie 7, 1972
Gary Nicklaus	1	Missed Cut, 2000
Jack Nicklaus	11	Champion, 1982
Mike Nicolette	2	Tie 40, 1984
Tom Nieporte	5	Tie 27, 1958
Frank Nobilo	5	Tie 33, 1998
Greg Norman	5	2nd, 1993
Tim Norris	4	Tie 11, 1985
Andy North	17	2nd, 1982
Vern Novak	1	Missed Cut, 1974
Arron Oberholser	2	Tie 21, 2005
*Alberto Ochoa	1	Missed Cut, 1997
Joe Ogilvie	3	Tie 14, 2004
Geoff Ogilvy	5	Tie 34, 2001
Brett Ogle	4	Tie 15, 1995
Mac O'Grady	6	Tie 16, 1988
David Ogrin	10	Tie 2, 1997
Aki Ohmachi	1	Missed Cut, 1988
Paul O'Leary	1	Tie 23, 1950
Ed Oliver	8	3rd, 1955
Mark O'Meara	16	Tie 4, 1985
Peter Oosterhuis	9	Tie 18, 1976, 1984
Steve Oppermann	1	Tie 53, 1968
Joe Ozaki	7	Tie 12, 1996
Roy Pace	5	Tie 47, 1972
Arnold Palmer	16	Champion, 1962
Johnny Palmer	18	Champion, 1954
Ryan Palmer	2	Tie 69, 2005
Rod Pampling	4	Tie 6, 2005
Brenden Pappas	2	Tie 62, 2003
Roger Parker	1	72nd, 1974
Jesper Parnevik	6	Tie 11, 2001
Craig Parry	10	3rd, 1995
Jerry Pate	12	Tie 2, 1978
Steve Pate	16	Tie 16, 1988
*Chris Patton	1	Missed Cut, 1990
Carl Paulson	4	Tie 24, 2000
Dennis Paulson	5	Tie 31, 2004
Corey Pavin	22	Champion, 1985, 1996
Bob Payne	2	Tie 34, 1975
Eddie Pearce	5	Tie 64, 1976
Calvin Peete	2	Tie 33, 1986
Toney Penna	5	2nd, 1947
David Peoples	6	Tie 33, 1991
Pat Perez	3	Tie 44, 2005
Craig Perks	4	4th, 2004
Tom Pernice Jr.	5	Tie 33, 1999
Chris Perry	6	Tie 23, 1991
Kenny Perry	16	Champion, 2003, 2005
Peter Persons	3	Tie 29, 1991
Tim Petrovic	3	Tie 5, 2004
Carl Pettersson	3	Tie 28, 2003
Mark Pfeil	7	Tie 4, 1984
Mark Pfingston	1	Disqualified, 1989
Henry Picard	4	Tie 5, 1946
Jerry Pittman	1	Tie 22, 1963
Gary Player	17	2nd, 1963, 1969
Dan Pohl	23	Champion, 1986
D.A. Points	1	Missed Cut, 2005
Don Pooley	7	Tie 35, 1985
Joe Porter	3	Tie 8, 1975
Johnny Pott	11	2nd, 1962
Greg Powers	1	Tie 28, 1982
Nick Price	17	Champion, 1994, 2002
Dicky Pride	1	Missed Cut, 1995
Dillard Pruitt	3	Tie 6, 1992
Ted Purdy	2	Tie 13, 2005
Tom Purtzer	25	Champion, 1991
Brett Quigley	6	Tie 5, 2001
Sammy Rachels	2	Tie 15, 1984
Dave Ragan	9	Tie 15, 1963
Ross Randall	1	Tie 57, 1974
Sam Randolph	4	Tie 52, 1989
Henry Ransom	3	Tie 5, 1946
Charles Raulerson	1	Tie 31, 2000
Mike Reasor	1	Missed Cut, 1975
Dean Refram	2	Missed Cut, 1969, 1976
Victor Regalado	9	Tie 36, 1980
Mike Reid	22	Tie 5, 1983
Steve Reid	3	Tie 46, 1968
Jack Renner	10	Tie 8, 1979
Rick Rhoads	1	Tie 70, 1974
Dick Rhyan	3	Tie 46, 1971
Tad Rhyan	1	75th, 1993
Robert (Skee) Riegel	2	Tie 19, 1951
John Riegger	1	Withdrew, 2004
Chris Riley	3	Tie 14, 2004
Larry Rinker	10	Tie 40, 1992
Lee Rinker	2	Tie 53, 1998
*Hillman Robbins, Jr.	2	19th, 1956
Loren Roberts	17	Tie 4, 1993
Phil Rodgers	14	4th, 1972
*Anthony Rodriguez	1	Missed Cut, 1995
Chi Chi Rodriguez	21	Tie 3, 1965
Bill Rogers	15	Tie 3, 1986
John Rollins	3	Tie 48, 2002
Bob Rosburg	15	Tie 7, 1971
Clarence Rose	7	5th, 1988
Justin Rose	1	Tie 13, 2005
Hugh Royer	1	Missed Cut, 1971
Hugh Royer III	1	Missed Cut, 1996
Mason Rudolph	13	Tie 4, 1975
Jack Rule, Jr.	3	Tie 12, 1964
Dave Rummells	8	Tie 22, 1988
Charlie Rymer	1	Tie 58, 1995
Rory Sabbatini	6	Tie 6, 2005
Ed Sabo	1	Tie 64, 1977
Bill Sander	4	Tie 37, 1987
Doug Sanders	18	Champion, 1961
Cesar Sanudo	3	Missed Cut, 1972-73
Gene Sauers	10	Tie 6, 1986
John Schlee	10	Tie 12, 1976
George Schneiter	6	8th, 1946
Steve Schneiter	1	Missed Cut, 1996
George Schoux	2	Tie 15, 1947
John Schroeder	13	2nd, 1977
Ted Schulz	3	Tie 45, 1993
*Juan Segura	1	42nd, 1951
John Senden	1	Tie 9, 2004
Bob Shaw	1	Missed Cut, 1972
Tom Shaw	8	Tie 7, 1970
Bob Shearer	4	Tie 14, 1979
Patrick Sheehan	3	Tie 28, 2003
Jack Shields	3	Tie 26, 1952
Tom Sieckmann	5	77th, 1990
Charles Sifford	8	Tie 15, 1973
Curtis Sifford	3	Missed Cut, 1973-75
Dan Sikes	8	Tie 8, 1967
R. H. Sikes	8	2nd, 1966
Tony Sills	4	Tie 4, 1984
Larry Silveira	1	Missed Cut, 1991
*Randy Simmons	1	Missed Cut, 1974
Jim Simons	11	Tie 15, 1974
Scott Simpson	17	2nd, 1994
Tim Simpson	12	Tie 3, 1989
Joey Sindelar	21	Tie 2, 1988
Vijay Singh	6	Tie 11, 1999
Heath Slocum	4	Tie 32, 2005
Jeff Sluman	18	2nd, 1996, 1999
Al Smith	2	Tie 27, 1950
Bob E. Smith	12	Tie 8, 1976
Chris Smith	3	Missed Cut, 2001, 2003
Mike Smith	3	Tie 11, 1985
*Reynolds Smith	1	26th, 1946
J. C. Snead	11	Tie 34, 1975
Sam Snead	4	Champion, 1950
Ed Sneed	12	Tie 6, 1977
Ansel Snow	1	Withdrew, 1953
Joey Snyder III	1	Missed Cut, 2005
*Jim Sorenson	1	Missed Cut, 1986
Annika Sorenstam	1	Missed Cut, 2003
Ramon Sota	1	Tie 42, 1964
Mike Souchak	15	Champion, 1956
Mike Sposa	2	Tie 11, 2001
Steve Spray	4	Tie 23, 1968
Mike Springer	3	Tie 30, 1994
Craig Stadler	15	Tie 10, 1992
Kevin Stadler	1	Missed Cut, 2005
Mike Standly	6	Tie 29, 1995
Paul Stankowski	6	Tie 66, 1995
Bobby Stanton	4	Tie 53, 1969
Nate Starks	1	Tie 55, 1975
Jerry Steelsmith	4	Tie 41, 1963
Earl Stewart, Jr.	18	Tie 6, 1968
Payne Stewart	15	2nd, 1984, 1986
Ken Still	13	Tie 13, 1968
Dave Stockton	28	Champion, 1967
Dave Stockton Jr.	7	Tie 30, 1994
Andre Stolz	1	Missed Cut, 2005
Bob Stone	2	Tie 52, 1972
Frank Stranahan	5	Tie 23, 1956
Curtis Strange	16	Tie 3, 1981
Ron Streck	8	Tie 11, 1981
Steve Stricker	4	Tie 13, 2005
Larry Stubblefield	1	Missed Cut, 1974
Mike Sullivan	12	Tie 6, 1986
David Sutherland	1	Missed Cut, 1998
Kevin Sutherland	7	Tie 20, 2000
Hal Sutton	16	Tie 5, 2003
Hidemichi Tanaka	1	Withdrew, 2004
Alan Tapie	6	Tie 20, 1979
Phil Tataurangi	2	Tie 5, 2002
Vaughn Taylor	1	Withdrew, 2005
Glen Teal	2	Tie 21, 1950
Brian Tennyson	3	Tie 7, 1990
Doug Tewell	18	Tie 4, 1980
Barney Thompson	2	Tie 57, 1981
Jimmy Thompson	2	23rd, 1946
Leonard Thompson	14	Tie 6, 1979
Rocky Thompson	6	22nd, 1968
Peter Thomson	9	Tie 6, 1956
Chuck Thorpe	1	Tie 60, 1972
Jim Thorpe	13	Tie 22, 1993
Harry Todd	10	2nd, 1946
Esteban Toledo	7	Tie 8, 2002
Tommy Tolles	4	Tie 6, 1996
David Toms	8	Tie 2, 2002
Bob Toski	5	Tie 17, 1951
Peter Townsend	1	Missed Cut, 1970
D.J. Trahan	1	Tie 38, 2005
Lee Trevino	21	Champion, 1976, 1978
Kirk Triplett	15	Tie 13, 2000
Mike Tschetter	1	Missed Cut, 1988
Bill Trombley	1	Tie 27, 1957
Ted Tryba	4	Missed Cut, 1994-95, 2000
Chris Tucker	1	Missed Cut, 1992
Murray Tucker	1	Tie 35, 1956
Bob Tway	20	Tie 6, 1997
Greg Twiggs	2	Tie 59, 1993
Howard Twitty	15	Tie 14, 1979
Tray Tyner	1	Tie 46, 1987
Tom Ulozas	1	Missed Cut, 1973
Wally Ulrich	4	Tie 11, 1953
Hal Underwood	1	Tie 60, 1971
Bob Unger	2	Missed Cut, 1974-75
Brett Upper	1	Missed Cut, 1986
Omar Uresti	5	Tie 38, 1996
Stan Utley	4	Tie 7, 1991
Tommy Valentine	3	Tie 34, 1982
Bo Van Pelt	2	Tie 5, 2004
Ken Venturi	10	2nd, 1958
Scott Verplank	17	Tie 12, 1995
Bob Verwey	4	Tie 35, 1970
Ellsworth Vines	3	Tie 13, 1946
*Mitch Voges	1	Missed Cut, 1992
Norman Von Nida	1	Tie 10, 1950
Ernie Vossler	19	Tie 7, 1959
Bobby Wadkins	19	Tie 5, 1983
Lanny Wadkins	22	Champion, 1988
Fred Wadsworth	1	Tie 18, 1987
Grant Waite	4	Tie 41, 1997
Duffy Waldorf	15	Tie 4, 1993
Art Wall, Jr.	19	Tie 11, 1957
Bobby Walzel	6	Tie 42, 1979
Fred Wampler	3	Tie 29, 1953
*Harvie Ward, Jr.	1	Tie 3, 1954
Charles Warren	1	Missed Cut, 2005
Nick Watney	1	Missed Cut, 2005
Denis Watson	11	Tie 43, 1986
Tom Watson	24	Champion, 1998
Brian Watts	5	Tie 11, 1999
DeWitt Weaver, Jr.	7	Tie 46, 1971
H. R. (Bert) Weaver	5	Tie 11, 1959
*Wilford Wehrle	3	22nd, 1946
D. A. Weibring	21	3rd, 1995
Mike Weir	6	Tie 8, 2000
Tom Weiskopf	20	Champion, 1973
O'Neal (Buck) White	4	Tie 17, 1952
Don Whitt	3	Tie 4, 1961
Mark Wiebe	11	Tie 6, 1988
Jim Wiechers	5	11th, 1973
Terry Wilcox	1	Tie 29, 1970
Jay Williamson	3	Tie 28, 2003
Garrett Willis	1	Disqualified, 2002
*Bob Willits	1	26th, 1947
Brian Wilson	1	Tie 62, 2001
Dean Wilson	2	Tie 21, 2003
Bo Wininger	14	Tie 6, 1956
Casey Wittenberg	1	Missed Cut, 2005
Bob Wolcott	1	71st, 1991
Randy Wolff	2	Tie 24, 1971
Willie Wood	9	Tie 7, 1985
Larry Wood	3	Tie 31, 1972
Jeff Woodland	1	Missed Cut, 1994
Tiger Woods	1	Tie 4, 1997
Jim Woodward	1	Missed Cut, 1992
Lew Worsham	1	Tie 12, 1947
Robert Wrenn	4	Tie 31, 1989
Bob Wynn	4	Tie 70, 1977
Mike Wynn	1	Tie 45, 1975
Dudley Wysong	4	Tie 9, 1968
Bert Yancey	10	2nd, 1971
Kaname Yokoo	3	Tie 55, 2000
Bruce Zabriski	1	Missed Cut, 1992
Kermit Zarley, Jr.	15	Tie 6, 1973
Bob Zender	3	Missed Cut, 1974-75, '79
Larry Ziegler	9	Tie 17, 1970
Al Zimmerman	1	38th, 1952
Billy Ziobro	2	Missed Cut, 1974
Fuzzy Zoeller	21	Champion, 1981
Richard Zokol	5	Tie 16, 1992

*Names in italics designate amateurs.

records AT A GLANCE

SCORING RECORDS

For 72 Holes

261 - Kenny Perry 2003, 2005
264 - Fulton Allem 1993
265 - Greg Norman 1993
       David Frost 1997
       Tom Watson 1998
266 - Corey Pavin 1985
       Keith Clearwater 1987
       Nick Price 1994
       Scott Simpson 1994

For 54 Holes

192 - Kenny Perry 2005
193 - Kenny Perry 2003
195 - Scott Simpson 1994
       David Ogrin 1997
196 - Tiger Woods 1997
197 - Fulton Allem 1993
       Greg Norman 1993
       Paul Goydos 1997

For 36 Holes

128 - Kenny Perry 2005
129 - Fulton Allem 1993
       David Frost 1997
       Brad Faxon 1997
       Paul Goydos 1997
130 - Corey Pavin 1985
       Dick Mast 1993

For 18 Holes

61 - Keith Clearwater..................... 1993
      Lee Janzen............................. 1993
      Greg Kraft 1999
      Kenny Perry 2003
      Justin Leonard........................ 2003
      Chad Campbell 2004
62 - Joey Sindelar.......................... 1985
      Gene Sauers........................... 1990
      Steve Elkington 1991
      Patrick Sheehan .... 2005\

Front Nine

28 - Wayne Levi............................. 1993
29 - Tom Watson 1985
      Scott Hoch............................. 1987
      Keith Clearwater..................... 1991
      Sergio Garcia.......................... 2001
      Kenny Perry 2003
      Justin Leonard........................ 2003

Back Nine

28 - Keith Clearwater..................... 1993
29 - Lee Trevino 1976
      George Burns 1984
      Mike Hulbert 1990
      Guy Boros 1994
      Greg Kraft 1999

THE TWENTY YEAR CLUB

Thirty-five golfers have played in 20 or more of the Colonial tournaments. These men have won a total of 29 championships at Colonial and have taken home more than $7 million in prize money.

PLAYER	YEARS	WINS	AVG.	MONEY
Ben Crenshaw	32	2	70.95	$478,747
Tom Kite	30	-	70.68	181,835
Rod Curl	30	1	74.55	65,314
Gene Littler	29	1	71.76	111,883
Dave Stockton	28	1	71.94	85,728
Bruce Lietzke	27	2	70.37	452,388
Julius Boros	27	2	72.13	62,815
Don January	27	-	72.23	81,034
Al Geiberger	26	2	71.72	133,808
Ray Floyd	26	-	72.23	71,331
Tom Purtzer	25	1	71.08	365,607
Charles Coody	25	-	72.33	43,063
Tom Watson	24	1	69.91	788,695
Peter Jacobsen	24	1	70.90	228,049
Dan Pohl	23	1	71.59	207,501
Corey Pavin	22	2	69.34	988,745
Lanny Wadkins	22	1	71.59	218,170
Gil Morgan	22	-	70.82	145,670
Hale Irwin	22	-	70.86	211,623
John Mahaffey	22	-	71.09	156,325
Mike Reid	22	-	71.01	106,386
Mark Brooks	22	-	70.88	297,682
Ben Hogan	21	5	71.11	47,664
Lee Trevino	21	2	70.69	162,576
Tommy Bolt	21	1	73.04	17,468
Fuzzy Zoeller	21	1	70.78	190,918
David Frost	21	1	70.44	560,132
D.A.Weibring	21	-	70.74	205,801
Chi Chi Rodriguez	21	-	72.00	33,533
Joey Sindelar	21	-	70.83	173,653
Tom Weiskopf	20	1	71.56	74,936
Bob Tway	20	-	70.26	344,522
David Edwards	20	-	70.53	341,604
Miller Barber	20	-	72.54	23,872
Lionel Hebert	20	-	73.72	13,237

TOP TENS

PLAYER	YEARS IN TOP 10	YEARS PLAYED	WINS
Ben Hogan*	15	21	5
Gene Littler	12	29	1
Tom Watson	11	24	1
Julius Boros	9	27	2
Gardner Dickinson	9	18	1
Ben Crenshaw	8	32	2
Lloyd Mangrum*	8	15	-
Gary Player	8	17	-
Corey Pavin	7	22	2
Lee Trevino	7	21	2
Cary Middlecoff	7	18	1
Don January	7	27	-
Jack Nicklaus	6	11	1
Bruce Crampton	6	16	1
Jeff Sluman	6	17	-
Ted Kroll	6	9	-
Tom Kite	6	30	-
Nick Price	5	17	2
Johnny Palmer	5	18	1
Tommy Bolt	5	21	1
Ed Oliver	5	8	-
Peter Thomson	5	9	-
Justin Leonard	5	12	-
Jimmy Demaret	5	10	-
Dow Finsterwald	5	13	-
Mark Calcavecchia	5	17	-
Payne Stewart	5	14	-
Jack Burke	5	15	-
Doug Ford	5	16	-
Bob Murphy	5	18	-
Byron Nelson	5	18	-
Hale Irwin	5	22	-
John Mahaffey	5	23	-

WHOS THE BEST

The charts below show the best lifetime scoring averages at Colonial, for players who have competed more than 10 years.

FOR 11-20 YEARS

PLAYER	YEARS	ROUNDS	STROKES	AVERAGE
Kenny Perry	16	60	4147	69.12
Justin Leonard	12	48	3323	69.23
Tom Lehman	11	36	2495	69.31
Phil Mickelson	12	44	3050	69.32
Jeff Sluman	18	66	4584	69.45
Fred Funk	15	56	3894	69.54
Kirk Triplett	15	58	4036	69.59
Nick Price	17	65	4531	69.71

OVER 20 YEARS

PLAYER	YEARS	ROUNDS	STROKES	AVERAGE
Corey Pavin	22	83	5755	69.34
Tom Watson	24	87	6082	69.91
Bruce Lietzke	27	97	6826	70.37
Tom Kite*	30	117	8269	70.68
Lee Trevino	21	77	5443	70.69
D. A. Weibring	21	70	4952	70.74
Fuzzy Zoeller	21	77	5450	70.78
Gil Morgan	22	77	5453	70.82
Hale Irwin	22	79	5598	70.86
Mark Brooks	22	73	5174	70.88
Peter Jacobsen	24	82	5814	70.90
Ben Crenshaw*	31	103	7308	70.95
Mike Reid	22	77	5468	71.01
John Mahaffey	22	80	5687	71.09
Ben Hogan	21	83**	5902	71.11

* includes amateur appearance(s)
** includes one 18-hole playoff round

COME FROM BEHIND

This table shows the greatest gaps Colonial champs have overcome during their climb to the title.

AFTER 18	SHOTS BACK	POSITION
Olin Browne, 1999	7	63T
Ben Hogan, 1946	6	12T
Ben Hogan, 1952	6	21T
Ben Hogan, 1953	6	9T
Mike Souchak, 1956	5	24T
Gardner Dickinson, 1969	5	18T
Gene Littler, 1971	5	35T
Rod Curl, 1974	5	14T
Tom Purtzer, 1991	5	44T
AFTER 36		
Olin Browne, 1999	7	30T
Sergio Garcia, 2001	6	16T
Roberto De Vicenzo, 1957	6	17T
Ben Hogan, 1946	5	14T
Johnny Palmer, 1954	5	7T
Mike Souchak, 1956	5	15T
Doug Sanders, 1961	5	9T
Keith Clearwater, 1987	5	25T
Tom Purtzer, 1991	5	20T
Bruce Lietzke, 1992	5	17T
AFTER 54		
Nick Price, 1994	7	4T
Ben Hogan, 1952	6	3
Phil Mickelson, 2000	6	8T
Sergio Garcia, 2001	5	7T
Gene Littler, 1971	5	12T
Gardner Dickinson, 1969	4	6T
Tom Purtzer, 1991	4	15T

TOURNAMENT PARTNERS

TOURNAMENT SUPPORTERS THROUGH THE YEARS

Colonial has been privileged to enjoy strong relationships with many sponsors, vendors, charities, and other supporters over the years. They have been integral to the success and growth of the event. Our supporters on the following pages chose to also specifically support this history book, and we thank them for helping make it possible.

-- Colonial Country Club and Tournament Committee

ABOVE:
A view of Colonial's clubhouse, overlooking the scenic 18th hole.

BANK OF AMERICA

Title Sponsor, 2003 - 2006

When Bank of America became title sponsor of the Colonial tournament in 2003, a bond of mutual sportsmanship and philanthropic interest was forged between the history-rich Colonial and the time-honored financial institution.

HERITAGE

From its beginning, Bank of America has sought to enrich itself with partnerships that share the same appreciation of heritage, and the desire to be part of a worthwhile charitable benefit. The Colonial golf tournament, the longest running event on the PGA Tour still being held at the original site, appealed to the financial institution as a natural match, garnering the company's title support in 2003.

WINNING

For 60 years, the Colonial tournament has showcased the power of the athlete's spirit. The historic Fort Worth country club, founded in 1936, has borne witness to this spirit. Whether challenged or lifted, the indomitable spirit of Colonial cannot be broken.

Ben Hogan personified the true spirit of Colonial. Even after he was told he may never walk again, much less play golf after his near fatal car accident, he never gave up -- spurred on by his love of life and of the game. As we know, not only did he walk again, but he went on to win at Colonial -- three more times, a record five times in all.

Bank of America established a significant hospitality program that is staged at several tournaments throughout each year, in addition to Colonial. Its theme, "Hogan's Alley," honors and salutes Colonial icon Ben Hogan. Bank of America enjoys giving individuals the opportunity to participate in the Colonial. That may mean bringing in national clients to play in the Pro-Ams or, on a local level, selling tickets to the tournament out of their Dallas-Fort Worth bank branches. Bank associates even get into the act by becoming volunteer bank "Ambassadors," working specific assignments at the tournament, to help stage the event and enhance the spectator experience.

ABOVE:
Annika Sorenstam, Hall of Famer, chips a shot in the 2003 Bank of America Colonial, making history as the first woman ever to play the tournament.

SPIRIT

In 2003, Bank of America was proud to share its "first" with another Colonial "first." Annika Sorenstam, showed us a new version of spirit as the first woman to compete in the history of Colonial's PGA Tour event, Sorenstam won a place in history and in the hearts of many aspiring athletes, both men and women.

HIGHER STANDARDS

As the old adage goes, winning isn't everything, but it certainly is the driving force responsible for the amazing feats Colonial has seen in its six decades. Although each year someone will be honored with the plaid jacket, the charities are the true victors at Colonial.

Bank of America was founded on an important ideal, the promise of higher standards: people are their best when they are striving to exceed accomplishments of the past. Ben Hogan once said, "I'm the sole judge of my standards." He set very high standards for himself, both as a golfer and an individual.

Bank of America looks to the integrity he displayed throughout his life as an example for their business ethic and philanthropic involvement. As title sponsor, Bank of America shares this outlook in serving its customers and shareholders. For Bank of America, an important part of delivering a Higher Standard is helping their communities and their neighbors.

Bank of America has made the largest commitment to community development by a financial institution -- $750 billion over ten years. In fact, in 2005, the Bank of America Colonial generated $1.6 million in community service and charity donations. $500,000 in contributions went to the tournament's main beneficiary, Cook Children's Medical Center.

Bank of America
100 North Tryon Street
Charlotte, NC 28255
www.bankofamerica.com

169

golf trip with two sons: $1,230

(showing them that they're still not too old to get spanked: priceless)

there are some things money can't buy.
for everything else there's MasterCard.® **MasterCard**

Preferred Card of the PGA TOUR.

ABOVE:
Part of the highly successful MasterCard "Priceless" advertising campaign.
OPPOSITE PAGE:
A close-up view of the floral logo at the 18th hole scoreboard.

MASTERCARD

TITLE Sponsor, 1996 - 2002

Like the Colonial PGA TOUR event, MasterCard International's rich history began in the late 1940s when several U.S. banks began giving their customers specially-issued paper that could be used like cash in local stores. Today, MasterCard cardholders can use their cards at more than 23 million acceptance locations around the world, including over 1 million ATMs and other locations where cash can be obtained.

Before entering the golf arena in the 1990s, MasterCard was solely focused on the FIFA World Cup. In looking towards different ways of delivering value to its critical audiences, MasterCard decided that the Colonial golf tournament presented the perfect opportunity to penetrate the affluent segment. One of the oldest tournaments on the PGA TOUR, steeped in history and rich in tradition, the Colonial was an attractive offering for MasterCard. Upon announcing its title sponsorship of the event in 1995, MasterCard also announced its sponsorship of the PGA Grand Slam of Golf year-end event.

Subsequently, MasterCard began partnering with other sports properties -- MLS, World Figure Skating, NHL, MLB, NASCAR, Formula 1 and NFL teams. This full array of sports properties provided MasterCard with an eclectic grouping of assets allowing the company, among other things, to deliver value to its customer financial institutions.

Sponsoring Colonial was part of MasterCard's synchronized global sponsorship and promotions strategy to reinforce brand awareness and generate business-building opportunities for MasterCard members and merchants. Value was also provided to its cardholders by creating a platform to form strategic alliances with key co-branders, through an extension of its media and advertising activities.

The Sponsorship also provided a fitting backdrop for its hugely successful "Priceless" campaign. The MasterCard award-winning Priceless® advertising campaign is now seen in 105 countries and in 48 languages, giving the brand a truly global reach and scope.

ABOVE:
The coveted Colonial tournament trophy.

ABOVE:
Olin Browne receiving credit card from Alan Heuer on the 18th hole
during the 1999 awards ceremony.

Since the beginning, the MasterCard Colonial always provided unique opportunities for client entertainment and business development over a week-long period. Both on and off the course, many important alliances have been formed, and countless existing business relationships were strengthened and renewed.

In 1996, MasterCard announced its sponsorship of the MasterCard Championship seniors event in Hawaii and a spokesperson agreement with hall of famer Tom Watson, who then won the 1998 MasterCard Colonial. MasterCard became further committed to golf by becoming the preferred card of the PGA, PGA TOUR, and LPGA. MasterCard truly is the card associated with professional golf, and continues to proudly support the Colonial and its many deserving charities.

"This is a very giving community," said 2006 Colonial President Bill Bowers, "and we are pleased the tournament is such a big part of it each year."

MasterCard
2000 Purchase St.
Purchase, NY 10577
www.mastercard.com

BAYLOR ALL SAINTS

Upon reflection of the history and philanthropic benefit the Colonial has contributed to Fort Worth in its 60-year history, Baylor All Saints Medical Centers have the distinction of sharing with the tournament a common bond. The hospital is also celebrating a huge milestone -- its 100-year anniversary as a trusted server of the Fort Worth community. Since 1906, the hospital has been committed to serving its neighbors in Fort Worth and the surrounding communities by providing quality care and advanced technology in a warm, caring atmosphere.

The hospital has grown dramatically in both size and scope over the past century. In 2002, the Fort Worth community and business leaders governing All Saints decided to become a part of the Baylor Health Care System, an extensive network of private, not-for-profit hospitals in the Metroplex area. The merge resulted in Baylor All Saints Medical Center at Fort Worth and Baylor Medical Center at Southwest Fort Worth.

Baylor All Saints excitedly looks forward to the $100 million campus expansion plan, including a state-of-art women's hospital which was announced in December 2005, and expected to be completed by March 2008.

Earlier in 2005, Baylor All Saints also announced a $29 million expansion in other health care services at the hospital, especially in organ transplant, oncology, and cardiology. The hospital is the only one of its kind in Tarrant County that is equipped to conduct pancreas and liver transplants.

For the past three years, the hospital has been honored to have a relationship with the Colonial, one of the most exciting and eagerly awaited annual traditions in Fort Worth.

"This is an exciting time for us at Baylor All Saints Medical Centers. Much like the Colonial Invitational Tournament, our future promises to hold much excitement and opportunity. The community can take pride in both of our commitments to continually make Fort Worth the best place to work and live," commented Steven R. Newton, president, Baylor All Saints Medical Centers.

Baylor All Saints
1400 8th Ave
Fort Worth, TX 76104
(817) 922-7760
www.baylorhealth.com

A Textron Company

BELL HELICOPTER

Sixty years ago, the Colonial Tournament joined the ranks of top-notch golf events, and today, the competition continues to draw raves from golf champions and fans alike.

In a serendipitous parallel, Bell Helicopter, the first company to get involved with the Colonial on a sponsorship level, is positioned at the top of the heap in terms of helicopter aviation. A leading producer of vertical lift aircraft, Bell has been a valuable part of Colonial's history for over 50 years, and the company's commitment to this first-class tournament has never wavered.

A look back at Bell's liaison with the Colonial reveals a bona -- fide partnership steeped in a legacy of charity and an authentic sense of community.

In the early 1950s, Bell public relations executive Jim Fuller spearheaded a sponsorship program of worthwhile Fort Worth activities.

Mr. Fuller established the Colonial tournament as one of the program's cornerstones, and that foundation still stands.

Today, all vending machine profits and other proceeds are converted to over $2 million worth of tickets and sponsorships annually, including the Colonial.

The company participates for the sole purpose of supporting its employees and the community of Fort Worth, and Bell's sponsorship has never been used as an advertising tool. P.D. Shabay, Executive Vice President of Administration and Chief Human Relations Officer, is intensely proud of the fact that this philosophy has not changed over the years.

Further, as part of the tournament, Bell acquires four pro-am spots, which are appropriated to four fortunate employees via a computerized lottery system. This approach ensures that all of Bell's employees have a shot at what many consider to be a once-in-a-lifetime opportunity.

Paul Bradtmueller described his pro-am participation this way: "What an experience it was, walking the fairways of Colonial that so many of the world's greatest golfers have walked before. The Colonial Pro-Am was fabulous from beginning to end. I didn't want it to end."

As the Colonial has risen from a modest invitational to a nationally televised event with an impressive field and a multi-million dollar purse, Bell Helicopter has consistently been by their side. One golf tournament. One Helicopter company. Two leaders.

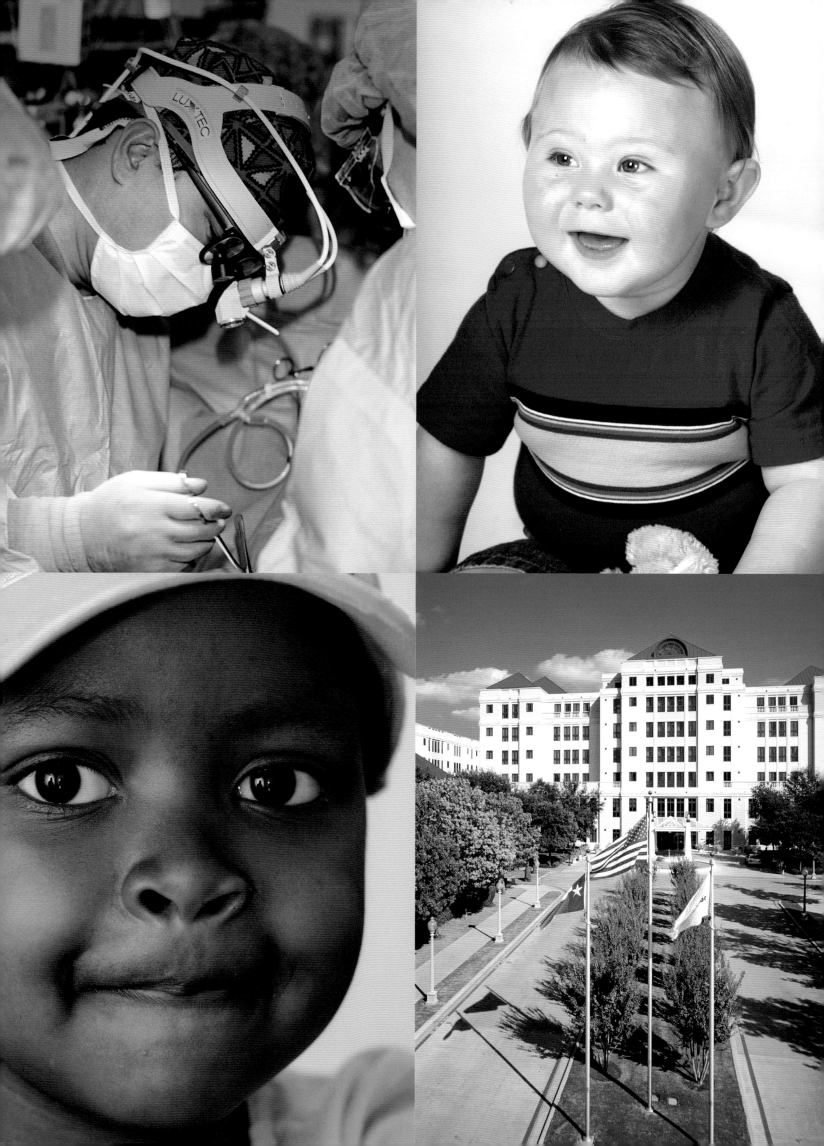

COOK CHILDREN'S MEDICAL CENTER

Cook Children's Medical Center is perhaps one of the most visible examples of how the Colonial golf tournament not only serves to showcase golfers at their competitive best, but that at the heart of it, the tournament's focus is on philanthropic endeavors.

Cook Children's has a long history of compassionately serving the children and families of Fort Worth and the surrounding counties. What we know today as Cook Children's Medical Center is the result of a merger finalized in 1985 between the Fort Worth Free Baby Hospital (later called Fort Worth Children's Hospital) and W.I. Cook Memorial Hospital.

Continuous improvement and expansion abound at Cook Children's Medical Center: in 2003, a $53 million, five-floor pavilion expanded critical care areas, and increased bed capacity to 282. In 2004, a fracture clinic, urgent care center, and heliport were added to the medical center campus, and in 2005, the heart center expanded catheterization and heart surgery facilities. The hospital provides more than 30 pediatric specialties and services.

Cook Children's Medical Center became a beneficiary of the Colonial golf tournament in 1997 through the efforts of G. Malcolm Louden, then chairman of the Cook Children's Medical Center board of trustees, and Carol J. Alexander, then president of Jewel Charity, and members of the Jewel Charity Ball board. In 2003, when Bank of America became the tournament sponsor, Colonial Country Club continued their support of Cook Children's Medical Center through Jewel Charity. The 2005 Colonial alone generated $500,000 on their behalf.

Through the generosity of Colonial sponsors and other donors, Cook Children's Medical Center continues to stay true to it's mission and values, to care for our future -- our children.

CookChildren's.
Medical Center

Fort Worth, Texas

Cook Children's Medical Center
801 Seventh Ave.
Fort Worth, TX
(682) 885-4000
www.cookchildrens.org

MERRILL LYNCH

The Colonial golf tournament has been a part of the Fort Worth community for years; it matches a great day of golf with a tradition of giving back. Merrill Lynch, one of the world's leading financial management and advisory companies, annually invites clients, families, and friends to this exciting event.

Merrill Lynch also looks for ways to provide its clients with unique experiences at events like the Colonial. It hosts breakfast and lunch seminars where guests can hear from financial pros in such areas as estate planning, credit and lending, and retirement planning before they head out to watch the PGA Tour pros. Alan Fonner, Merrill Lynch Managing Director in Fort Worth notes, "Our guests appreciate the opportunity to watch the players, but they also appreciate group settings to hear how we can help them develop strategies to reach their goals."

Through the Total Merrill platform, Merrill Lynch Financial Advisors customize financial strategies for each client. By looking beyond stocks and bonds, clients can optimize all the components of their financial lives. And just like a golfer on the first tee, having a plan to achieve your goals is essential.

It's also essential to be charitable, and Merrill Lynch has been a responsible corporate citizen in Fort Worth for more than 40 years. Its longstanding relationship with the Colonial tournament presents a valuable opportunity to give back to the community through the organizations it benefits.

MERRILL LYNCH SALUTES THE COLONIAL
GOLF TOURNAMENT ON ITS 60TH ANNIVERSARY

TOTAL MERRILL

201 Main Street, Suite 2100
Fort Worth, TX 76102
(817)-877-9610
www.ml.com

ABLe
COMMUNICATIONS

Growing up on the west side of Fort Worth, Rick and Hiram Lopez were always taken in by the city's anticipation of the Colonial tournament and the history associated with it. It was that spark of excitement and city pride which made the Lopez brothers know they had to be a part of it.

In 1994, the brothers founded ABLe Communications, Inc., a voice and data cabling solutions contractor located in Grapevine, Texas. Able Communications offers full-service telecommunications network infrastructure support. Thorough knowledge of advanced fiber optic technology enables ABLe team members to assist in design, implementing, and managing both inside and outside installations. The company is recognized as a Registered Communications Distribution Designer (RCDD). This certification is awarded to companies that maintain their prominence through continuing education, innovative design, proficient installation, and the implementation of newly developed technologies.

As their business grew, the brothers were eventually able to fulfill one of their many business and personal goals by becoming a Colonial Golf Tournament sponsor. "It became the perfect opportunity to show appreciation to our customers and

vendors," noted Rick Lopez. "With our business in Grapevine, we do not have the pleasure of running into our Fort Worth friends on a regular basis. We always enjoy a week of getting reacquainted with everyone at the tournament."

ABLe's involvement has grown from daily tickets, to a Sponsor Table for ten on the indoor tennis courts, to where they are today in the Colonial Club.

Beginning with the 2005 Colonial, they had the great opportunity to sit on the veranda overlooking their favorite spot, the 16th hole. "We had a fantastic week and so did our customers and vendors. We look forward to many more years of support and partnership with the Colonial and the good it does for our hometown."

ABLe Communications
753 Port America Place, #104
Grapevine, TX 76051
(817) 488-2253
www.ablecomm.net

ATC LOGISTICS & ELECTRONICS

Growth has been a defining theme for ATC Logistics and Communications for the past decade, one that fits right in with the company's involvement in the Colonial tournament.

Headquartered in Fort Worth, Texas, ATC began in 1994 and employs about 1450 in the Dallas/Fort Worth area. In the last year alone, the company has experienced an astounding 45% increase in growth. It is the company's mission to put their "people, processes, and technology together to deploy smart, focused, and complete solutions." ATC's strategic methodologies have provided its clients with positive results, extraordinary benefits, and lasting business success. In fact, companies such as Cingular, Nokia, Motorola, GM, and Ford have relied on the expertise and direction of ATC.

Two years ago, President Bill Conley felt that as his company continued to experience the rewards of fortunate growth, he had a responsibility to his employees, shareholders, and the community to share that good fortune by becoming increasingly involved in civic-minded events. Already a past supporter of Party Fort Worth, City Sister, and other philanthropic events that are unique and tied directly to the area, the Colonial tournament was a natural addition. The rich history and integrity of the Colonial offered the perfect blend of showcasing Fort Worth, a charitable involvement, and a fun platform for an employee recognition program.

Bill Conley envisions future Colonial tournaments to serve as the backdrop for his company to host an annual weekend event and offer a taste of Fort Worth. "Our involvement in the Colonial will continue to grow and evolve as our company does. As our key annual event, it will also serve as the perfect vehicle for ATC to show off the rest of Fort Worth's one-of-a-kind attractions to our clients. It's a great mix of business and pleasure."

ATC Logistics & Electronics
13500 Independence Parkway
Fort Worth, TX 76177
(817) 491-7727
(800) 466-4202
www.atcle.com

AUTOBAHN
MOTORCAR GROUP

Sixty years ago, ladies and gentlemen might have confused the meaning of the words tee time with tea time. Not today. More men, women, and children of all ages are enjoying golf, "the greatest game ever played."

Even auto manufacturers are designing SUVs and other vehicles with golf clubs in mind. This is evident when you look around the parking lot of any golfing facility in America. If you check the nameplates on the vehicles at the Colonial, where excellence is a standard and quality a tradition, you'll find that many of the new BMWs, Jaguars, Volvos, Porsches, Land Rovers, and Volkswagens come from the neighboring AUTOBAHN MOTORCAR GROUP in Fort Worth.

Of course, being close may be one of the reasons. But being the best in Customer Satisfaction with the utmost professionalism, personal care, added conveniences, and state-of -the-art facilities is the number one reason Autobahn customers come from near and far. That's why John Chase, president, and Chad Chase, vice president, and the entire award-winning AUTOBAHN staff are dedicated in their effort to provide you the best possible ownership experience.

Since 1979, AUTOBAHN has been setting the pace in the Fort Worth-Dallas Metroplex, constantly improving and expanding into one of the top, most honored dealership groups in America. In this respect, as a leader, Autobahn is somewhat unique. It is one of the few independent, family-owned, authorized dealership groups where all important decisions are made at the local level -- and not by an out of state investment conglomerate.

So whether you're driving golf balls at the beautiful, world famous Colonial Country Club, or world-class vehicles from the AUTOBAHN MOTORCAR GROUP, it doesn't get any better than this.

Autobahn Motorcar Group
3000 White Settlement Rd.
Fort Worth TX 76107
(817) 336-0835
www.shopautobahn.com

BARLOW GARSEK & SIMON, LLP

arlow Garsek & Simon, LLP, is a full-service civil law firm whose first priority is its clients. Barlow Garsek & Simon's roots date to 1978, when three partners from two large Fort Worth law firms decided to form a practice that would "hold its members to the highest professional and ethical standards while fostering a strong sense of camaraderie and client commitment."

That spirit still guides its practice and outside business partnerships today. As a telling extension of that commitment, the firm has been a sponsor of the PGA event held at Colonial Country Club since 1989. The firm of about 20, including six partners and nine lawyers, is "incredibly generous, giving of their time and energy to make the event better each year."

As Mr. Garsek has stated, "it is easy to get involved in something you truly believe in and are enthusiastic about such as the Bank of America Colonial. The philanthropic support that results from so much work and the combined efforts of so many people is something of which we're all very proud."

As a Colonial Country Club member for the past 28 years, a past President of Colonial, and the current Bank of America Colonial Tournament Chairman, Elliott Garsek holds this monumental event close to his philanthropic and personal interests. He and other members of the firm also support the Jewel Charity which benefits Cook Children's Medical Center, the primary beneficiary of the Tournament, as well as numerous other charities supported by the Tournament.

The lawyers and staff of Barlow Garsek & Simon, LLP enthusiastically support the Bank of America Colonial.

Barlow Grasek & Simon, LLP
3815 Lisbon Street
Fort Worth, TX 76107
(817) 731-4500
www.bgsfirm.com

BEN E. KEITH COMPANY BEER DIVISION

Ben E. Keith Company is the exclusive distributor for Anheuser-Busch beers in 60 counties across North Texas, and is fortunate to have enjoyed a strong business and sponsorship relationship with the Colonial for many years.

Founded in 1906, Ben E. Keith Company began as a fresh produce company. During Prohibition, Anheuser-Busch sought a business relationship with Fort Worth businessman Benjamin Ellington Keith. The relationship continued beyond Prohibition, and flourishes today under owners Robert and Howard Hallam. Ben E. Keith Company is distinguished as the largest distributor of Anheuser-Busch beers in the United States.

John Pritchett, General Manager for the Ben E. Keith Company Beer Division in Fort Worth, appreciates the brand availability and association they have had with Colonial over time. "It is important to Ben E. Keith Company, and important to the success of the Anheuser-Busch brands in Fort Worth to be associated with a tradition rich event like Colonial. We have greatly appreciated having product availability at Colonial for many years, and plan to continue the relationship into the future."

Ben E. Keith Company annually entertains clients at the Colonial, participates in the Wednesday pro-am, and works diligently to satisfy the many product vendors on the course throughout the week with sufficient supply of cold Budweiser beer.

Says Mr. Pritchett, "The Colonial is an integral part of Fort Worth's diverse culture, and a revenue builder for the community. Fort Worth is a great city because of events such as Colonial, and we are very fortunate to distribute beer in such a market. We will work hard to be a part of Colonial and Fort Worth's continued success."

Ben E. Keith Company
Beer Division
7001 Will Rogers Blvd
Fort Worth, TX 76140
(817) 568-4000

BJ SERVICES

BJ Services has been supporting Colonial's professional golf tournament for nearly 50 years. Starting their first year back in 1957, the oil and gas services company was known as the Western Company and gave their support by purchasing what was then called the Super Saint Package.

The oil and gas industry is known for its commitment to local communities. BJ Services uses its sponsorship to entertain customers, especially in the pro-am. The company has always bought a pro-am package, and back in the late 1960's early 1970's they also hosted corporate hospitality at the Colonial swimming pool overlooking the #1 tee during the golf tournament.

Local BJ Services executive Dale Haley, who has been a tournament volunteer since the mid 1980s, said the company has been a long time supporter of the Colonial golf tournament.

BJ Services Company
309 W. 7th Street Suite 1520
Fort Worth, TX 76102
(817) 877-3725
www.bjservices.com

CARTER & BURGESS

For Carter & Burgess, Inc., the Colonial tournament has always been about establishing and enriching relationships. The Fort Worth-based engineering and architectural firm, begun in 1939, formed its long-standing relationship with the Colonial almost from the tournament's beginning. It seemed a natural pairing because, as Ben Watts, President and CEO of Carter & Burgess, says, "The rich history and family atmosphere of the Colonial tournament mirrors our own company culture."

Carter & Burgess cofounders, Gene Carter and John Burgess (photo circa 1980s), became involved with the Colonial through their personal association with Colonial Country Club founders O.B. and Marvin Leonard. Such personal relationships in business have always been valued by the company as it has grown from a local into a national organization.

In the last 15 years, Carter & Burgess has grown substantially to include some 24 major office locations nationwide. Their multidisciplinary teams of architects, engineers, planners, and program/construction management personnel serve a broad diversity of market sectors. Today, Gene Carter and John Burgess' legacy continues through the company's "commitment to excellence, desire to provide meaningful work for employees, and passion for involvement in significant projects."

By far the largest event the company is involved in locally, each year the Colonial has proven the perfect venue to bring in clients from all over the country. Business relationships are renewed face to face and both Carter & Burgess clients and employees have a great time while doing it, and from the veranda over the 18th green no less. As Ben Watts sums it up, "I don't think any of us at Carter & Burgess have anything *but* fond memories of the Colonial. We look forward to it every year both personally and professionally."

Carter▪Burgess

Carter & Burgess
777 Main Street
Fort Worth, TX 76102-5304
(817)-735-6000
www.c-b.com

COCA-COLA COMPANY

The name Coca-Cola needs little introduction. The soft drink, introduced in 1886, has become the beverage staple no party or event is complete without. The Fort Worth Coca-Cola facility began operation in 1906 with 2 wagons, 4 mules, and 50 employees.

In 1946, Fort Worth became home to the Colonial National Invitational Tournament, where Ben Hogan, a Fort Worth native ,won top honors. Coca-Cola's partnership with the Colonial began with that inaugural tournament in 1946 and continues today.

Coca-Cola chooses events carefully based on many defining factors. Any event that represents as much unwavering prestige, rich history and integrity as the Colonial has had from the beginning, is something with which we are proud to be associated.

The fact that the Colonial is such a family-oriented event made it a natural choice for Coca-Cola. It was important to have a place where the company's family and clients could gather. Consequently, it was only natural that we were the first company to host a corporate hospitality tent at the Colonial tournament.

Through the years, Coca-Cola family members have many fond memories of the people that make the Colonial happen. It's their hard work that makes the Colonial golf tournament one of the biggest events in Fort Worth and the golfing community.

It has been an honor to be part of the Colonial Golf Tournament over the past 60 years ... The Coca-Cola Family looks forward to a continued partnership over the next 60 years.

Coca-Cola Company
3400 Fossil Creek
Fort Worth, TX 76137
(817) 847-3010
www.coca-cola.com

DEHART CROCKETT, P.C.

As one of the many Colonial volunteers, Craig Crockett (pictured left), along with his Fort Worth law firm, Dehart Crockett P.C., knows firsthand what makes the tournament a philanthropic and sporting success year after year. It is about the volunteers who unselfishly give of their valuable time to support Colonial and its charitable efforts.

Craig, a member of Colonial Country Club and volunteer Chairman of the Scoring and Shotlink Committee, is responsible for overseeing 150 dedicated volunteers who use revolutionary technology to record and transmit player group information -- including time, stance, lie, and results for every tournament shot. Like the players and volunteers, Craig must be prepared and at the top of his game throughout the tournament. Preparation, the use of state-of-the-art technology, and management of personnel required by his Colonial position are things Craig excels at in his law practice and allow his firm to achieve superior results.

DeHart Crockett P.C. focuses on trial law, including business, commercial, class action, and product liability litigation. Craig and his partner, J. Cort DeHart (pictured right), have achieved Martindale Hubbell's AV rating, the highest rating for legal ability and ethical standards based on peer evaluations completed by local attorneys and judges.

For Craig, "Meeting such great people: the volunteers who work so tirelessly toward the same philanthropic goal; that's the most rewarding aspect of the tournament. Our law firm is honored to be a part of the rich tradition and contributions that the Colonial brings to the Fort Worth community each year."

DEHARTCROCKETT PC
ATTORNEYS

DeHart Crockett, P.C.
3340 Camp Bowie Blvd., Suite 100
Fort Worth, TX 76107
(817) 810-0400
www.dehartcrockett.com

FIRST HORIZON BANK

Relative newcomer to the Colonial and to the Dallas/Fort Worth metroplex is First Horizon Bank. The 2005 Colonial tournament marked the bank's first year as a sponsor.

In the past, First Horizon had been known in the metroplex only through its mortgage company name, First Horizon Home Loans. However, today it is exporting its highly successful personal and commercial banking strategy to Texas and other principal cities across the country where it is has a high concentration of mortgage customers, beginning with four branches added to the metroplex in 2005. With several more branches planned for 2006, First Horizon Bank is on its way to becoming a very visible presence in Fort Worth/Dallas.

Sponsorships such as the Colonial golf tournament are important to First Horizon Bank and its partners for many reasons, such as building brand awareness. But more importantly, these events offer the opportunities to deepen and strengthen relationships with clients and co-workers in a fun, non-work environment.

"As a long time Tarrant County banker, the Colonial has always been a special event to me that I have enjoyed sharing with many friends and clients throughout the years. The Colonial is not only the greatest golf event in the country, but it is also the social event of the year. To miss the Colonial would be like skipping Christmas," says J. Scott Jones, Senior Vice President, Tarrant County Commercial Banking Manager.

Although 2005 was the first year First Horizon existed as a bank in the Metroplex, the employees hired were seasoned banking leaders who had great memories of the Colonial tournament and immediately recognized the importance of First Horizon's partnering in the event. First Horizon looks forward to growing and making history with the Colonial.

First Horizon Bank
201 Main St, Ste. 1300
Fort Worth, TX 76102
(817) 333-0200

12400 Coit Rd., Ste. 1100
Dallas, TX 75251
(972) 788-9700
www.firsthorizon.com

GREG NORMAN COLLECTION

The Greg Norman Collection launched in 1992 beginning as a golf-inspired knitwear line designed exclusively for men, developing into a complete lifestyle brand for every enthusiastic golfer today.

GNC is a leading marketer and distributor of golf-inspired sportswear and accessories targeting active, sophisticated men and women who range in age from 35 to 55. With the introduction of its notable, moisture-wicking PlayDry® technology in 1998, the Collection set an unprecedented standard for performance golfwear and continually answers the demands of those on the course. The sensible combination of performance, luxury, and style within GNC adds a new element of fashion to the golf world, while remaining to draw its inspiration from the game and Greg Norman himself.

The Greg Norman Collection, in keeping with its golf heritage, is proud to support The Bank of America Colonial event - long considered a premier stop on the PGA Tour.

As a player, Greg Norman has two top 10 finishes at Colonial and finished second by a shot in the 1993 event. The owner of 20 PGA Tour victories, and 68 other wins worldwide, he was elected into the World Golf Hall of Fame in 2001.

GREG NORMAN

Greg Norman Collection
1309 Juneau Ct
Fort Worth , TX 76116
P: 817.731.0743
www.shark.com/
gregnormancollection/

HARRIS METHODIST FORT WORTH HOSPITAL

Harris Methodist Fort Worth Hospital's first aid tents are just what the doctor ordered at the Bank of America Colonial Golf Tournament

The latest spring fashions, a great round of golf, friends gathering for long overdue visits, and smiles all around. For the most part, the Bank of America Colonial Golf Tournament is enjoyed by all and is a wonderful and memorable experience.

But sometimes the hot Texas sun gets the best of the game's enthusiasts, and a visit is in order to one of the five Harris Methodist Fort Worth Hospital first aid tents, each conveniently located around the golf course.

Since 1987, doctors, nurses, emergency medical technicians, and other clinical staff from Harris have staffed the tent throughout the weeklong tournament. Each year, they care for hundreds of golf fans for such ailments as heat exhaustion, dehydration, falls, and more. In addition, advanced life support is provided at each station, and CareFlite crews are on-hand as well. Most people who visit the tents stay for just a few minutes and then return to the golf camaraderie, often after a quick rest on a medical cot.

However, each year, approximately half a dozen people require a quick dash to the 710-bed flagship facility -- Harris Methodist Fort Worth Hospital, a part of Texas Health Resources (THR).

Congratulations, Colonial!

"Harris Methodist is proud to be associated with the Bank of America Colonial Golf Tournament and as the tournament celebrates its 60th anniversary, we congratulate all involved," said Barclay E. Berdan, president of HMFW.

"Providing needed health care services through these on-site first aid tents is the ideal way for us to reinvest in building healthier communities, give back to Fort Worth's residents and visitors, and help improve the health of the people in the communities we serve," Berdan added.

HARRIS METHODIST
Fort Worth Hospital
Texas Health Resources

Harris Methodist Fort Worth Hospital
1301 Pennsylvania Ave.
Fort Worth, TX 76104
(817) 250-2000
www.HarrisMethodistHospitals.org/hmfw

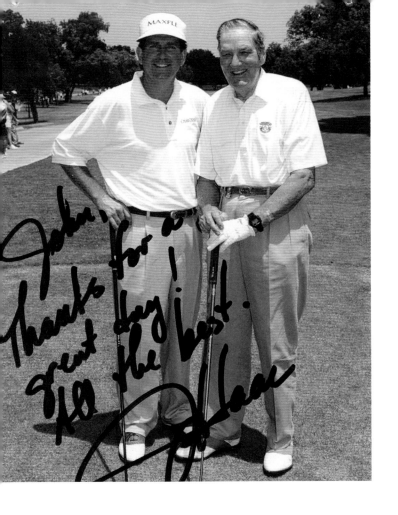

HOWELL
INSTUMENTS,
INC.

Testing in the aircraft industry began with the development of the JETCAL® Analyzer. In meeting the challenges of today's changing world, the people of Howell Instruments, Inc. consistently ensure that the demands of our military are met, keeping alive the spirit of excellence on which the company was founded.

While a successful business took much of his time, John Howell still made time for the important things in life -- family and of course, golf. In fact, the beloved father of four was an avid golfer and a member of Shady Oaks, Ridglea, Rivercrest, and Colonial Country Clubs in Fort Worth.

Mr. Howell truly cherished his membership in the various clubs, particularly Colonial Country Club where he was a member from the 1950s until his death in 2002. From its beginning, Mr. and Mrs. Howell were part of the history most of us only read about today.

He was fortunate enough to count Ben Hogan among his dear family friends and they shared many rounds of golf together. The two were playing partners from 1962-1967 at Shady Oaks Country Club. An accomplished golfer in his own

right, Mr. Howell got a hole-in-one during the 1961 Colonial pro-am and usually bested his Pro.

One of the things that delighted Mr. Howell the most was his Company's involvement in the Colonial PGA Tournament every year. This also allowed the employees to be a part of the rich history of Colonial Country Club.

A number of his employees have been and are still members of the club today, because of the great opportunity he provided to those who may not have been able to join without a corporate membership.

Howell Instruments, Inc.
3479 W. Vickery Blvd.
Fort Worth, TX 76107
(817) 336-7411
www.howellinst.com

JPMORGAN CHASE

When the Colonial golf tournament began in 1946, so did its long relationship with Fort Worth National Bank, a JPMorgan Chase predecessor. Fort Worth National was the first bank of the Tournament, and the bank has been a sponsor of the Colonial for the Tournament's entire 60 years.

From people like Marvin Leonard, who took an idea that grew into greatness, to bank employees who have served as committee members and volunteers, the Tournament is an ingrained part of the Fort Worth community.

Chase in Fort Worth is part of JPMorgan Chase & Co., a worldwide banking leader with more than $1 trillion in assets and operations in more than 50 countries. As the largest bank in Fort Worth and in Texas, Chase operates more than 150 bank branches in the Metroplex, manages retail and commercial banking operations nationwide from a state-of-the-art data center in Tarrant County, and employs nearly 8,700 area residents.

Chase has a long history dating back to its Fort Worth National Bank roots of serving as one of Fort Worth's leading corporate citizens. The bank has supported countless organizations and events in Tarrant County, and the Colonial golf tournament is among the largest. The Colonial has provided the opportunity for us to renew relationships and begin new ones in a relaxed, fun atmosphere that is always present at the tournament.

From Ben Hogan to Ben Crenshaw, the Colonial is synonymous with the history of golf, and Chase is honored to have played a key role in the tournament's development. As Fort Worth National was there in the beginning, Chase is here now and will be in the future as the tournament moves towards its seventh decade of entertaining golf fans worldwide.

JPMorganChase ◖

JP Morgan Chase
PO Box 2050 MC TX1-1260
Fort Worth, TX 76113
(817) 884-4151
www.jpmorganchase.com

KELLEY INSURANCE AGENCY, INC.

I. Lionel Kelley's personal and professional life has been entwined with the Colonial since 1974 when Lionel and his family, wife Gaynelle, and two children, became members of the country club. In 1978, Lionel became part of the members' volunteer ticket sales force and his life insurance business, Kelley Insurance Agency, Inc., became a long-time sponsor.

A proud Fort Worth native and lifetime resident, Lionel began his life insurance business in 1959 after graduating from TCU. Some of his proudest career highlights have been the Career Service award he received from the Fort Worth Association of Life Underwriters in 2001 and his 2003 induction into Gen America's Hall of Fame (a MetLife affiliate). These accolades speak volumes of his reputation in the insurance business.

Lionel participated in the Wednesday pro-am for 14 years, but now passes that great opportunity to his lucky clients. During those years Lionel had more than a few "once-in-a-lifetime" opportunities of playing with some of the game's legends. The consistent luck of his chance pairings even turned into a running joke among friends each year and led to his favorite Colonial memory. During the 1982 Colonial, Lionel was paired with golf great Jack Nicklaus. Although they didn't win the pro-am, Nicklaus did go on to win the Colonial that year.

Each year, both personally and professionally, Lionel Kelley looks forward to his continued involvement in this premiere Fort Worth event.

Kelley Insurance Agency, Inc.
I. Lionel Kelley, CLU, Chfc, CFP®
1200 Summit, Suite #510
Ft. Worth, TX 76102
(817).335.1465
www.kelleyagency.com

NORTHMARQ CAPITAL, INC.

NorthMarq Capital, Inc. has proudly partnered with Colonial since 1992. Phillip Askew, SVP/Managing Director, feels the company's partnership with Colonial is a very special one. "Just to be part of something like this and be able to support the Colonial in its mission is an honor for us". Askew/Reese Investment Company was purchased by NorthMarq Capital in July 2000, and Phillip, Ron Reese, and NorthMarq gladly continue their association with Colonial.

NorthMarq is a national real estate investment banker providing financing for commercial real estate, including office, retail, industrial, and multifamily developments. Since August 2000, the Dallas operation has originated over $5 billion in real estate financings in the Texas market.

Mr. Askew notes that one of the most enjoyable benefits of Colonial is to invite a client to play in the pro-am. "We don't do it just to strengthen client relations; we truly enjoy the excitement our clients feel in participating in the pro-am."

For the past seven years Mr. Askew has invited client Dick Sullivan of Legacy Bank to play in the Monday pro-am. "It has been great fun over the years to play in the Colonial pro-am in what is a very traditional and terrific golf venue. There is so much to be said for such a well organized and respected golf tournament as Colonial," cited Mr. Sullivan.

As of last year NorthMarq had earned its way to the Wednesday pro-am and had Frank Miller, President/CEO, of the JPI Companies participate. He states, "I started playing and following golf at age 10. It is an honor to have played at Colonial, a course steeped in rich tradition and historic memories of professional golfers, like Ben Hogan."

Phillip Askew, Ron Reese, and Bill Jackson of NorthMarq plan on continuing their support of Colonial and being a part of its fine tradition.

NorthMarq Capital, Inc.
4890 Alpha Rd. Ste. 200
Dallas, TX 75244
(972) 392-3366

PROGRESSIVE CONCEPTS, INC.

Progressive Concepts, Inc. (PCI) and Hawk Electronics proudly celebrated their 30-year history in 2005. From humble beginnings installing car stereos in a converted service station, PCI and Hawk have grown into a diverse sales and service organization employing more than 350 people and 12 retail locations. Today, PCI is focused on wireless communications, mobile electronics, and security.

The company's success is the result of its officers: Robert M. McMurrey, Chairman and CEO, George J. Hechtman, COO, and Keith H. Cole, Sr. Vice President and CFO -- and their management philosophy: "To market reliable products and services, support what we sell, and focus on our most important asset -- the customer."

Emphasis on the customer continually reminds PCI that the company, its customers and community are one. PCI and its employees are active in the community through numerous corporate contribution and volunteer efforts. Through the fund-raising activities of employees, PCI has been a generous contributor over the years to numerous charities throughout DFW. Since 1984, PCI has pledged the use of temporary cell phones, service, and two way radios during the Colonial's annual event. As the Colonial looks back on its history of accomplishments, PCI looks forward to the future -- refining and developing its services and programs to better serve the community. Says Robert McMurrey, "The Colonial is one of the biggest events in Fort Worth every year, bringing international attention to our city. As a business founded in Fort Worth and Tarrant County, our involvement in the Colonial is a public service to our community, and beneficial in exposing our products and services to key decision makers."

A Division of Progressive Concepts, Inc.

Progressive Concepts, Inc.
Hawk Electronics
5718 Airport Freeway
Fort Worth, TX 76117
(817).831.6789
www.hawkelectronics.com

PHOTOGRAPHY CREDITS

PHOTOGRAPHY CREDITS

AUTHOR ACKNOWLEDGEMENTS

Having grown up in Fort Worth, and been directly involved with Colonial's annual PGA TOUR event in some capacity for roughly 25 years, it was a thrill and a privilege to oversee this 60th anniversary book project. Never before has such an extensive history of the tournament been published, and yet there are countless more photographs and stories for which we didn't have room in this book. Nonetheless, Colonial members, volunteers, sponsors, players and tournament fans should enjoy the many memories relived here. What a wonderful legacy Marvin Leonard has given us.

I wish to thank the additional three writers that contributed to this project. Not only do they each have a long history with Colonial, they share a deep admiration and respect for the tournament and Mr. Leonard's legacy. They all jumped at the chance to contribute to this book. It was important to bring in these other writers' perspectives, in addition to my own and those of the many Colonial personalities included here.

Fort Worth's own Dan Jenkins is one of America's most acclaimed sportswriters. He attended the first Colonial tournament in 1946, and he knew Ben Hogan better than any other journalist. First as a Paschal High School and TCU golfer, and then as a friend of Hogan's, he walked Colonial's fairways countless times. Jenkins contributed to this project the chapter about Colonial's golf course in the early years.

Freelance writer Russ Pate attended the tournament for the first time in 1964 and later authored The Legacy Continues, a 50-year history of Colonial Country Club. For this project he wrote two chapters: one on Marvin and Marty Leonard ("Remembering Marvin") and one on the priceless contributions of tournament volunteers. Also, much of the opening chapter and some information from the 1941 U.S. Open chapter, first appeared in The Legacy Continues.

Mike Rabun recently retired from United Press International after more than 40 years of covering and editing news and sports events. Prior to becoming UPI's Southwest Sports Editor in 1972, Rabun's uncle took him to his first Colonial tournament in 1955 and he has not missed many since. He first covered the event as a writer in 1965. For this project, he visited anew with many Colonial winners and wrote the Wall of Champions chapter.

On behalf of these writers and myself, I wish to thank all the champions, players, sponsors, volunteers and Club members who shared their memories with us. It seems like you could just mention the word Colonial to someone, and they would happily stop what they're doing and share at least half an hour of story-telling with you. We wish we could have included them all here. Each of these groups of people, including the Colonial Country Club staff, is a huge, indispensable component of this great event. We hope that the stories we have included will help rekindle your own special memories of this tournament.

I especially wish to thank Marty Leonard, with whom it is a constant joy to share Colonial stories and photographs. She is always supportive and willing to assist in any way. When she told me last May that she had never had her picture taken with the tournament's Leonard Trophy, I couldn't believe it. You'll see the first such picture in this book, Marty with two-time champion Kenny Perry and the trophy, on page 53.

I wish to thank the many sponsors who helped make this book possible. You will tell from reading their profiles in the Tournament Partners section just how lucky our tournament and our city is to have them. There are many more corporate partners out there who make the event happen each year.

Thanks also go to our publisher, Panache Partners and its talented staff, who embraced this project from the beginning and worked hard to make it happen. I would like to thank the tremendous, loyal individuals I have worked with on the Tournament Staff over these many years: Jimmie Whitt, Tracy Childers, Sue Ann Hoad, Judy Gordon and Eckie Lynch. Finally, I would like to thank the Club and Tournament Committee for entrusting me with this project. The longest-running PGA TOUR event on the same course needed its own book. I'm proud to have helped make it happen.

Dennis Roberson